The Actors Studio

The Actors Studio

A History

by

SHELLY FROME

McFarland & Company, Inc., Publishers

Jefferson, North Carolina, and London

ALSO BY SHELLY FROME

Playwriting:
A Complete Guide to Creating Theater
(McFarland, 1990)

LIBRARY OF CONGRESS CATALOGUING-IN-PUBLICATION DATA

Frome, Shelly, 1935–
The Actors Studio : a history / by Shelly Frome.
p.   cm.
Includes bibliographical references and index.

ISBN 0-7864-2320-X (softcover : 50# alkaline paper) ∞

1. Actors Studio (New York, N.Y.)—History.   I. Title.
PN2078.U62 N37   2005   792'.028'097471—dc21   2001031610

British Library cataloguing data are available

Manufactured in the United States of America

On the cover: *"Times Square"* by Frank Federico

McFarland & Company, Inc., Publishers
Box 611, Jefferson, North Carolina 28640
www.mcfarlandpub.com

For Susan
and the days of Brando and Dean

Contents

Acknowledgments

I would like to thank Phoebe Brand, Frank Corsaro, Julie Harris and Elizabeth Stearns for deepening my understanding and to express my gratitude to the following people for also sharing their experiences and furnishing me with invaluable new information: Arthur Bartow, Robert Brustein, Keir Dullea, Dick Franchot, Andre Gregory, June Havoc, Israel Horovitz, Fred Kimball, Martin Landau, N. Richard Nash, Estelle Parsons, Bob Reynolds, Sam Schacht, Brett Somers and Rip Torn.

I am also grateful to the Research Foundation of the University of Connecticut for supporting my firsthand observations in New York and the U.K., and to Richard Fennegar, Tana Sibilio, Chilton Ryan and Nafe Katter for acting as an intermediary on my behalf. Lastly, I am especially grateful to my wife, Susan, for typing the final draft, dealing with a new and frequently problematic word processing program, and helping me keep a sense of balance.

Prologue

It's been said that America is a clash of ideas and personalities, a contest between insiders and outsiders, a freewheeling quest for attainment. Firmly rooted in this tradition is the Actors Studio, a secluded workshop that in one way or another has had a marked influence on the stage and screen. Unfortunately most accounts have been fraught with so many overstatements, it's become difficult to sift through all the hyperbole and find the linkages and the vital interplay. Over time the significance and the true stories seem to have been lost.

As a case in point, at the turn of the 21st century a television program focused on Lee Strasberg, a longtime artistic director. Part of a series on the Arts and Entertainment network, "Biography" was immediately preceded by a promo on secret societies. Modulating his voice, the announcer declared that "membership has its privileges and its price." Ostensibly, viewers were being induced to stay tuned to two similar shows: Strasberg and the Studio and the exposé which followed—both investigating mysterious and notorious practices. Presently, the same announcer intoned that Strasberg was a god who held the keys to stardom; proclaimed a genius by some and a madman by others. His celebrated pupils had been nominated for over a hundred Academy Awards, all due to his method which was responsible for a new kind of acting (cut to film clips from the movies of Marlon Brando and James Dean and, momentarily, shots and clips of Marilyn Monroe).

Early on there was a glimpse of Strasberg at work in the recesses of a small converted church in mid-town Manhattan. Here, for about forty seconds, he was shown performing some kind of psychotherapy, attempting to draw out a past experience from an actress' life. In a later segment, Monroe, "Hollywood's greatest star," was featured, reportedly seeking acting lessons from the world's "greatest teacher." In so doing, she was compelled to dredge up painful memories from her hazy past and "suffered tragic consequences." In this same portion Strasberg was characterized as a person "intoxicated by adulation and publicity," relinquishing his prior high-minded elitism in favor of Hollywood commercialism. As

a direct result, he left the mark of the Studio on the cinema and an enduring legend—all of this as an outsider who wished to achieve more and, thereby, became
a "patron saint."

     After an hour of these overblown claims and misleading shot sequences, the
viewer was left with a mix of inconsistencies. The viewer was also left with false
impressions, including the mistaken belief that actors like Brando and Dean
learned their craft at the Studio under Strasberg's guidance, as did all the other
celebrities, most of whom were unnamed. Moreover, neurosis was linked with the
theories of the great Russian actor, director and teacher Constantin Stanislavsky,
labeling Stanislavsky as "Strasberg's hero." This particular diffusion of fact and
fiction only added to the conundrum. Except for a fleeting mention of the debate
between Stella Adler and Strasberg, the true clash of ideas and personalities within
the context of changing times was bypassed in favor of sensationalism.

     Then again—all considerations of viewer entertainment aside—a major rea-
son for the misinformation and confusion may stem from the fact that the Studio, like its predecessor the Group Theater of the 1930s, does function like a secret
society behind closed doors.

     Another difficulty lies in contradictory acts of self-promotion. As it happens,
another program entitled "Inside the Actors Studio" ran simultaneously on the
Bravo channel. At first glance the opening credits seemed promising. A pair of
oversized blue wooden doors opened out invitingly. The doors did belong to the
actual Studio on West 44th St. (although they are white, not blue). Images of James
Dean, Marilyn Monroe, Paul Newman, Dustin Hoffman and other idols flashed
by, followed by a glimpse inside the same theater space where Strasberg was
glimpsed holding court in the "Biography" profile. A sign read: "Quiet. Work in
Session." Suddenly everything switched to a large auditorium at the New School
of Social Research at the opposite end of town. Seated in the packed house were,
predominantly, a group of students from a three-year M.F.A. program.

     On stage, a moderator introduced the celebrity of the week. Speaking in
hushed, reverential tones, he recounted the guest's awards and accolades, showed
film highlights and sought out telling events that shaped his or her career. The interview was followed by a previously taped question-and-answer session in progress.
The students' queries focused mainly on practical matters—e.g., working in movies,
how do you handle this situation or that?, what are the opportunities? etc.

     Subsequent airings proved that many, if not most, of the personalities who
continued to appear—like Jack Lemmon, Steven Spielberg, Lauren Bacall, Carol
Burnett, Meryl Streep, Anthony Hopkins, Julia Roberts, Jerry Lewis, Sylvester
Stallone, etc.—were not associated with the workings of the Studio or its forebear. In fact, during one questioning session the comic actor Nathan Lane made
fun of animal exercises attributed to Method actors. During another segment,
John Hurt, the noted British actor, imitated Dame Edith Evans, stating, "I pretend, dear boy. I pretend." Counter to an approach that supposedly insists on emotional recall and living the part, Hurt spoke of sophisticated pretense, text analysis,
visual imagery, vocal adjustments and the extraordinary as opposed to the real.

Admittedly, from time to time you might come across a rerun featuring a seasoned Studio member or someone who had taken Strasberg's private classes. You would then have discovered, say, the actress Sally Field talking about forgoing her commercial career, going into therapy and reveling in self-disclosure. You would have also caught her during the question-and-answer period chiding a young actress for her reluctance to expose her private and deepest feelings.

During another of these tapings, you might have also noted the host nodding toward the student audience every time a Studio guest uttered a key phrase like "using that side of me" or "stretching myself a bit." In those moments, wearing the mantle of the dean of the school, the host made comments like, "You see? What did I tell you?" In those same moments, he seemed to be promoting a particular philosophy of acting and one could have hoped that the title of the program held some promise, that some aspect of the controversy would be further disclosed. But nothing of the kind was allowed to take place. When, for example, the actor Paul Newman actually mentioned his admission to the Studio on the basis of acute anxiety mistaken for talent, Newman's remarks were disregarded. When Newman dismissed his work in the film *The Left-Handed Gun* as misguided, his comment was sloughed off.

Undaunted, an intrepid viewer could have rented the video. As it happens, this particular movie was made during the heyday of the Method (1958). It was also Studio director Arthur Penn's first feature, loosely based on Billy the Kid's career. Here you find Newman sitting still as the camera moves in, wrinkling his brow, straining his eyes as if in deep thought as a voice off-camera reads a passage from the bible. In another sequence, he slows down the delivery of his lines, gazing past two other actors as though in a trance. Another time, in the aftermath of an aborted fast-draw contest, Newman smiles, suddenly draws his six-shooter, clenches his fist as he screams, drops his voice to a whisper, glares, and pauses. Then, deliberately spacing each of his lines, he unclenches his fist and lets the gun slip to his side. At the opening of another scene, Newman doesn't just wait in the doorway and listen to the conversation in the foreground. Instead, he raises one knee, drops his head, closes his eyes, crosses his arms and holds this pose until the end of the exchange. A moment later, he returns to his trance mode outside the shack, holding onto the dangling rope above him, swaying slowly back and forth, muttering to himself, "Go on ... run ... I don't need you..." as if playing only to the camera.

The point is, it was this kind of stylized acting that Newman was trying to disown, a topic the host-producer deftly avoided. Issues could have been addressed, students in the audience and viewers at home could have been notified of an actual process: a collaborative effort by a Studio director and actor to graft a 1950s brand of behavior on a legendary figure of the Old West. The conversation could have led to Newman's far superior effort years later in *The Verdict* and his honest, understated and thoughtful portrayal of the failed lawyer Frank Galvin and his search for redemption. The discussion could have included the marked difference between performance and private experience. Lee Strasberg's techniques might have been mentioned. In a sense, the interview could have actually taken viewers "Inside the Actors Studio."

Regrettably, this program, like the "Biography" profile and so many writings on the subject, has something else in mind. Which leaves us with the same inklings of a method without a significant end; an amorphous Studio without distinction or heritage; a notorious guru without virtues, flaws and human dimension; a role call of stars whose true affiliations are unknown; and an obscure Group Theater hovering in the background.

Also among the missing is, perhaps, the most influential figure of them all: Elia Kazan, the founder of the Studio. And what of the Russian master Constantin Stanislavsky and all the other notables in between? And what of the Studio for the new millennium? Is it really passé, as an article in *The New York Times* intimated, hopelessly out of touch with the changes and fractured nature of contemporary life? Is it true that "after all, the Method is useless … the Group is dead" and actually going "inside the Actors Studio" doesn't matter very much?

For my part, there has always been this sense of unfinished business, like coming across a provocative mystery whose meaning lay hidden beneath the lines. My first involvement centered entirely on acting technique. I was a fledgling actor lost in the maze of the New York theater scene. The only thing I had going for me, it seems, was some kind of lively believability. I was therefore billed by agents as a Method actor. The only trouble was that I didn't have a clue what the Method was. Rumor had it that it emanated from the Actors Studio. After a preliminary audition, I was called back because they liked my flair but wanted to see "something else." I assumed they were looking for total relaxation and naturalism. I guessed wrong. The secret keys to the art of acting remained concealed behind those white doors.

Later on, in an encounter with Elia Kazan I hoped to be cast in his Broadway production of Tennessee Williams' *Sweet Bird of Youth*. Williams had used me during the original tryout in Coral Gables, Florida. It was a bit part and he liked my laugh. Kazan demurred, holding out for a true southerner well over six feet. I was two or three inches too short. It was type-casting. I had assumed the so-called internal approach used a different set of standards. Once again I was wrong.

Studying with Uta Hagen and Gene Frankel kept me on the periphery: quasi–Method acting exercises (endowing an empty suitcase with weight, trying to conjure up the sensation of warm bath water, etc.) with no discernible application. Roles Off Broadway didn't help. I was "performing," my fellow aspiring actors advised me. Performing was not the object. To audiences I was an effective Method actor; to those who knew better, I had missed the mark. The elusive way supposedly used by the likes of Brando and Dean continued to elude me.

On the second pass over a decade later, I found myself inside the Studio conducting research for a graduate thesis. Although my perspective had broadened considerably, I was still seeking the path to that realm they had called "something else." During the twice-weekly sessions I witnessed many things. A woman removed her clothing and paraded around aimlessly; an actor renowned for his comic timing focused solely on mundane tasks, completely oblivious of the Studio members in attendance; couples engaged in scenes they had written with no beginning or end. In response, I heard Strasberg wearily ask for intentions. Then, using the word "we" to indicate that all present surely must agree with his pronouncements, he asserted that either the intentions weren't fully carried out or "the work" was not understood. When I tried to pin Strasberg down about his own intentions, I was given short shrift. As if I were a novice. Looking back I see that, essentially, he was right.

However, while I was observing I thought of the great plays of Williams and Miller that went beyond the purely natural and crossed the artificial boundary between the real and the poetic. Plays that embraced big audiences, addressed to anyone; not overly intellectual but struggles that met you on your own terms. The closest I came to this ideal was a critique by Harold Clurman on an evening in March. The occasion was a showing of a work in progress by the actor/playwright Michael Gazzo. As I recall, the proceedings took place around a living room table in a sparse area of the Studio. In response, Clurman (the spiritual founder of the Group Theater) questioned the purpose beyond the display of authentic working class dialogue and a family's typical behavior. How did it transcend the real into something more vital and meaningful we can all relate to and understand?

When I asked the same question of Studio members, their answers inevitably shifted to their own individual quirks, expressive difficulties and, in one instance, a need for an authoritarian father figure. Nothing cohered. I found myself inside a members-only-club, a place to hang out between acting jobs, a shelter from the wind, snow and rain. There was no sign of the vibrant immediacy that I had found in the films of my favorite actors, John Garfield, Montgomery Clift, Julie Harris, Brando and Dean. No hint of the influence of Kazan. No trace of the volatile excitement that had inspired me in the first place and prompted me to try my hand. I was in the right place at the wrong time. Or perhaps I was just standing too close.

After a time, while grappling with Kazan's rambling autobiography, I came upon a passage that struck a chord. Among his recollections was an image of Strasberg strutting past the TV camera on a variety show called "Night of 100 Stars." A chorus girl was attached to Strasberg's left arm, his right arm left free to doff his top hat, his features somber and tense. To Kazan, what registered across Strasberg's face was denial and disapproval of what he was doing for publicity's sake. For Kazan, the moment was also a betrayal of the spirit of the Studio and the memory of fervent years long since past.

Kazan's notation of this moment of regret led me to accounts of the history of the Group Theater and their revolutionary ideals. From there I secured an interview with Phoebe Brand, an integral member of the legendary Group. The Brand interview led me back to the linchpin, the Group's guiding light.

The Moscow Art Theatre

In my reexamination of the Moscow Art Theatre under Stanislavsky's leadership, I came upon the prototype of the non-method Method actor and the source of it all: the First Studio—Stanislavsky's experimental arm, the spiritual ancestor of my subject. What the Actors Studio was supposedly all about.

It appears that at the outset Stanislavsky was pursuing the freshness of inspiration, a certain spark that would insure the illusion of the first time: every occasion actors and audiences came together, every instance a director attempted to bring a playwright's vision to life performance after performance. He found this kind of total absorption watching children at play. He found it watching Isadora Duncan dance when she visited Moscow—barefoot, daring and dynamic, freely moving to strains of classical music and her intuitive response to images of ancient Greece. He discovered it watching street performers cavorting and improvising. He experienced this intense, expansive state when he, himself, was in love. All tension disappeared. He merged with any role he played. Through faith, imagination and complete naiveté he seemed to radiate with this special energy. As did Duncan, the incomparable Salvini, and Stanislavsky's own protégés like Vakhtangov, Meyerhold and Michael Chekhov in subsequent experimental studios attached to the parent company.

His methods altered in pursuit of this heightened state. As he pointed out in *My Life in Art* (1924), he had "lived a variegated life" during the course of which he found himself impelled "more than once" to change his ideas in pursuit of this fundamental goal. As a teenager, he noted that what the actor may feel is not always what the audience sees. He also realized that actors are more effective when they play parts that are the opposite of their own personality. When he began his first theater he discovered that in playing opposites—an evil man looking for goodness, a young man searching for signs of decrepitude and illness, etc.—characterizations became much fuller and unpredictable.

The first of the studios, in short, was a workshop dedicated to the extension of his theories, a testing ground to find solutions to new styles and philosophies (like symbolism) in order to bring them to life. Underscoring the true nature of his work was his association with a free spirit by the name of Leopold Sulerzhitsky. Because of his open, childlike nature, this non-actor became irreplaceable and was affectionately dubbed "Suler." Together they experimented. When realism and naturalism were deemed too superficial for the times, only capturing the obvious (what everyone could see and hear), Suler and Stanislavsky sought a spiritual depth, a deeper communication with the audience. Yoga came into play with its resultant calm, certainty of purpose, as did the Hindu Prana (invisible waves of energy). They engaged in vocal and movement explorations for their beauty, truth and logic. Believing more and more that the imitation of everyday realities was a facade hiding deeper longings, they continued to explore. Through these probes, they looked for ways to delve beneath the self-deceptions and masks people exhibited in public, to expose them and reveal life's hidden agenda.

In the plays of Chekhov, Stanislavsky found undercurrents of melancholy in keeping with the Russian soul. But, then again, through Suler's warm and energetic personality, the opposite was found: the surprises, the contradictions that were part and parcel of the Russian temperament as in their joyful adaptation of Dicken's *The Cricket on the Hearth*.

Under the auspices of the MAT all of these ideas were tested, always in flux, evolving and subject to change. Ever seeking a balance between realism and poetry, always looking for that special communion through inspiration and audience response, and always serving the author's vision.

With these principles in mind, I began to piece the puzzle back together. I soon realized that, like trading goods, aspects of Stanislavsky's work were imported to America, exchanged, mixed and blended. Transactions were sometimes heated as personalities clashed, new alliances were formed and cultural products and commerce became intertwined. Most of these personalities were outsiders trying to become insiders, caught in the context of their times and their view of the American dream.[1]

This understanding was then deepened through probing conversations with additional key figures: people who had been involved in this interplay, individuals who represented a broad range of viewpoints and experiences. What follows is an attempt to set the entire dynamic in motion in order to capture what was gained by the Americanization of Stanislavsky's legacy and what was lost. What follows is a search for engaging ideas, life stories, the give and take of the creative process and something of value at every turn.

1

Beginnings

For Americans in the arts, the 1920s were heady years. Intellectuals discovered and nurtured an authentic native voice in literature, music, and photography. Expatriate life in Paris for F. Scott Fitzgerald, Ernest Hemingway and others included concerts by the avant garde composers Schoenberg and Stravinsky, the radical innovations in painting by Picasso, Matisse, and Duchamp, and the theatrical experiments of Jean Cocteau and Jacques Copeau.

Back at home, Manhattan alone had well over two million people riding subways and streetcars uptown and downtown till all hours of the night, feeling safe to walk anywhere and everywhere through Harlem or the dimly lit stretches of the Lower East Side. For all kinds of news and views there were 250 weeklies, 450 monthly journals and magazines. For immigrants there were dailies in French, German, Italian, Bohemian, Croatian, Serbian, Arabic, Yiddish, Ukrainian and at least a dozen other languages. Political views were reflected on the right by *The Globe*, *The Mail* and *The Herald Tribune*; in the middle by *The Times*, *The World* and *The Sun*; *The Evening Post* represented enlightened liberal opinion while the tenets of socialism were advanced by *The Call*.

As always, New York was indifferent to the lives of its inhabitants but—again, as always—its aloof laissez-faire was liberating. It was within this exuberant, blunt, boisterous city during this era one could find an unrivaled concentration of genius and a whirligig of ideas about politics, art and life—a virtual melting pot that never stopped bubbling and reinventing itself, seeking old connections while experimenting with new variations. It was a time and a place right after the Great War where, for a decade at least, opportunity was everywhere. It was around the corner. There were issues under debate in the lecture halls; there was talk of change in and around Washington Square. Creative activity was homegrown and, at the same time, sparked by notions and explorations from across the sea.

Part of this ferment was the explosion of theatrical energy called the "little theater movement" which experimented with different forms in search of audiences for serious drama. Eugene O'Neill, Maxwell Anderson, Elmer Rice, Sidney Howard, Paul Green and John Howard Lawson were among those who were writing plays about the American Scene, honing their own distinctive native style. In Greenwich Village, the Provincetown Players staged the early works of O'Neill in a small rented space on Macdougal Street. A host of pocket theaters flourished throughout lower Manhattan as well, offering plays in English and other languages.

Solidly situated within this ambiance lay The Neighborhood Playhouse, with its insistence that the theater had a vital role to play in the community. Inspired by its thrust and example, smaller ventures began to blossom like The Students of Arts and Drama Club at the Chrystie Street Settlement House. Through these social outlets young immigrants and first-generation Americans who thought they had no connection with American culture became part of the excitement of the little theaters. And it's within this backdrop that the Americanization in question began to unfold.

At places like the Grand Street Theatre on the Lower East Side, the Yiddish theater brought productions of classic drama (Shakespeare, Tolstoy, Chekhov and Gogol) to life in performances of extraordinary realism by actors like Jacob Adler, Boris Thomashevsky and David Kessler. Their work featured outpourings of emotions and a vital "full acting style" along with an intense relationship among actors and between audiences; creating a special sense of theatre as a gathering place for the community; unconsciously reflecting a portion of Suler and Stanislavsky's dream.

Adding a jolt to this fermentation, the Moscow Art Theater arrived on the scene in 1923 and presented a series of productions at Al Jolson's Fifty-Ninth Street Theatre. In two seasons in New York, the Russians presented over a dozen plays from their repertory—original productions with most of the original casts including Gorky's *The Lower Depths* and four Chekhov plays: *The Three Sisters*, *The Cherry Orchard*, *Uncle Vanya* and *Ivanov*. On display was the same ensemble effort of the Jewish Art Theatre but much more: a seasoned three-dimensional sense of living the part by every one of the actors. Maria Ouspenskaya in the minor role of the governess in *The Cherry Orchard* had the same conviction and inner truthfulness as Stanislavsky, who portrayed Gayev; Leo Bulgakov playing a small role in *The Sea Gull* was in no way inferior to Vassily Katchalov as the Baron in *The Three Sisters*.

By implication, there had to be some singular process or procedure that made these results possible. It was obviously a band of players who had the benefits of similar training, years of practical experience in working together. It was a group that enjoyed the luxury of time to work on a body of distinguished native plays. It was a company that reveled in agreed-upon aims and ideals.

In marked contrast, the Broadway scene at the time featured stars: Katharine Cornell, the Barrymores, Laurette Taylor, Helen Hayes, the Lunts, Ina Claire, Jeanne Eagles, etc. They embodied glamour and exhibited ready-made personalities. They appeared in hit-or-miss shows supported by a great deal of money and technical know-how—lavish displays like *No, No, Nanette, Showboat, The Ziegfeld Follies, George White's Scandals* and Irving Berlin's *Music Box Revues*. In short, there were "names" and would-be "names" appearing in open-ended runs, lasting as long as the market would bear. There were no fundamental, sustaining ideas about theater, no system of training, no disciplined ensemble devoted to their art. It was all about product and marketing.

To some who viewed this contrast between the MAT and the present state of affairs, it was the difference between capitalism and something much more profound. Members of the audience found moments and scenes especially haunting in *The Brothers Karamazov*. For example, Katchaloff as Ivan suffers through an extended monologue in which he pits two sides of his soul in a tortured debate; Moskvin as Smerdyakof, after losing his integrity over money matters, painfully attempts to retain one last, tragic claim to honor. In these instances, the actors seemed to be submerging themselves in their parts, transforming themselves physically and spiritually. Unlike the stars of the American stage who put on a prefabricated persona from role to role, these actors appeared to remake themselves and literally lose themselves in the given circumstances of each play.

One critic of *The Times* referred to the acting as "an intense revelation of the soul ... a characteristically Russian quality, a Slavic gift of the persistently illumined countenance."

This was the positive general impression at the time. It was startling compared with what passed for the norm to see actors working with their backs to the audience. It was unnerving to see performers so engrossed behind an invisible fourth wall.

On the other hand a number of critics found it degrading, a total departure from the American ideal of decent lives where no one carried on. For a body of theatergoers the Russian repertory was immersed in neuroses, fixating on the inner demons of troubled characters indulging themselves in emotional displays. These audience members couldn't relate to the messages beneath the lines and spontaneous outbursts. They also couldn't relate to a closely knit group that seemed to be living their own private lives, at times remaining so absolutely still, so deep in concentration, that they made the onlookers feel as if they were intruding.

From another point of view all of this was old-fashioned. In the years leading up to and following the Revolution, Russian theatre diverged into different camps. Meyerhold's extreme forays into theatricality—theater not as life but as spectacle, carnival and bacchanal—were in opposition to his mentor Stanislavsky's preference for some retention of lifelike behavior. And, by 1922, Vakhtangov had already modified his master's original precepts in a few notable productions in which he fused Meyerhold's use of physicality, gesture and mime and Stanislavsky's inner work. In essence, each effort was given Stanislavsky's blessing. After all, he himself worked in everything from Shakespeare to opera. In point of fact, he set up a series of studios beyond his own First Studio in order for others to explore—where anti-realist ideas could be tried out, abandoned or absorbed into the parent company itself; where styles like impressionism, which in 1905 was already established in the other arts, could be tested and applied. Nothing was to be regarded as fixed, rigid or defined.

Besides, everyone in the touring company realized the style they were using reflected the old realism. They had played these parts for years. It was like a concert of old favorites.

To illustrate, we can look at Vakhtangov's work shortly before his death in 1921, two years before the tried-and-true work of the MAT reached American shores. Vakhtangov was Stanislavsky's favorite student. Through a captivating staging of Carlo Gozzi's *Turandot* in the Third Studio in Moscow he captured the essence of Stanislavsky's quest. To begin with, *Turandot* utilized multiple acting styles, alternating between open sincerity to ridiculous clowning and improvisation (both feigned and real), social parody and a high degree of theatricality. Vakhtangov explored the entire gamut of Stanislavsky's love of heightened states of expressiveness. The theater became an event, like going to a fine restaurant. No fourth wall, no attempt to hide the setting, doormen, chefs and inner workings. On the contrary, the theater afforded the customer-spectators with a complete festive experience. The theater was a place for joy and celebration.

In keeping with this often childlike "fantastic realism," the actors made their costumes out of simple materials: a tennis racket for a scepter; a torn towel for a beard. And when a performer professed that her evil character in this Mandarin court of ancient China went against her own nature, Vakhtangov told her to fantasize that she was not Adelma but a Commedia performer playing Adelma. In like manner, the actors greeted the audience near the cloakroom and in the aisles, commenting on the show and the day's events. To assure the audience that nothing would be hidden, the actors donned their costumes and put on their makeup in full view. During an emotional monologue about the death of a parent, a second actor ran on stage to collect the tears and showed them to the audience.

To demonstrate further the lengths to which Vakhtangov took his master's teachings, he once changed his physical stance and sank ball after ball while playing billiards. When his roommate, Michael Chekhov, asked how he managed this feat, Vakhtangov simply replied that he decided to imagine that he was the greatest pool player who ever lived and took on that posture, attitude and manner of play.[2]

Michael Chekhov, in turn (who, as it happens, was the nephew of the MAT's favorite playwright Anton Chekhov and, according to the master, a brilliant pupil) devised a super-imaginative approach to characterization, altering each character he played through movement, makeup and extraordinary psychological gestures. For instance, in playing an alcoholic, Chekhov imagined that each part of his body was dying in a separate, agonizing way. Inspiration was derived from imagery and the charged almost mystical atmosphere of the stage itself: a bewitching aura fused with fictional, external stimuli outside one's personal experience.

All of these examples point up the fact that what New Yorkers were witnessing at the Fifty-ninth Street Theater in Manhattan was not, in fact, revolutionary.

And anyone would be remiss to capsulize Stanislavsky the actor/director/theorist/teacher on the basis of this one phase of his work.

Understandably however, for those who hadn't grown up in Russia, hadn't experienced its Golden Age of theater and weren't privy to the Russian love of dialectic and counterpoint—e.g., modernistic and traditional, logical and emotional, realistic and extraordinary—the performances by the MAT were not a throwback. For a few particular first-generation Americans avidly involved in the theater whose world consisted of Broadway, the pocket theaters and the Yiddish theater, the MAT was the wave of the future. And it's here, through their eyes—taking into account what they understood and felt—that our story actually starts.

The one most taken by Stanislavsky's troupe was, arguably, Harold Clurman. Tall, gregarious, the son of Russian Jewish immigrants, he was more privileged than most of those in his circle and a step ahead. He had taken a break from his studies at Columbia and traveled to Paris in 1921 with his friend, the musician and composer Aaron Copland. There he encountered firsthand that special time and place where so much experimentation was going on all at once. Among his many delights was the opportunity to hear Cocteau lecture. He also managed to see touring productions by the Moscow Art Theatre before they reached New York.

After writing a thesis for the Sorbonne on French drama, he returned to Manhattan in the summer of 1924 seeking the kind of stimulation and interplay Copland and his fellow musicians found in the rhythms of modern life. Clurman wanted to link this energy to the teeming realities he discovered on the streets of New York. He recalled Jacques Copeau's unified theater and actor training and what Copeau perceived as a common artistic language. Clurman also thought of the fervent unity of the Yiddish theater in his old neighborhood. He longed for an Americanization built of the same tradition. He was taken with the emotional intensity of Jacob Adler, the renowned Yiddish actor. He admired the expressive work of Adler's daughter Stella and soon found himself romantically involved. All of what he perceived and longed for served as a prime catalyst.

At the same time, Stella Adler's perception and experiences as a professional actress enhanced Clurman's understanding. The Yiddish theater was a self-contained subculture. Stella performed in any venue, equally at home in an American drama at the Neighborhood Playhouse in the Village as she was in a sentimental comedy featuring her father Jacob on the Lower East Side.[3] She was flamboyant but could also adapt to a Copeau and MAT-like ensemble that reflected the upbeat tempo and tone of the twenties. Through his relationship with Miss Adler, Clurman was beginning to see possible applications, fusing his abstract notions of fervency, unity, and tradition with a contemporary, fresh relevance injected into the American theater.

Because he was worldly and articulate, and because theater is a collaborative art, there was no one more suited to inspire potential collaborators than Harold Clurman. What he needed next, even more than Stella Adler's example of exuberant professionalism, was someone who understood exactly how Stanislavsky's acting system worked, could train Americans and was serious and dedicated enough to share in his vision.

As it happens, the key person Clurman would align himself with had other qualities which would prove to be problematic. But for this moment in time, it was Clurman, the hope of a romantic/professional liaison with Stella Adler, an aim that had yet to be clearly formulated, and a controversial and highly enigmatic figure waiting in the wings.

Lee Strasberg

In a sense, there is a great similarity between the Lee Strasberg who appears as Hyman Roth the gangster in *The Godfather Part II* and the person Harold Clurman began to associate with in the mid–1920s. It's as if the director Francis Ford Coppola had followed Elia Kazan's dictum of finding a person who, in essence, is the character because the camera is so penetrating it exposes everything. There, projected on the screen, is a small, slight figure with a guarded look in his eye— plainspoken with a disregard for intonation, pitch, or the rhythmic possibilities of speech. The voice is harsh, flat, tired and wary, tinged with a distinct New York accent; picked up, perhaps, from the days he manufactured women's hairpieces and learned that business was business and time was money. Here also is a paternalistic coolness, employed to gain dominance and respect. Along with the coolness is a palpable threat of anger which is barely contained: the demeanor of a man who, unlike Clurman, had never gone to college, never finished high school for personal reasons, but was bound and determined to carve out a niche for himself through sheer determination.

As a result, Strasberg, in life as well as on the screen, generated an aura about him, an intimidating force. As Bobby Lewis (the future cofounder of the Actors Studio) tells it, it was immediately apparent the moment anyone encountered him. For Lewis, it happened during the first days of the Depression. He was basking in the glory of favorable notices for his "tender and sincere" portrayal of the anarchist Vanzetti, when Strasberg arrived backstage at the Provincetown Playhouse in the Village. Strasberg's question was delivered through taut lips and clenched teeth. "What—were—you—trying—to—do?" said Strasberg. Lewis was struck with guilt even though he had no idea what Strasberg was talking about. "Do you think that was real emotion you felt up there?" Strasberg continued. "You were just indicating."

"Indicating" Lewis discovered was a crime in the Strasberg lexicon. It meant you were acting, faking, not fully and personally involved. The accusation in that moment at the Provincetown Playhouse was so compelling that Lewis accepted him as an authority figure then and there.

Returning to the Godfather movie, the gangsters are as dutiful toward Strasberg-as-Roth as Bobby Lewis was years before, fearful that his temper might flare up perhaps, or simply afraid of the unknown. Roth lectures, makes pronouncements and then pulls back and lies in wait, as though trying to see through everyone's facade.

The contradiction (according to his son John) is that Lee Strasberg was never capable of expressing his own feelings and, therefore, became fixated in his desire to have others express theirs. An administrator who worked under Strasberg in the 1960s referred to this trait as "burning ice." On the other hand, if you run his initial scenes from the movie again, you can catch a glimmer of affection for the actor Al Pacino who secured the role for him. There is also a flicker of calm satisfaction when he portions out slices of his birthday cake. Like many a provocative and obscure personality, it takes an awareness of his background and way of processing information before one can begin to understand the nature of his effect on others.

An immigrant who came to America at the age of seven from the village of Budzanow (then part of Austria-Hungary), Strasberg was first exposed to the rich emotionality he coveted while watching the Yiddish theater on the Lower East Side. Later, in his early twenties, he began slipping away from his job in the ladies' wig business to join in theatrical projects at the Chrystie Street Settlement House. He also secluded himself in the world of books, becoming a self-taught scholar in the field of theater. Having no credentials (he never went beyond the 10th grade due to family needs), his apparent objective was to combine practical experience with enough knowledge to compensate for any of his shortcomings.

He fastened onto passages and phrases. He was especially taken with the dedication noted in Gordon Craig's *On the Art of the Theater*: "To the courageous individual in the world of the theatre who will some day master and remold it." He was also impressed with William Gillette's concept of the illusion of the first time; an historical account of the English actor Edmund Kean who was said to have had wild emotional power; and articles about Stanislavsky and his troupe which foretold of a unique seriousness, cohesiveness and aliveness on the stage.

By the time the MAT came onto the New York theatrical scene in 1923, Strasberg was totally predisposed. To his delight, their performances embodied his own concept of theater: a group of actors easily given to emotion, living truthfully behind an imaginary fourth wall. It was at this point that Strasberg began to separate the internal from the external. It may have been that Strasberg was not aware of the Russian love of dialectic, evolution and change; or Stanislavsky's work with Suler and his great appreciation of Vakhtangov's, Meyerhold's, and Michael Chekhov's sheer theatricality. Be that as it may, upon witnessing the MAT performances firsthand, Strasberg was convinced that Stanislavsky had formulated a unique way to stimulate and reveal innermost feelings on stage as if the actors were in the privacy of their own home. He felt there had to be a system, a practical approach. If only someone from the MAT were accessible and could show him the way.

Fortunately for Strasberg, because of the success of the MAT performances through May of 1924, the American Laboratory Theatre was founded on MacDougal Street by a group of wealthy American patrons. Their aim was to encourage, develop and implant a similar cultural force in the United States. To this end, Richard Boleslavsky (a former member of the MAT who had fled the Russian Revolution) and Maria Ouspenskaya (a current member of the troupe) were enlisted to inspire talented American students and urge them to develop their skills at the highest and deepest levels. To Strasberg, these two figures represented the key to the MAT's style of acting.

Like an impatient pragmatist, Strasberg enrolled for one semester and took what he needed. He zeroed in on Boleslavsky's lectures and Ouspenskaya's techniques. From Boleslavsky he took the concept that actors have one of two choices: they can either skillfully imitate or live their parts. This idea confirmed Strasberg's belief in the split between inner work, which was truthful, and outer work which was artificial. It was the difference between right and wrong.

Strasberg also learned that acting was an exacting art that demanded control in order to tap the desired authentic feelings. Even more importantly, he discovered that it was possible to systematically hone a sensory and emotional technique. By doing so, a teacher/director could lay the groundwork for a disciplined, collective effort—a facsimile of the MAT.

From Ouspenskaya's acting class, Strasberg acquired the specific tools and a role model. "Madame" was slight of build and, with one piercing look, could take total command of a situation. Her intense and vehement criticism often brought her students to tears. In this way she broke through habitual defense mechanisms and provoked or released any given individual's emotionality. If you view this approach positively, it was an effective way to overcome fearfulness and self-consciousness and induce unforced truthful responses. Moreover, Strasberg felt that her powers of observation were astonishing along with her uncanny ability to put her finger on the solution to any actor's emotional blocks.

Evidently she didn't follow any prescribed routine but selected exercises to either stimulate her students or overcome their individual problems. Her devices included sense memories of meaningful past experiences, concentration exercises, and methods of physical relaxation. This work was carried out in the belief that an actor who can stand in an imaginary snow-drift with full conviction, and make an audience shiver as well, has mastered his art.

In these classes there was no mention of the gentle, free-spirited Suler, the range of Stanislavsky's explorations including his love of the Commedia, or Vakhtangov's belief in theatrical fantasy coupled with complete conviction and a joyous interplay with the audience. In Ouspenskaya's approach these considerations either didn't exist or weren't basic and fundamental.

With Strasberg focused on Ouspenskaya's techniques, we can turn back to Stella Adler as a third force in this emerging dynamic. As indicated, unlike Strasberg, she was a formidable professional when she enrolled at the Lab during this same period. In addition, she was outgoing and expansive. As a Russian Jew, she felt that the size, spirit and strength she admired in her father's performances were, by dint of genetics and her own work by his side, naturally flowing through her veins. Most importantly, she was able to incorporate the entire range of the

Lab's training including intensive work on the voice, body and intellect, and the incorporation of acting and movement through ballet adaptations called Plastique and Mimeodrama.

In Adler's mind the reality Ouspenskaya was looking for was an expression of Russian theatricality, which meant the submerging of one's identity into the demands of the role. The Boleslavsky lectures she attended emphasized the given circumstances of the play, not the actor's own circumstances. At the Lab, an actor was an artist who had developed all resources, both inner and outer, and could translate the training into expressive dramatic action. An actor was a performer who knew that the snow-drift was imaginary but could summon up the energy, feeling and technique to induce an audience to accept the illusion. In other words, Stella Adler's impressions of acting and the Stanislavsky system were quite different than Lee Strasberg's.

And so the stage was set for an eventual clash between two volatile personalities who had backgrounds and aspirations that were both similar and at odds. But for now these underlying issues were not an operative factor. By the spring of 1925 all was rife with promise and possibility fostered by the irrepressible spirit of Harold Clurman.

It was at this same time that Clurman met Strasberg at a casting call for the Theater Guild's *Garrick Gaities*. Both men wanted work in the theater, were drawn to Broadway where the action was, and disparaged the superficiality of it all at the same time. They found themselves debating over what could be done to redeem what they felt was a sorry state of affairs. In sharing their ideas, a fusion began to take place incorporating the notion of a company that was close in spirit to the MAT while growing out of native soil.

Needless to say, if the Theater Guild had been a true guild, a union of artisans banding together to promote and uphold common interests, Clurman and Strasberg would have taken their blossoming ideas to the board of directors for consideration. However, although the Guild aligned itself with well-crafted continental plays, its governing principle was commercial necessity. It mattered not that the themes of selected works were often pessimistic, the scripts unrelated to the times, the roles primarily frothy vehicles for stars like the Lunts. It mattered not that the actors only came together for rehearsals; the playwrights were distant literary figures; and ideals, a common way of working and a chance for continuity and growth were nonexistent. The Theater Guild offered polished production values and limited runs and that, for the most part, was that. As far as Clurman's wider vision and Strasberg's concept of realism were concerned, both men would either have to make do or put their ideas to the test.

Their exchanges continued. Through Clurman, Strasberg began to consider the influence of current social and political issues on new plays. Through Strasberg, Clurman began to perceive how the particular working process of actors and directors could impinge upon the staging of a playwright's work.

Soon Strasberg was exploring alternatives to the Guild, trying out and modifying Ouspenskaya's techniques on amateurs at the Chrystie Street Settlement.

The Group's founders: Cheryl Crawford, Lee Strasberg and the guiding spirit, Harold Clurman. (From the Billy Rose Theatre Collection, NY Public Library.)

There he employed what he called "adjustments"—ways of inducing people to personalize their parts. For example, to play Biblical kings and queens, he would tell his charges to think of themselves as priests or nuns, to consider how adapting themselves to that more familiar lifestyle would affect their behavior. During this same exploratory stage, Strasberg returned to the Lab (accompanied this time by Clurman) to study directing with Boleslavsky. However, since Boleslavsky was often absent and the course of study was disorganized, there is no telling what either of the two gained during this short course of study. The only significance being that the two were clearly eager to apply their budding theories.

A bit later, in 1927, Copeau came to New York to direct and lecture at the Lab. Clurman was finally inspired to stop his hedging and found a theater of his own. He and Strasberg then began discussing prospects in earnest: how exactly to form a company which, while drawing on primarily Russian sources, would become uniquely American. But they needed an interim step, some way to test the waters.

They continued to vacillate between stints as bit players and stage managers (plus playreading for Clurman) mainly for the Theater Guild, and privately seeking after some exploratory venue. The gregarious Clurman began talking openly about the need to start a new venture with anyone who would listen. One member of his audience was Cheryl Crawford, the Guild's casting director. Calm, sensible and efficient, with origins a long way off from the Lower East Side (Ohio and schooled at Smith), her interest in Clurman's opinions provided a vitally needed new dimension to the evolving enterprise. She brought to it a practical know-how and an administrative business sense. She could make something happen.

Still, the guiding light was Clurman. It was his Jazz Age optimism; his keen awareness of cultural influences; his critical understanding of dramatic literature; and his sensitivity to the fact that regardless of rampant artistic expression in New York, something essential was missing. He sensed a pervasive hunger for something deeper and cohesive, much bigger than the artist and his private world. He was aware that the little theater movement was fading and nothing being produced related to the realities of people's lives. As part and parcel of this widening gap, there was a fundamental lack of a common artistic language serving a unified cause and tapping the raw energy of the struggle and confusion of American life.

Through Crawford's intervention, and in deference to Clurman's fervor and Clurman and Strasberg's insistence, the Theater Guild allowed the triumvirate to experiment with special Sunday performances. Subscribers were given the option of sampling works beyond the Guild's usual fare of sophisticated comedies and arty American tragedies. But Clurman's choice of a soviet play with political overtones, the poor box office receipts coupled with the stock-market crash closed the project down. Ironically, it was these very same conditions and failure of the Sunday venture that thrust the Group Theater into being.

By 1930 everyone everywhere was restless. After the crash of '29, business underwent a series of declines. Production levels and commodity prices sank steadily. The people who still had jobs wondered how soon they might join the six million on the bread line. The banner of self-reliance quickly faded. The notion of shared feelings, thoughts and needs had great appeal. Any outlet that promised to transform isolation, anxiety and frustration into significant action was almost irresistible.

At the Steinway Hall, after all the Broadway shows had let out, twenty-seven actors (including Stella Adler) were mesmerized by Clurman's fervent talks. Unlike the hit or miss of the commercial theater and the fear evoked by the current conditions, Clurman's concept of a group theater offered the promise of continuity, artistic development and the possibility of changing people's lives. All the actors had to do was find the right material and work together.

Now, at last, after all the preliminaries, the stage was set. Not for a Sunday series, a workshop or another branch of the American Lab. The time was ripe for a theatrical revolution and a profound change of consciousness. Like the MAT, which provided a home for its actors and solace for its audiences during turbulent times, the Group Theater in America was born of necessity.

2

The Group Emerges

At first glance, the composition of this collective was highly diverse. Many, like Clurman, Adler and Strasberg, were children of immigrants; some were from the heartland of the Midwest; a few were from affluent East Coast families. In terms of theatrical experience, there was a marked disparity as well, with Stella Adler among the most professional and future playwright Clifford Odets listed among the bit players and beginners.

Even among those with similar backgrounds—like Robert Lewis with his foreign-born parents and his admiration of Jacob Ben-Ami, the great Yiddish actor—perceptions were not quite the same. For young Bobby it wasn't just Ben-Ami's deep, emotional expressiveness that was so captivating. To Lewis, the mystery and "greatness" of his performances emanated from his ability to be theatrical without losing his sense of inner truth. Ben-Ami's graphic choices, such as slowly, in a great sweeping arc, pointing the muzzle of a revolver toward his temple, illuminated the essence of his character—a weak man who was a failure even at killing himself—and manifested authentic feelings as well. In essence, Lewis's views were more aligned with Stella Adler's love of theatricality and acting with one's "blood and soul" than with Lee Strasberg's insistence on deep personal responses.[4]

But Lewis, the youngest member of the troupe at twenty-two, was still in awe of "General Lee." He recalled Strasberg's indictment of indicated emotions at the Provincetown Playhouse a short time before. Even though Lewis valued style and a melding of meaning and sincerity, he hadn't formulated any definite theories and was willing to go along for the greater good. He played small parts, helped stage-manage and stayed more or less in the background for about three years.

By the same token, at the outset the majority of the original twenty-seven were swept up in activities and rehearsals. By and large, everyone was studious, curious and eager to learn and grow: artistically united in their preference for unconventional forms, politically leaning toward the left. There were no foreseeable

The Group Theater company with (foreground, left to right) Lee Strasberg (glasses), Sandy Meisner (shins showing), Bobby Lewis (white shoes), and Harold Clurman (white pants). John Garfield (directly behind and between Lewis and Clurman) is directly in front of Elia Kazan (beside woman in white hat). (From the Billy Rose Theatre Collection, NY Public Library.)

problems. Clurman had raised money from sympathizers, even from the Guild itself. Everything was positively in motion.

There were, of course, strains of ambivalent behavior and tension. The matinee idol Franchot Tone often became aloof and went off on his own, caught between his liberal politics, his preference for a sophisticated life style and the call of Broadway and Hollywood. In addition, according to Clurman's account, Strasberg was a fanatic on the subject of emotion: "an inquisitor who was outraged by trick substitutes. Emotion was almost holy and Strasberg was its prophet."

Any strains, however, were balanced by those who were seasoned and were able to remain both clear-eyed and devoted. One of these was Phoebe Brand. Born in Syracuse, she had been encouraged since the age of four by a mother who was a producer of children's theater. Her initiation came by way of a "spectacular, magical and gorgeous" production of *Snow White*. At the Princess Theater in New York, she actually played a princess and copied her teacher Clare Tree Major because she was "worth copying." She also loved her British teacher of Shakespeare and resisted when Strasberg (whom she met at Major's school) quit in favor of the American Lab. She felt that Strasberg, with his raspy, New York accent and lack of theatricality, was unsuited for a life on the stage. And when the MAT came to town, her beloved Shakespeare teacher advised her that the work was too coarse to be worthwhile. In deference, Phoebe did not attend. But, by nature and through experience, she could appreciate both of these seemingly disparate worlds.

One strong linking element was the fact that Phoebe and many of her cohorts in the Group had worked for the Theater Guild. They had all agreed with Clur-man that there was something shallow about appearing in hit or miss shows that had nothing to do with their lives or the times. They appreciated the slick and charming technique and style of the Lunts. They admired their work ethic. But they too had wanted an American theater and a way to make a social statement. Drawn in by Morris Carnovsky, Sandy Meisner and other on-again off-again Guild actors plus the Sunday experiments, they liked the idea of living together for this first summer in Connecticut to forge a common technique.

Accepting Clurman's precept that any component of Stanislavsky's System was a means not an end, they gave themselves fully to exploring a new set of atti-tudes. Everything and everyone must serve the Group and, by extension, serve the play. In that bucolic enclave in Brookfield, Connecticut, they accepted Clur-man's analogy of the differing pursuits of Bach and Tchaikovsky—the former mak-ing the world's suffering his, the latter making his suffering the world's. In the back of their minds they were always on the side of Bach. But, also in the back of their minds, they knew they could only go so far. For the sake of their own integrity, each one reserved the right to have a mind of his own.

With the overall objective firmly understood, Strasberg was given a free hand to mold them into an ensemble. In this formative stage, it was forgivable that Stras-berg treated them like lazy students who had to be coerced. In order for the col-lective experiment to succeed, they needed to believe in their leaders. The new life they envisioned required that all and sundry devote themselves to the work. By and large, Strasberg's bouts of rage were discounted, the occasional heated dis-agreements overlooked. By and large, the first summer would be recalled as a har-monious success.

Utilizing what he had gleaned from Ouspenskaya at the American Lab and applied to amateurs at the Chrystie Street Settlement House, Strasberg stressed concentrated relaxation, improvisation, sense memory and affective (emotional) recall. He termed these techniques the heart of the Stanislavsky System—the way to authentic acting through the truthful response to imaginary stimuli.

Although Group members thought it humorous for Strasberg to yell at them while urging them to relax, they readily accepted the basic premise. They realized that while under stress they resorted to copying and relying on their old tricks. After all, imitation was all people like Phoebe Brand knew. It was the only way they knew to suit the expectations of a Theater Guild audience. But it had no cur-rency in dealing moment to moment with the realities of a situation. The char-acter was going through this for the first time. The character had no right to know. This concept was all so exciting and different.

To enhance this "truthful awareness" once they had reached the optimum relaxed state, Strasberg had them recreate everyday events through their senses—e.g., recall the taste and odor of a morning cup of coffee, the warm feel of the cup, the texture of the handle and saucer, etc. And, in turn, as they went through each of these acting etudes, the members kept in mind that the goal was to reach people with an appropriate play. Unique and interesting as the exercises were, the entire approach had no meaning unless the procedures amounted to something and were applied.

For *The House of Connelly* by Paul Green—a drama about the decline of the Old South, an aristocratic family fallen on hard times and the rise of the tenant-farmer class—Strasberg devised improvisations (just as he had done with his amateur group) based on situations surrounding the play. By engaging in farm work, digging imaginary potatoes and so forth as preparation, every part, no matter how small, was invested with some kind of worth in terms of the whole. Spontaneity and a sense of the life were continually stressed. Pushing the concept even further, Strasberg had the actors put their lines and stage directions aside, ad-libbing the scenes to break down verbal patterns and preconceived ideas. Only afterwards were they to learn the actual lines.

The most provocative technique was his insistence on affective memory, a device he claimed was the cornerstone of Stanislavsky's system. Before each entrance and prior to any peak moment, an actor was to "take a minute." Choosing a potent and appropriate memory from his or her private life, the actor was prompted to retrace, step by step through the senses, the actual occurrence: what do you see? what sounds do you hear? are there any distinct odors? The theory was that emotions could only be induced indirectly. When it came to strong emotions, for Strasberg nothing less than the real thing would do.

Again, since it was all so novel and because Strasberg insisted it was the key to the essence of the MAT, everyone went along. One could "take a minute" for a longer period offstage or, for the sake of expediency, narrow the sensory springboard down to one or two.

To broaden their training, Clurman made certain that the actors were provided with other tools, other classes given by other teachers during this intense first summer: vocal exercises, a form of modern dance to free the body, etc. But the primary focus was on Strasberg's teaching and preparation for his professional directorial debut.

Because it was their initial production and because Clurman wanted to give hope to people during the Depression, he persuaded playwright Paul Green to change his gloomy ending and transform the final scene into a cry of affirmation. Clurman claimed that even though the play was of a bygone era, to be of any worth it had to speak to the present time and enable the actors to make a statement they could fully support. And because the play extolled the virtues of youth over age, the young triumphing over the old order, the actors also needed to tailor their roles to their own lives in keeping with Strasberg's technique. Even Stella Adler (with her rich background and training) and Eunice Stoddard, who equally had had a great deal of training and experience, freely lent their expertise to this radical way of dealing with a text. So did Phoebe Brand. So did they all: caught up in a world seeking a form of politics, arts and letters—any kind of ideology that had the potential to revitalize and sustain.

Encouraged by their collaborative spirit, Strasberg extended the improvs and "personal adjustments." In a climactic second-act scene, he directed Franchot Tone to wait in the wings until he heard the gunshot signaling his uncle's death. At the same time, actors offstage who had been "taking a minute" to personalize their response to the woeful news were to begin keening and crying out. Tone was then free to run on at will; sometimes spotting the "farmers" in time to recoil back into the room; at other times finding himself shoved back by the force of the people carrying Uncle Bob's corpse.

On balance, however, something was amiss. For one thing, it was a stretch for many of the actors to convincingly play southerners. It was especially difficult for those who had to portray aristocrats from the Old South enraptured with a bygone culture and lost causes. Moreover, Strasberg's approach couldn't accommodate Paul Green's employment of field hands as both symbolic figures of doom hovering over the house and representations of the rhythm of life. Nor could his way of working deal with other emblems of fate, ecstasy and prejudice. Lastly, by convincing Green to alter the ending in which the tenant farm girl Patsy is strangled to death by two old maidservants portraying remnants of the slave past, Clurman undermined the integrity of the play.

No matter. As far as the Group was concerned, the mounting of *The House of Connolly* was an auspicious beginning. The perfect combination of an ideal play for their company and the times and an exhilarating audience response was on the horizon.

For the time being however, the more they believed in their identity as a true collective, the more their dutiful attitude began to shift as a matter of course. Members became reluctant to leave all decisions in the hands of the leaders. Under the influence of organizations like the Theatre Union and Theatre Collective, an actors' committee was formed which sought democratic procedures. President Roosevelt urged all citizens to rise up and do their part, take some initiative in pulling America out of the Depression. Clurman had spurred the troupe with talk of artistic freedom and growth. They were no longer commodities but thinking people with a voice. By the summer of 1933, some had defected, gone to Hollywood or taken roles in Broadway shows. By that same summer, new people had come into the fold. Hardly anyone was still intimidated by the possible anger or presence of Lee Strasberg.

Given all these factors—including the goals of the Group, the particular mix of temperaments and the allegiance to Clurman as the leader and mediator—it was inevitable that Strasberg would be unable to maintain his role as a parental authority. Perhaps if he had felt less pressure to prove himself as a director and top his success as a man who could mold an ensemble, he might have been able to pull back. Perhaps if he hadn't tried to combine his notion of Broadway success with his understanding of the techniques of the MAT there wouldn't have been the contradiction between relaxation and submitting to his will, inspiration and the imperative to "take a minute" no matter how personally painful or inhibiting. Perhaps if there hadn't been the threat that others might follow Franchot

Tone seeking the lure of fame and Hollywood, Strasberg might have been content to loosen the reins. By all accounts, however, loosening the reins under any circumstances was not in Strasberg's nature.

To be fair, there are indications of possible moments of release. For instance, during one production he asked Bobby Lewis to be funny at several intervals. (Strasberg knew of no sensory or personalized way to derive laughter and had to rely on Lewis' innate sense of humor and style.)

Nevertheless, as things progressed from production to production, the tension between Strasberg and the actors began to proliferate. He became furious when Phoebe Brand refused to call up delicate memories from her past. The technique not only unnerved her, it kept throwing her out of the reality of the play in question. He became more and more indignant at any sign of insubordination. By this stage the ideals of collective harmony and artistic freedom and growth while making a significant impact on people's lives was tangled up with the problems of dealing with their difficult teacher/director.

At one point, during a rehearsal of *Gold Eagle Guy*, Beany Barker, an actress from an affluent family, rose from her seat during a party scene to help a woman who had fainted. Although this was a natural impulse given her nature, Strasberg's direction called for Barker to serve tea, oblivious of the plight of the fallen guest. Strasberg stopped the scene and demanded to know what Barker was doing. Even though Barker tried to slough the incident off and asked if they could go on with the scene, he kept badgering her. Barker was brought to tears. To many it was another instance of his need to reassert his authority, to make everyone wary lest they might displease him. In this particular case, Ruth Nelson, the Group's self-appointed Good Samaritan, came to Barker's aid. The incident was just one more in a long line of volatile encounters.

The first signs that things were reaching a turning point came from bit player Clifford Odets. Clurman admitted Odets to the Group solely on the basis of his enthusiasm and humanity. He seemed to love everything—buildings, the subway and any chance to pound on a piano. He was also troubled, suffering psychic wounds from his parents' unhappy marriage that eventually inspired him to write. He also garnered what he could from observing bits and pieces of Strasberg's teaching, became an integral part of the collective and, early on, began challenging Strasberg's ideas. When Strasberg told Odets that he wasn't interested in Odets' thoughts on the subject, Odets yelled back that he wasn't interested in Strasberg's opinion. Granted that in every group dynamic there is an uneasy balance between the needs of individuals and the plans of the leaders to steer the group. But when you take into account the range of artistic temperaments and power of will within this particular company, you quickly realize that something, as they say, had to give.

The role of this particular leader, while it was to become crucial during the peak years of the Actors Studio, was not crucial to its forebear. What was crucial was the directorship of Harold Clurman. What was also crucial was the nurturing of playwrights like Odets to provide the material through which the Group's ideals and goals could be met.

The difficulty, in terms of the Group, is to put Strasberg's contributions in perspective. He was a teacher of fundamentals, a man who initiated actors into aspects of Stanislavsky's world. He instilled a sense of dedication. More importantly, he imbued everyone with the belief that their individual response system was a powerful source of expression. And his direction of plays like *The House of Connolly* and the innovative drill he put the actors through in the operating scene in *Men in White* gave them all a deep sense of living through an experience on the stage. Strasberg's efforts provided an essential stepping stone. They served as a point of departure. What was still missing was a means for Clurman, Odets and the Group to realize their deeper purpose.

Once Odets had passed his formative stage he was able to clearly articulate the task: to show people everywhere that there was a way out of their trying times. To speak fervently of the pressing realities of the here and now, mine the hidden poetry of everyday life and, impossible as it seemed, change the whole basis of society.

By 1933, following Clurman's advice, Odets began writing about people he knew, trying to capture the edgy, anxious atmosphere of the Depression. At the start he called the work *I Got the Blues*. He centered it around a Jewish family in the Bronx, struggling for economic survival and emotional fulfillment in a chaotic world. He drew on his own family, his anger and fear over a bleak future, certain members of the Group, people he met on the streets of New York, overheard dialogue, the rhythms of Jewish lower-middle-class speech, and the urban immigrant experience.

During this same transitional phase, the Group began to learn of Stanislavsky's continuing work. In turn they learned of Russia's state-supported theater, that it was diversified and designed to serve everyone, especially the common man. In contrast to the failing banks and uncertainty in the United States (where it seemed the propertied class had bungled everything), Russian culture and society appeared to be a model of coherence and viable solutions. It was in this milieu that Odets and Clurman, writer and director, found themselves walking the streets together, reflecting on conditions, forging an artistic bond. Clurman gained a great deal from Odets' liveliness and contact with the down-to-earth realities of the Depression. In turn, Clurman's intellectual clarity infused Odets' sprawling prose.

Soon Odets began coming into his own. He taught his own version of the system he had picked up from Strasberg. His students were novices enrolled in the leftist Theatre Union's free workshop. In contrast to Strasberg, he approached the subject with an infectious warmth and enthusiasm that captivated people like young Julie Garfinkle. Julie then became a member of the Group and went on to exert a great influence in films under the name of John Garfield.

The keynote was sounded. Everything was now subject to evolution and change in keeping with the tenor of the times. Everything was like New York itself: restless, infused with a charged energy, ever seeking, in constant flux.

During this same pivotal stage, more members joined the ranks including Elia Kazan. He was a tireless "opportunist" in Phoebe Brand's eyes, always trying to assimilate and overcome his immigrant experience as a second-class Greek citizen in a land ruled by Turks. Ever the outsider trying to please and repress his anger and resentment over his roots, Kazan's experiences with the Group would shape his own vision of theater and film, lead to his creation of the Studio, and leave a legacy as teacher/director which, in the eyes of many, surpassed them all.

And it was here, with this addition of yet another strong personality that it was no longer possible to put a frame around the composition and activities of the Group. It was becoming more like a campaign, with many ups and downs, maneuvering in response to the political climate, struggling through encounters that led off to other crossroads and issues, continually hunting for just the right agenda.

As a new addition to the movement, Kazan brought with him a broader view. Educated at Yale, he had learned from the professor of directing, Alexander Dean, that stage positions and movements could enhance the telling of a tale. He observed that Strasberg's notion of directing actors was a limited approach in terms of relation to the overall task. Kazan appreciated the musical theater as well as stars like Jeanne Eagels who expressed great depths of feeling. He also brought with him an edgy enthusiasm and irrepressible strength of purpose. With the addition of Elia Kazan, the former collection of young visionaries was turning into a seasoned force which insisted on experimentation as a means of individually and communally finding their own way.

Bobby Lewis, believing more than ever in a heightened theatrical style, explored a choral approach to a simple play about coal miners. Morris Carnovsky conducted a workshop exploring fresh interpretations of Shakespeare. Retaining his strong love of verse as well as realism and leftist politics, he urged his charges to discover the meaning of every line and the application of each message to both Shakespeare's time and the present day. Sandy Meisner, an original member of the Group from the Theater Guild, began looking for a simpler and more direct way of approaching a play.

The days of Strasberg as the sole arbiter of technique had clearly passed. In point of fact, Clurman was often called upon to act as a buffer in dissentions over choices of material and during other power struggles—a role he was, by nature, unequipped to play.

In one instance, Stella Adler was in conflict with Strasberg over his direction of the play *Gentlewoman*. Strasberg wanted the emotionalism curbed in the portrayal of the central character, a socialite who didn't give vent to her feelings. When he was unable to devise an alternative to Adler's natural exuberance, she became stifled. She began to hate acting—unable to connect with the role, groping with his arbitrary and contradictory employment of externals such as imposing carefully worked out gestures and rhythms of speech and grafting them onto her own experiences which she found inappropriate to the play. As a result, author John Howard Lawson pointed out that Adler's character became "pitiable" instead of cold, sophisticated and incapable of love. He also intimated that sophisticated drawing-room manners, underpinned by leftist political sentiments against the bankruptcy of the idle rich, was obviously not Strasberg's forte.

By the spring of 1934, all of this disjointed interplay of material, political agenda, the turbulent times and Strasberg's directing came to an impasse. Oddly enough during this same interval Strasberg accompanied Stella Adler to Moscow to view the Russian theater firsthand but was somehow unaware that Adler's main reason for the trip was to bring back "the word." The Group sorely needed a remedy for Strasberg's overbearing interventions and obsession with affective memory and Adler personally needed to resolve her disenchantment with Stanislavsky's system as promulgated by Strasberg. Not only had she become tied in knots over playing characters by producing feelings from her past, others had become so anxious over constantly "taking a minute" to placate the director's views that they couldn't act at all. After so many skirmishes and deflections there was no way out. The Strasberg issue had to be confronted head on.

As would be expected, Adler was impressed with the range of classes and styles she discovered. Born in Odessa, brought up in the Yiddish theater, her original impression of the MAT—truth from the soul not self, plus an exuberant theatricality—seemed to be validated during her stay in Moscow.

Strasberg, in turn, translated what he saw in terms of his own filtering system. Meyerhold's revolt against naturalism through the use of pure theatricality and movement became "life-activity." A love scene staged acrobatically on a pair of swings was decoded as a way to capture "life's richness more fully." When Strasberg and Adler visited Vakhtangov's widow, Strasberg took certain letters from Stanislavsky as a validation of his own "adjustments" (taking every stage task personally). Apparently, Strasberg was never fully aware of Vakhtangov's "fantastic" vision of theater and never apprised of the fact that when a part went against someone's nature, Vakhtangov prompted the actress in question to re-imagine herself as a theatrical performer playing a role in front of an audience.

Be that as it may, the definitive answer to the dilemma was waiting in the wings in Paris. When Strasberg returned to America, Clurman joined his on-again off-again love interest (Adler), took her to Paris and—through the intercession of his former teacher Jacques Copeau—introduced her to Stanislavsky. Stanislavsky immediately advised Stella Adler to discard any device like affective memory that wasn't useful. Adler was further instructed to give up all concerns over emotion. Feelings were the natural result of the character's action within the given circumstances of the play. He also revealed that his theories had evolved significantly since the days when Boleslavsky and Ouspenskaya had worked with him.

In essence, the search for truth was in the play, not in the actor's personal history. It was the result of engaging in an appropriate set of tasks in order to realize a character's overall objective. And this objective must coincide with the author's central purpose.

Needless to say, Adler was overjoyed, reworked her present role for four weeks under Stanislavsky's guidance and returned to the Group's summer retreat. Her news provided her fellow actors with relief and renewed vigor.

Strasberg countered by declaring that Stanislavsky didn't know what he was talking about. He, Strasberg, had improved upon Stanislavsky with a method that incorporated the work of Vakhtangov and Meyerhold. Strasberg's arrogance severely damaged whatever prestige he had left. No longer were the actors willing to be judged by how well they could make themselves suffer and cry. They were eager and determined to apply Stanislavsky's "true" method of physical actions in its stead.

Soon afterwards, Stella Adler began giving classes. She emphasized the concept of the will and mind in service to the style and objectives of the play: to understand and do, to make the words come alive for a higher purpose in the here and now.

Undaunted, Strasberg began to impose athletic movements in the manner of Meyerhold, employing platforms and various levels for the new period play *Gold Eagle Guy*. (Strasberg had commissioned the work the previous spring and ostensibly wanted to demonstrate his newfound flexibility and understanding of all aspects of Russian theater.) Set in 19th century San Francisco, the episodic piece covered a period of forty years during the rise of a ruthless shipping magnate. The huge cast contained only one life-like character, the protagonist. The theme was dated and ran counter to the spirit of the times. And no matter how much he tried to incorporate a physicalized abstract style—making Julie Garfield perform a spectacular leap down a flight of stairs, drilling the actors in speech tempos and movement to reflect the rhythms of an old way of life, inserting the dancer/choreographer Helen Tamiris' dances—Strasberg was in over his head. With no training in theater movement and only a cursory understanding of Meyerhold's use of "externals," he subjected audiences to what Kazan termed "heavy-handed, turgid, clumsy and boring" sequences. The play closed after an extremely short run.

To cap off the entire misguided experience, Kazan's stage management of the final scene—a symbolic San Francisco earthquake replete with rope tricks, lighting effects and the release of snow bags full of rubble—was brought into question as Strasberg chastised Kazan in front of the whole company. In Kazan's view, Strasberg always relieved himself of responsibility by blaming those who were too vulnerable to fight back (like the episode with Beany Barker, badgering her to tears).

The whole event served as a catalyst, the proverbial last straw. The membership was more than ready for a venue independent of Strasberg and to show its true colors and take a stand. As though answering the call, a leftist organization known as the New Theatre League needed a script to fill out a program of revolutionary pieces. Odets proposed a strike story, created a structure and wrote parts with specific actors in mind. The actors adjusted the lines in keeping with their overall frame of mind: anger over existing social conditions, belief in collective action, wanting the theater to be a force for change. They also expressed their lighthearted exuberance, camaraderie and love of the kind of open improvisational scenes Odets had devised. Odets titled the piece *Waiting for Lefty*.

In their enthusiasm they invited Strasberg to a final rehearsal. His response was a cool shrug which only served to widen the gap and strengthen everyone's resolve. One way or another, the theatrical fellowship known as the Group would never be the same.

3

Days of Glory and Beyond

In performance, the bare portable setting serves as a springboard for the action: a meeting of taxi drivers addressed by the head of their corrupt union. Actors seated in the audience are intimidated as the proceedings commence. The call goes up for a "damn Red" to reveal himself. One of the committee members onstage protests, claiming that there are no Reds, only "black and blue boys because we've been kicked around so long." He goes on to tell why his wife called for a strike. Five scenes are then dramatized showing the plight of the cabbies, including Phoebe Brand and Julie Garfield as young lovers, typifying those who can't make a living, marry and support a wife because of the corruption and graft that has infested their union.

During opening night, the audience responded to every jab and goad. In a scene where a wife threatens to leave her ineffective husband, everyone clapped. When Bobby Lewis did one of his patented turns as a villainous character named Clancy—sidling up from the audience, face wrinkled in a grimace of cunning in keeping with the propaganda devices of the day—the audience jeered. When Kazan bolted out of his seat and exposed him while acknowledging that he was his brother, the audience exploded and Bobby ran off.

The cheering and booing proliferated during each ensuing encounter. There is a speech about how the cabbies' ancestors froze at Valley Forge, honest workers were sold out and the Constitution applied only to the rich: "The meek shall not inherit the earth. Only the MILITANTS!" A character who has lost an eye in an industrial accident defends the "comrades" who picked him up when he was down and bleeding. Someone rushes up the aisle onto the stage and announces that Lefty was found behind the car barns with a bullet in his head. The messenger then implores the audience, asking, "Well, what's the answer?" A handful of actors planted in the audience call out, "Strike," just as they rehearsed. When the messenger asks them to say it louder, 1400 people in the audience suddenly rise and yell, "Strike! Strike! Strike!"

During this same opening night, most of the actors wept, overwhelmed by the standing ovation. When Clurman brought Odets out onto the apron, the audience stormed the stage and embraced the playwright who had voiced their hopes and fears. They remained, still dazed, talking to one another, then spilled outside, waiting for the actors to reappear. Deeply moved, Odets felt that the true essence of theater had been realized. The proscenium arch and the imaginary fourth wall had dissolved and the audience and actors had become one.

Finally parting company from their well-wishers, the actors straggled outside as stunned as the audience—Harold Clurman among them—remaining together till almost dawn. Kazan and Odets sensed that they had all, at long last, attained respect. Each and every member of the cast now embraced acting as a means of communion (shades of Suler and Stanislavsky). Theater mattered; it could touch people's lives and give everyone involved a sense of meaning and dignity.

Waiting for Lefty would continue to stimulate audiences and go on to be produced in theaters across the country and affect countless others in the British Isles as well. Critical reviews were glowing, extolling the fact that the Group had finally found an outlet for their "maturing revolutionary convictions." Strasberg's aside to Clurman, "Let them fall on their faces," rang especially hollow in the light of this remarkable achievement.

After its successful run, the actors were champing for a new challenge. Two out of the three administrators however (Strasberg and Cheryl Crawford) were ready to call it a season. Discounting "Lefty," they pointed to the overriding failure of *Gold Eagle Guy.* The actors turned to Clurman, only to discover that, though he was a master at exhorting people to action, he still couldn't handle any situation where he might be caught in the middle.

With her paramour (Clurman) reluctant to take a stand, Stella Adler stepped in. She brought up the fact that it was January, the dead of winter. Quitting would throw all of her colleagues out into the cold, unemployed without money for food or rent. Odets spoke up, informing all assembled that his "blues" play—now called *Awake and Sing* was ready to be put into rehearsal.

Countering, Strasberg replied, "You don't seem to understand, Clifford. We don't like your play." (By all accounts, the word "we" in Strasberg's lexicon meant a tacit agreement by all present with his statements.) When he repeated his assertion, the actors overruled him and embraced Odets' play. As everyone knew, the work was written especially for them and was infused with the animating force of their lives. Presently Clurman, who had helped to nurture the manuscript over its trials and errors, took a stand, broke openly with Strasberg and announced that he would direct. Soon after he obtained financial backing from Franchot Tone (one of the original members, now a featured player in Hollywood) and the project was on its way.

During rehearsals of this full-length play, all the elements came together. Concentration, a sense of truth, depth of feeling, ensemble playing and a work ethic—the basics learned from Strasberg—were retained. But the focus, spirit and essential

Top: A moment from *Awake and Sing* (1935). Stella Adler is standing, Morris Carnovsky is seated far left, Pheobe Brand is seated opposite Adler as Sandy Meisner (seated next to her) tries to get her attention. Bottom: Elia Kazan, third from left with his arms raised in defiance, calls on the audience to strike at the climax of *Waiting for Lefty* (1935). (From the Billy Rose Theatre Collection, NY Public Library.)

way of working were transformed. Gone were the improvisations linked to the actors' lives, circling around the given situations in the play. Gone also was the tension produced by an autocrat, overseeing each and every step of the actors' internal work, confronting them with their inadequacies, imposing the stamp of his will.

In its place was the joy of working with a high spirited leader who saw himself as a guide and a partner alongside the writer, actors, designers and technicians. Gregarious as ever, Clurman encouraged the actors to find their own way. He instilled in them the courage to try, reminding them that in every creative venture one is bound to fail as often as not.

This time the playwright's lines and themes were a primary concern. Odets' message—that there's a way out of the present conditions if you search hard enough—was the main focus. In Clurman's approach each character's function was to build toward this ultimate understanding.

More specifically, the play was set in the Bergers' overcrowded Bronx apartment. The exuberant messiness of life, ebbing and flowing as characters kept engaging each other, echoed the rhythm of the New York streets. The daily events outside the windows, the actual relationships among the actors, and many other things Odets had experienced firsthand came into play. He utilized his intimate knowledge of tenement life, his intolerable childhood, his encounters with the downtrodden and his walks with Clurman. He also incorporated his dreams and fears and overriding need for self-realization. Even the set was prompted by designer Boris Aronson's visit to Julie Garfield's family apartment. A calendar, sentimentalizing the romantic pull of faraway places, was placed in a prominent position in stark contrast with the Bergers' living conditions. The walls between the rooms were removed, a device that generated continual movement and a sense of overlapping lives, often working at cross purposes.

In effect the company was again giving vent to their radical feelings: refusing to remain victims of a demeaning society and depressed economy; insisting on wringing optimism from defeat; agreeing with the Hebrew prophecy that called on people to "awake and sing."

Articulating the dynamic that fueled the play, Clurman found realism pitted against idealism, memory against hope, rebellion against the acceptance of middle-class values. He also found poetry arising out of everyday speech; the aspirations and restlessness of a generation given a voice and an escape route from a failed materialism. Producing the play, therefore, was tantamount to issuing a proclamation that the basis of society had to change, Freud and Marx had to be taken into account, and ordinary people had greater depth than they were given credit for. It also proved that Clurman was right when he declared that any good play is a propaganda play. Odets felt that he was simply telling the truth; but the truth to Clurman was always revolutionary.

As for the characters, Stella Adler played the mother, Bessie—the constant caretaker, afraid of poverty, telling jokes, struggling to hold on. Because Odets envisioned his characters whole, Bessie had her contradictions and failings, manipulating her son Ralph, keeping him from the girl he loves and discrediting his dreams of a future, justifying her actions through a misplaced passion for money, security and togetherness.

Another primary character was Hennie, Bessie's self-reliant daughter. Phoebe Brand invested the part with a sardonic wit that held the fear of being trapped at bay. Sandy Meisner played Sam Feinschreiber, lonely, a foreigner, always sensing that others are laughing at him. But he too, along with all the others, managed to buffet an agonizing desire through humor and or anything else at hand that might enable him to survive.

The heart of the play is embodied by Julie Garfield as Ralph. In his exchanges with his grandfather, Jacob (played by Morris Carnovsky), we can readily detect both Odets' own hopes and fears and an indication of Carnovsky's personal fondness for the much younger Garfield. We can also sense Odets' understanding of the drives and sensitivity of Garfield, his star pupil, friend and neighbor from the Bronx. The dialogue also exudes Odets' love of the syntax and rhythms of everyday speech taken to poetic heights:

> RALPH:　I wanna make up my own mind about things … be something. I don't know … Every other day to sit around with the blues and mud in your mouth. What's life for?
>
> JACOB:　Boychick, wake up. Be something. Make your life something good. For the love of an old man who sees in your young days his new life, for such love take the world in your two hands and make it like new. Go out and fight so life shouldn't be printed on dollar bills.
>
> 　　　　　　　[to BESSIE about her son]
>
> Ralph you don't make like you. Before you do it, I'll die first. He'll find a girl. He'll go in a fresh world with her. This is a house? Marx said it—abolish such families.
>
> 　　　　　　[about the times and Ralph]
>
> In my day the propaganda was for God. Now it's for success. He dreams all night of fortunes. Why not? Don't it say in the movies he should have a personal steamship, pajamas for fifty dollars a pair?

The play see-saws back and forth but always returns to the prospects of the young and their plight. Hennie, Ralph's sister, finds herself trapped in a loveless marriage with Sam (Sandy Meisner), the well-meaning but hapless refugee. But she never ceases to look for a way out. And time and again, the primary focus returns to Garfield and the urgings of Jacob, his grandfather. In this final example, Ralph learns that his girlfriend is being coerced by her parents to leave the city and seek a husband who will bring her economic security.

> RALPH:　When I was a kid I laid awake at nights and heard the sounds of trains … faraway lonesome sounds … boats going up and down the river. I used to think of all kinds of things I wanted to do. What was it, Jake? Just a bunch of noise in my head?
>
> JACOB:　You wanted to make for yourself a certain kind of world.
>
> RALPH:　I guess I didn't. I'm feeling pretty, pretty low.
>
> JACOB:　You're a young boy, and for you your life is all in front like a big mountain. You got feet to climb.
>
> RALPH:　I don't know how.
>
> Jacob:　So you'll find out. Never a young man had such opportunity like today. He could make history.

RALPH: I'd fight the whole goddam world with her, but not her. No guts. The hell with her. If she wants to go—all right... She'll see what I can do. No one stops me when I get going. [near to tears] I don't know what to do.

JACOB: Look on me and learn. Look on this failure and see for seventy years he talked with good ideas, but only in the head. It's enough for me now I should see your happiness. This is why I tell you—DO! Do what is in your heart and you carry in yourself a revolution.

In approaching these roles the actors followed Stella Adler's lead and Stanislavsky's emphasis on physical action: concentrating on their character's intentions, dealing with the objects and stimuli within the environment, working off the immediacy and the moment to moment give-and-take. Phoebe Brand, for example, discovered that frequently working on her nails energized her, reinforced her resolve and prepared her for a new life far away from her stifling existence. Morris Carnovsky relied on his natural expansiveness plus relating to Garfield, Stella Adler, the other characters and the objects on stage. In this way he was able to pair the immediate truth and the larger-than-life truth he'd always sought. And whenever Carnovsky needed to deepen his characterization, Clurman would come up with an improvisation like sewing a button on his coat while recounting a boyhood episode—from Jacob's memory, not Carnovsky's.

Taken together, the overall effect was positive and significant. For the first time on Broadway (according to writer Alfred Kazin) general audiences of ordinary people discovered that culture was meant for them. Through the prism of the Bergers they saw their own mothers, fathers, uncles and aunts occupying the stage with as much right as if they were Hamlet and Lady Macbeth. As with "Lefty," actors and audiences came together with shocking immediacy. The energy triangulated from Stella Adler's Bessie beyond the footlights, through the spectators and back again. Carnovsky's ardent passive socialist from the old country touched a chord with all those immigrants struggling to put children through school on meager working-class incomes. The reviewers recognized this phenomenon, the play had a most successful run, the actors became solvent and secure. It was 1935, soon to be known as the year of Odets.

With Clurman as director and one of their own providing vehicles of poetic-realism, the Group realized its potential. Providing drama with a message to make life more meaningful for audiences was tangible. So was the sense of harmony, joy and fulfillment for one and all. Now open to all possibilities, they envisioned adding Michael Chekhov (who had emigrated from the Soviet Union in 1928) to their ranks as an instructor, impressed by his use of the "psychological gesture" to expressively externalize inner states of being.

However, in the transitory world of American success and the nature of changing times, there were factors that mitigated against this kind of creative euphoria. How could things continue in this vein, especially when you take into account Odets' mixed feelings about revolutionary drama on the one hand and a desire for recognition on the other? True he loved the security, camaraderie and artistic dedication of the Group. But that love was tugging against a yearning for fame and fortune in the movies, a longing barely disguised in this play. And it wasn't just Odets. The struggle against war, fascism and economic instability was wearying, especially when you consider the pull of an easier life in Hollywood, an enticement most of the company had been attempting to shrug off for some time. What's more, the odds were stacked against any continuing endeavor of this type on Broadway. Everyone knew the rules of the game: you're only as good as your last show; all your gains can evaporate overnight in the aftermath of one batch of mixed reviews.

With these factors in mind, the completed runs of *Waiting for Lefty* and *Awake and Sing* can be marked as a pinnacle and the beginning of a last chapter. As mentioned, success evoked dreams of the addition of Michael Chekhov along with a school, a studio—a Moscow Art Theatre of America completely subsidized. The realities signaled the advent of a juggling act which would carry on for less than four more years, replete with hard lessons to be learned and one more triumph, albeit much more commercial and costly in other ways.

Wavering but still attached to the Group, Odets wrote his next play *Paradise Lost* as a reflection of his concern over prospects for the future, to let everyone know that things weren't as promising as they seemed. His characters may have been better off but they were blind to the true nature of their circumstances, spending time escaping into fantasies and weaving unrealistic strategies.

Picking up on this premise, Clurman's direction mixed tragic farce, naturalism and social realism. The social realism was indicated by Odets' familiar elements of activism like the use of a homeless man shouting, "You're all sleeping! All over the country people are sleeping!" Also interspersed were the hints of a better tomorrow within everyone's grasp: "There is more to life than this. The past was a dream but this is real... The truth has found us. Everywhere men are rising from their sleep ... The world is in its morning."

The elements of tragic farce were exemplified by two stylized turns. In a tour de force, Bobby Lewis played Mr. May, an arsonist who proposes to burn down the central character's factory. Stylizing the role to the hilt, Lewis dyed his hair red, combed it straight up and affected a strange accent to punctuate the bizarre nature of his role. Odets created another two-dimensional character by the name of Kewpie especially for Kazan. As a person who relentlessly pursues success, Kewpie was a mirror image of the "hungry wolf" aspect of Kazan's personality.

Unfortunately none of this juxtaposition of styles and messages jelled. Middle class audiences found the combination confusing. They balked at being depicted as a group of people who were cavalier about their allegiances and unable to cope with real life. The wealthy in the audience were distressed over the social and political implications, and the critics were baffled.

If that wasn't unsettling enough, some Group members were disgruntled for personal reasons. There weren't enough roles and opportunities for continued creative growth. Accusations were made that major parts were given to established "stars" like Luther Adler (Stella's brother) who had played Phoebe Brand's love interest in *Awake and Sing* and flitted between much more commercial ventures as well. The realities of maintaining an artistic collective set against the backdrop of Broadway came sharply into focus, a dilemma that would play itself out in the 1950s when the Actors Studio would repeat the same pattern.

In order to continue the successes of 1935, Odets would have to keep furnishing topical and successful struggle-for-better-lives plays with challenging parts for all. He would have to accept that he was relied upon as the Group's voice. He would have to remain true to his talents and forego the ever-pressing lure of Hollywood. What was heretofore sensed but unspoken became painfully obvious.

In addition, during the second part of the decade in question, the impending threat of fascism overseas overshadowed everything. Group members became even more political, actively engaged in fringe-like Communist activities. They also brought this orientation and Socialist doctrines into Group procedures. Within this framework—breaking into cells, consorting with outside factions, dickering with the leaders (mainly Clurman) under the banner of the Actors Committee—Kazan's opportunism became much more serious. To some he was regarded as a foreman type, trying to curry favor with the bosses, willing to do anything to get ahead. It was as though they wanted to reinvent *Waiting for Lefty* and play it out for real.

In this highly problematic atmosphere, radio and movie money was proposed as a solution to administrative problems. A permanent theater and basic security was spoken of in the same breath as making do with any script available to placate the smash-hit psychology of the Great White Way. Ideals, the political climate and practicality became all mixed up.

As this juggling act proliferated, a few took whatever odd roles they could find in other productions. For Odets, the possibility of reaching millions through film was now irresistible. Playing both ends against the middle, he promised another play while frequenting the Hollywood hot spots and falling in love with the Vienna-born screen actress Louise Rainer.

Stella Adler stayed on a while longer, coaching the women who had leading roles, offering workshops in interpretation and characterization through the use of scenes from classic and contemporary plays. Morris Carnovsky offered sessions in vocal characterization and dealt with problems of speech and language in poetic drama. But all of this was just a shadow of the great promise of '35. The thrust and cohesiveness were gone, replaced by a breakdown in discipline, personal, professional and political discontents. The realization sunk in that they couldn't change Broadway, couldn't be a force if they lowered their sights and operated on the fringes of the theater district. They also weren't in their early twenties anymore, willing to pin their hopes on a fervent dream.

In this same period of encroaching disenchantment, Lee Strasberg reentered the picture. Clurman persuaded him to direct a poetic American folk tale entitled *Johnny Johnson* despite the fact that his cachet was in question and no one was enthusiastic about the material. Despite these qualifying factors, Clurman felt this new work had the potential to rekindle nationalistic spirit and boost the Group's morale.

Strasberg, however, wasn't up to the project. He gave the renowned set designer Donald Oenslager free rein while he himself toyed with an amalgam of fantasy, music and homespun life. Finding his authority on shaky ground, he was unable to make his customary demands or follow Clurman's lead and come up with a compelling theme. Nor was he either willing or able to provide individual actors with insights. The only creative force was Oenslager, whose overpowering setting dwarfed the entire enterprise.

Unwilling to take constructive criticism, Strasberg found himself barely on speaking terms with Clurman. Consequently, all relationships were strained and the production elements were incongruous. Nothing quite fit together.

When the critics called the show amateurish, the membership became visibly agitated. Shortly thereafter the Actors Committee felt compelled to issue a paper detailing the low state of morale and placing most of the blame on Strasberg. His "doggedness, necessity for being right, cold scorn of artistic compromise, removal from life, hysterical force and psychotic domineering ... were unhealthy and apt to destroy every breath of theatre love that he ever called forth." Carrying on, the Committee reiterated the familiar wish: to become the Moscow Art Theatre of America with a similar experimental studio and a subsidized repertory company. Regardless, as anyone could have predicted, this outpouring of dismay and desire had little effect.

By 1937, Odets had married his movie star; Stella Adler, Clurman and Kazan had set off for Hollywood with Luther Adler, Phoebe Brand, Morris Carnovsky et al. to make screen tests. Those who remained joined the ranks of their colleagues scrambling for roles in other venues. In March of that same year Strasberg officially resigned. There was no chance of recreating the Group as he had known it. Or, as Phoebe Brand put it: "If he couldn't have it his way, he couldn't deal."

After a time, Kazan succeeded in convincing Clurman to return to New York and reclaim his rightful place as the heart and soul of the Group. New actors were brought in and old stalwarts were reassembled.

Odets followed suit, armed with a new play—*Golden Boy*. But the script didn't exactly spring from the depths of his being. In the vernacular of this boxing saga, Odets pulled his punches and used what he had picked up from the movies— e.g., a Hollywood style with a central character and a formulaic set of plot twists until the inevitable point of no return, climax and fade. In point of fact, it was constructed quickly to generate seed money for the reemergence of the company.

Still the play had its merits. Beneath the surface of the familiar tale of a prizefighter gone wrong there is a deeper meaning, a theme that continues to slip in and out of this evolving dynamic: the artist tempted from his true nature. Like Odets, the character of Joe Bonaparte is essentially "a violinist," a person with a creative soul. But, at the same time, he yearns to escape from the ranks of the poor and gain recognition. He wants "to be someone." Lured by Eddie Fuseli (another part tailored for Kazan), an insidious predator who will "shoot you for a nickel, then for fifty bucks send you flowers," Joe Bonaparte weakens. He allows Fuseli to buy his marketability as a boxer in exchange for some "good times and silk shirts."

Echoing Odets' dilemma, Joe proclaims that he's "out for fame and fortune, not to be different or artistic," but then cries out, "I don't intend to be ashamed of my life."

In playing out this struggle, Odets surrounds Joe with two-dimensional characters like Siggie, his none-too-bright brother-in-law and his sister "Anna Banana," a part invested with crowd pleasing comic turns by Phoebe Brand. Filling out the cast are stereotypes like Joe's maudlin, sentimentalized Papa (played by Morris Carnovsky) and the denizens of the fight world—all of whom illustrate how little Odets knew about boxing and Italian-Americans and just how hastily the work was constructed.

As though taking their cue from the nature of the script, the Actors Committee decided on a new production tack: combining the slick Broadway mode of box-office appeal with "Group content" and social comment. In another nod to expediency, they mounted the show in six weeks. Gone was the full exploration of background material and concern for ensemble work and the living-through of the given circumstances. There wasn't time. The old devotion to artistic integrity and attention to detail was unnecessary and impractical. Simply put, the notion of becoming the Moscow Art Theatre of America was completely set aside. Compromise was the order of the day.

The new guidelines carried over into matters of casting as well. Gone also was the practice of affording members challenging parts. Even the ethic of keeping one's word was subject to change. Odets had promised the role of Joe to his friend and former student, Julie Garfield. After all, Garfield possessed all the necessary attributes: the ideal age (24), a tough childhood and adolescence as a street kid from the Lower East Side and the Bronx, a natural animal magnetism and an uncompromising sense of truth. But he wasn't a star. Luther Adler had more credits and notoriety. True, Adler was ten years older than Garfield, jowly and a bit paunchy, but his name above the marquee would boost ticket sales. Clurman justified the tactic claiming that Adler would bring a certain pathos to the role, a sensitivity and a search for philosophical meaning. Without putting up much of a fuss, Odets went along.

Time and again, it appears that much of the foundation for what was to follow was laid during the evolutionary ups and downs of the Group. As the old saying goes, "Past is prologue." There was never a Constantin Stanislavsky who was in a position to take a sabbatical and objectively reevaluate what had transpired. More often than not, the key figures in this chronicle seem to have been continually caught between desires and the push and pull of the changing tide.

Continuing in this new vein, Clurman assigned the second leading role to the attractive young movie star Frances Farmer. Although her well-bred speech wasn't appropriate for "a tramp from Newark," Clurman felt that her spontaneity would spark the necessary chemistry between her and Luther Adler. Clurman handed out parts to other newcomers under the rationale of instilling new blood into the organization. In the wake of all this reshuffling, Garfield reluctantly accepted the demeaning role of Siggie, the brother-in-law; some were duly satisfied, many were visibly upset.

On the positive side, Clurman discovered a directorial metaphor. Life was a prize ring. Every scene was a round as the actors battled opponents seeking their place in this world. Taking a page from Vakhtangov (à la Stella Adler), he also instructed everyone to find their own "fantastic" solutions to emotional blocks. As June Havoc would later point out, there were many who always felt that "what one used to get there was your own private business." The specific "fantastic" solutions were never discussed.

Again the results were mixed. The production, liveliness of the acting, salty dialogue and rapid action were praised by the critics. Luther Adler's sensitive portrayal was praised. But Odets' rendition of the boxing world was unconvincing and the structure of the play was considered trite. Despite all this, the play found favor with the public. The show ran and made money. In terms of commercial success, the new policy had paid off. In terms of the Group's origins and fundamental values, nothing would ever again be the same.

After the opening, a sign on the office door declared that no one belonged to the Group Theater except the cast of *Golden Boy*. Shortly after the sign was posted, leftist groups proclaimed that the Group had lost its social impact. It was no longer a force for change.

In store for the modified Group were a few more sporadic highs and lows until it all imperceptibly faded as a distinctive entity. The high point was the enthusiastic reception *Golden Boy* received during its London engagement. Phoebe Brand remembers how much the British audiences and press were taken with their energy, immediacy and ensemble playing; how they loved her devil-may-care attitude and reckless portrayal of Joe's sexy sister. "Lefty" had already been mounted by local amateurs in social clubs throughout the U.K. but nothing had prepared the general public for the audacity of the Americans. It was startling to see actors who appeared to be experiencing imaginary circumstances rather than playacting, impersonating characters and intoning their lines. As far as the English were concerned, the Group offered a refreshing alternative.

On a low note, Julie Garfield was no longer playing Siggie. He had signed a two-picture deal with Warner Brothers. Morris Carnovsky was upset, recalling their close relationship in *Awake and Sing* and hoping that "young Ralph" would stick it out as he had in the play. On the other hand, Carnovsky and the others had been tempted by their stay in Hollywood and knew full well that Garfield had been turning down movie offers for three years. They also must have known that the betrayal by his mentor Odets (and by extension Clurman) over the lead in *Golden Boy* had been the last straw. Discussions over right and wrong, good and bad no longer applied.

On another low note, after all the talk about Michael Chekhov as a source of renewed vitality, Bobby Lewis had the opportunity to view his work at Dartington Hall during the same London engagement. He found emphasis on movement and visual stylization but a total lack of conviction. This realization, coupled with the ambivalence over Garfield's career move and the new commercial policies, prompted Lewis to leave the U.K. Disenchanted, he made his way back home.

The core of the Group after the shake-up (1937). Seated left to right: Luther Adler, Phoebe Brand, Eleanor Lynn, Frances Farmer, Bobby Lewis, and Art Smith leaning in front of Elia Kazan. Standing: stage manager Bill Watts, Irwin Shaw, Sandy Meisner, Ruth Nelson, Lee J. Cobb, Harold Clurman, Leif Erickson (behind Clurman), Roman Bohnen, Morris Carnovsky, Michael Gordon and Kermit Bloomgarden. (From the Billy Rose Theatre Collection, NY Public Library.)

Lewis' departure signaled a continual downward spiral. Odets' next Broadway play, *Rocket to the Moon*, depicted the abandoned dreams of listless characters who drift in and out of a stifling dentist's office, haplessly searching for love, reflecting Odets' rueful state after the breakup of his marriage to his movie queen.

This time the rehearsal period was cut down to three weeks. Clurman again sought new faces. Sandy Meisner disliked his small dreary part as a womanizing dance instructor; the mature Morris Carnovsky was miscast as the boyish Ben; and few in the audience could relate to a drab, trivial affair between a dentist and his secretary while Hitler was encroaching on Czechoslovakia.

By the time the production of Irwin Shaw's *The Gentle People* was in full swing, Phoebe Brand perused the assembly of actors and realized she had come full circle. Casting was no different than it had been in the Theater Guild. Sylvia Sydney, who assumed she had traded Hollywood for art, found herself playing her usual role. Franchot Tone was brought back from Hollywood to complete the box office draw. Kazan was enlisted to revise the staging because of Clurman's new cavalier attitude. In point of fact, Clurman intimated that theater didn't matter all that much in the face of the darkness that was closing in as world affairs ominously took a turn for the worse.

The last straw was Stalin's non-aggression pact with Nazi Germany immediately after Hitler marched into Poland in August of 1939. The concepts of the commune, Russia as artistic and spiritual forebear, and the Soviet Union as a political model in the fight against German oppression were no longer tenable.

Paradoxically however, as the Group slowly dissipated and seemed to fade from memory, two from its ranks grew in stature and spread its influence. Their impact on the world of stage and screen was immeasurable. Their names were Garfield and Kazan.

4

Garfield and Kazan: Variations on a Theme

By 1938, the millions who flocked to the movie theaters had simple expectations. The stars, studio and genre always went hand in hand. Paramount turned out comedies about the idle rich. Action-adventures abounded starring Clark Gable and Spencer Tracy, and Ginger Rogers and Fred Astaire danced and sang their way through a white-tie-and-tails world for RKO. There were DeMille spectacles, James Cagney gangster movies and cute, bouncy vehicles for Shirley Temple at 20th Century–Fox. Predictably that same year Bette Davis played a tempestuous Southern belle opposite mild-mannered Henry Fonda in the costume drama *Jezebel*. And Franchot Tone, displaying not the slightest hint that he had worked under Strasberg, portrayed his usual earnest swain to Katharine Hepburn's customary bright and intrepid gal in *Quality Street*. Hollywood was a factory town providing consumers an escape from the harsh realities of life—a dream journey to a time and place that bore no resemblance to their own. Cocky James Cagney went too far, crime didn't pay, his environment and upbringing were to blame, moviegoers left the theater satisfied.

John Garfield

Starting with the opening shot, *Four Daughters* appears to fit some safe and predictable mold. There is a white picket fence bordering a flowering tree. A tracking shot sweeps the viewer inside a cozy home where four young women play their instruments beautifully for their crusty but benign father. Their features are ideal, their hair is flawlessly coifed. Everyone is jaunty and good-natured. One sister's "heartthrob" lives next door and delivers her orchids. The "clever" sister asks for help in cooking supper for rich Mr. Crowley as a ploy to entice him to propose.

43

John Garfield in *Four Daughters* **(1938, Warner Bros.).**

There is chatter among all four sisters about marriage for love, good looks, money
or laughs, as bubbly violin music wafts in and out on the soundtrack. A potential
beau swings on the front gate. A perfect picnic follows in perfect weather as three

of the daughters are courted by the stock characters assigned to them. Ann, the fourth and youngest, played by Pricilla Lane, bides her time as she flirts with the young man who swung on her front gate. During all this, Aunt Etta remains affable, cooking whatever food is required and Dad remains crusty and benign.

By this point, there could be no doubt of the genre. The only story question might concern the youngest daughter's marital future and the chances for a multiple wedding in a make-believe American smalltown.

Surprisingly, into this artificial world steps John (né Julie) Garfield (né Garfinkle) fresh from the Group Theater. His appearance is startling. He shambles into the house—a well-worn fedora cocked back, hair mussed up, tie dangling loose below a frayed collar, rumpled jacket and pants. His build is rugged and stocky, his nose looks broken, his features dark and Semitic. He puffs on a cigarette, blowing smoke into the foyer as if pitching it at the fastidiousness of the décor. The smile on his face is wry, surly, defiant. As soon as he utters his first lines, his Bronx accent with Lower East Side shadings accentuates his attitude.

He speaks to the carefree young man smitten with Ann, the youngest daughter. Expressing his outlook on life, he informs this comfortably situated acquaintance that it's "a poor man's privilege" to poke fun at the well-to-do. He also informs him that he was just evicted and needs a room "on the wrong side of the tracks" because he's not used to breathing clean air.

As it turns out, the young man is a composer and Garfield is a wayward musician whose only motivation for entering the scene hinges on some vague reference to an orchestration. But it's readily apparent that Julius Epstein, the screenwriter responsible for Garfield's dialogue, had much more in mind. In some uncanny way, Epstein appears to be picking up where Odets left off: writing roles tailored for actors he knew intimately; reflecting his own philosophy of life while exposing the shallowness of formulaic films and, possibly, the motion picture industry itself.

When pleasant Aunt Etta greets Garfield, he asks what type she is: "The sweet simple land-sake's-alive aunt or the one with the gruff voice and I-smell-something-burning?" Each thrust and parry pokes holes in Hollywood's version of the middle-class fantasy and establishes Garfield as the eternal outsider: a romantic rebel hero from the urban ghetto.

Priscilla Lane's portrayal of the youngest daughter makes the contrast between fantasy and reality even more pronounced. In trying to deal with Garfield, her delivery suddenly becomes less assured. Her gestures are hesitant as she attempts to light his cigarette while he plays the piano. She tells him that his composition is beautiful. He replies, "It stinks." As the scene continues, she reads her lines like an ingenue in a school play. Garfield, on the other hand, cuts through all the pretense. He is totally present, totally there. And it's not just Garfield's honesty and naturalness. Cagney and Spencer Tracy had both qualities. Garfield was displaying an organic style of acting millions of moviegoers had never seen.

We can attribute part of Garfield's impact to his training and experience. He had learned from Odets and Stella Adler to play the moment and use objects, like the cigarette, as a filtering device for characterization, improvising with whatever was at hand. But more importantly it was the effort to repress the feelings percolating underneath that was so unsettling. In his instinctive act of self-parody, he attained a special depth and resonance. By playing the opposite color—laughing at himself instead of revealing his pain—the emotional colors were revealed through his eyes because of the camera's ability to penetrate and magnify the subtlest nuances on the screen.

Fastening on the eyes, intonation and brief references to his background as clues, urban viewers could, no doubt, guess at the rest of the story. Born on the Lower East Side, his immigrant parents lived under constant pressure trying to survive. There was no time left to supervise young Julie. He was loose on the city streets, his delinquent peers his only guides and family. Any one of these selfsame viewers could appreciate the kind of knowledge you gain firsthand through the frustrations of the ghetto: the simple lesson that success was the one and only objective, the only way out.

What the viewers couldn't guess was the way this hard-edged education was tempered by Julie's sense of inclusion and belonging thanks to the Group. How he let down his guard because (as Odets describes him through the role of Ralph Berger) he was at heart a "boy with a clean spirit who wants to learn—ardent, romantic, sensitive, trying to discover why so much dirt must be cleared away before it's possible to get to first base." No one could know that his one defining moment was the occasion when, just before a final performance, Clurman came into his dressing room and told him he'd been accepted as a full member. Then and there Garfield broke down and cried. What could, however, be sensed up there on the screen was that somewhere along the line (after believing in the cause, acknowledging that he was deficient in "cultural things" and always showing his amiable and playfully spontaneous side) he had been betrayed.

By the same token, Garfield's unique hardened-yet-sensitive presence gave Epstein the chance to give voice to a heretofore unspoken American theme. There was a sharp line between those who had been brought up by immigrant parents and those who were part of the established order; between those for whom everything came easily and those for whom everything came hard. This script, taken from a mawkish Fanny Hurst short story with Garfield playing the pivotal role, gave Epstein the opportunity to appeal to all those who had streamed into the crowded tenements and found themselves on the fringes of society, hungering for a romantic image of themselves.

Clouding this image, however, was the issue of assimilation. What part does a young man from the ghetto play in the small-town America Hollywood dream? In movie terms of the day, it had to be fate, not prejudice, which does him in. Priscilla Lane had no real chance at reforming him and Garfield had no real chance at changing the natural scheme of things and coming between perfectly matched partners. And so the character who had changed his name to Mickey Borden drives his car over a cliff during a snowstorm. As if nothing had happened, the movie returns to its original mode and Priscilla Lane is safe once more, swinging on the front gate with the nice young man.

But even though one of the scriptwriters attempted to erase Garfield's troubling presence in favor of a Hollywood ending, the damage had been done. Garfield had made an indelible impression. By some stroke of irony, in breaking away from the Group and giving up his need to belong he became an outsider again—this time on the screen. In so doing, he found universal acceptance.

Unwittingly, he also established a prototype, leading the way for the likes of Clift, Brando and Dean. Kazan defined this exemplary quality in terms of "a final intimacy" that "spoke to an audience's secret self, the one you hide ... giving the world some genuine thing beyond the limits of civilization ... unpredictable and dangerous."

For some, this gave rise to a moral dimension, a duty actors had to reveal their own undercurrents of feeling, an obligation of self-exposure. Garfield's passion and innate lyrical sadness became a model of truth.

His work on the screen also reflected the restrictive nature of the movie business and the limitations of his training. His Bronx accent and distinctive mannerisms were exploited by Warner Brothers in a number of "fate-dogged boys from the wrong side of the tracks" potboilers. His overly energetic portrayal of Porfirio Díaz, the revolutionary general, in *Juarez*; his inability to sustain an accent in *Tortilla Flat*; and his labored attempt to play an articulate, stylized reporter in *Between Two Worlds* revealed his limited background as an actor. Only when given appropriate material was he able to realize his unique potential.

One opportunity came his way in the mid-forties when he was reunited with Odets. Although the story becomes totally implausible with Joan Crawford's contrived suicide, Odets' screenplay of *Humoresque* gives Garfield a chance to explore Ralph Berger's dream coupled with Joe Bonaparte's predicament, caught between art and success. Once again Odets succeeds in melding the role, current social conditions and the expressive capacities of the actor in this tale of a poor boy from the ghetto who becomes a violinist. Only this time by latching on to a wealthy dilettante, he discovers that culture corrupts as much as the commercial marketplace.

By this stage Garfield and Odets had more or less come to terms. They both knew by now that in the motion picture industry one had to make compromises: make do with movie actors who were content to remain one-dimensional or capitalize on their forte, and change the script for the sake of expediency or to meet commercial demands. The process was made up of bits and pieces, shot out of sequence, assembled later into a coherent mosaic or altered according to the whims of a producer. It couldn't compare to the integrity and the continual triangulation of energy during the live stage experience of *Awake and Sing*.

But the spiritual ties to the Group were still there. And in 1947 it became possible to recapture on screen what Garfield had once been denied on stage. In a sense, he was given the perfect way to make up for lost time.

In securing the lead in *Body and Soul*, Garfield was called upon to reenact Joe

Bonaparte's dilemma. A boxer at last, Garfield employed the cocky, wound-up-all-the-time side of his personality. In this acting stint he discards the values that he himself once believed in while working with his old compatriots, sacrifices his family, friends and the woman he loves for material gain, status and, as it turns out, a numbing alienation.

Testing limits again, he took on the leading part of a syndicate lawyer in *Force of Evil*. This time the character uses socially acceptable values to corrupt others, trying to convince himself that everyone is tainted, even the decent common working people he knows so well. He justifies his use of the ruthless tactics of a ghetto achiever but, as always in a meaningful role, is barely able to conceal the suffering he feels as he attempts to keep his sickly older brother out of harm's way and fails. Filmed on location in Manhattan, it's readily apparent that the locale and the circumstances hit very close to home. On the screen, Mickey Borden returns to his old stamping ground, older, wiser, jaded and, ultimately, bereft.

A retrospective of Garfield's better films shows a willingness on his part to share the self-destructive side of his personality and his battle with conflicting moralities. An ambitious, hard working, enthusiastic family man who believed in the promise of America and its ideals, he was also infatuated with celebrity, bitter over the machinations of the entertainment business and ashamed of his infidelities and the occasions when he sold out. It could easily be said that the latter three films gave him an arena in which to come to terms with troubling aspects of himself.

Cast as a Jewish soldier by Kazan (his old colleague from the Group) in the film *Gentleman's Agreement*, Garfield reaches a point when he no longer even attempts to act. He simply draws on his knowledge of ostracizing hotel managers, medical school quotas and country club exclusiveness—yet even more sources of disenchantment, made even more unbearable in the light of the recent horrors of Nazi Germany. In a scene with the genteel movie actress Dorothy McGuire and wearing his character's soldier's uniform, Garfield cuts through McGuire's airs and graces. As she relates how outraged she was at a dinner party where a wealthy man dropped anti–Semitic slurs, Garfield looks her directly in the eye and firmly strips her of all pretenses:

> GARFIELD: And what did you do?
> McGUIRE: I despised him. I wanted to yell at him. I wanted to leave and tell everyone at the table, "Why do we sit here and take this?"
> GARFIELD: And what did you do?
> McGUIRE: We all sat there. And I felt sick all through me.
> GARFIELD: I wonder if you'd feel so sick now if you'd nailed him. There's a kind of elation about socking back.
> [McGuire avoids his gaze, unable to reply.
> She puts her hands over her eyes.]

Considering a return to the stage, Garfield was given the impression that he could work once again with Elia Kazan. After all, they had so much in common, struggled and paid the price but still found themselves (in Kazan's parlance) "outside the limits," always striving for a venue to help come to terms with their anger and disenchantment. But somehow Garfield never got to play Stanley Kowalski in *A Streetcar Named Desire*. In his version, he turned the part down, rationalizing that he would be overshadowed by the character of Blanche and that Kowalski represented another in a long line of ethnic types he had played in the movies. In actuality, Tennessee Williams' world was too far beyond "the limits" and his range as an actor. Kazan had someone entirely different in mind, someone who, ironically, wasn't a star and had a wilder, more unpredictable way of working than any graduate of the Group.

Garfield did, finally, return to the stage. He teamed up with his friend Odets in a new play entitled *The Big Knife*. As Charlie Castle, he extended the downward spiral of his prototypical characters even further: portraying a film star trapped in a life that is destroying him; unable to face his youthful ideals which are mirrored by the presence of his wife whom he cares for and constantly betrays; vacillating between philosophizing, groveling, play-acting and hypocrisy.

There were a few more opportunities in the theater including a stint with Bobby Lewis. And just before his premature death, he, at last, got to play Joe Bonaparte.

However, by this stage of the game Garfield's "animal verve and immigrant chagrin" were no longer remarkable. He was the first of the rebel males and his influence was significant. But, as always, changes were taking place. Kazan, through his growing notoriety as a director, was redefining the demands of the craft. Soon, of all the Group alumni, he would have the most pervasive impact of them all.

Elia Kazan

By his own account, the various nicknames Elia Kazan was given by his Group cohorts—"Gadge"…"hungry wolf"…"the opportunist"…—were justified. "Gadge" was short for gadget and referred to the skills he had acquired at the Yale Drama School which enabled him to build, light or rig anything a director desired. The fact that he was also a seasoned stage manager only added to his indispensability. Kazan "the opportunist" was apparent at the outset when he informed Strasberg that his objective was to take over his job. Anytime an opportunity presented itself Kazan could be found latching on to it, even if it meant switching gears or siding with the powers that be rather than the rank-and-file—exactly as his comrades in the Group contended.

Another part of his strategy was to capitalize on his "external" training when called for, like the times when Harold Clurman needed help in blocking a scene. As indicated, Kazan had gleaned a certain directorial know-how from Yale professor Alexander Dean, one of the leading figures in the field. There he had learned the art of orchestrating stage pictures and movement and utilizing rhythm and pace, "builds" and "drops." Like his friend Bobby Lewis, he appreciated style and

the elements of design and felt Strasberg's preoccupation with emotional memory was overextended. But he apparently never confronted Strasberg directly. Like
any strategist, it was all a matter of timing.

In combination with a love of musical comedy, choreography and the fluidity of dance, his external preparation included an admiration of actors who were
consummate professionals. He had noted this quality while playing small parts at
Yale, at work back-stage, and sitting in the audience. These craftsmen would never
dream of "taking a minute" to evoke a painful experience. They took that time to
make certain all their props were in order and used their vocal and physical skills
to execute stage business with precision.

Keeping his options open, Kazan went along with the anarchistic notions of
taking on the establishment. But he also valued clarity, symmetry and the most
telling form. He wholeheartedly embraced Group undertakings like *Waiting for
Lefty*, generated out of a leaderless fervency, but, then again, there were many
more times when he stood back, sometimes angry, often detached. Like Garfield,
he was an outsider who learned about life the hard way. But unlike Garfield he
made certain that he had a wealth of experience and education so that he could
distance himself and, simultaneously, stay on top of the seesaw of idealism and
success. This stance was due to the early lessons that shaped his life and equipped
him to best capitalize on the Group experiment.

As a child, an Anatolian Greek in a land ruled by the Turks, he discovered
one had to be crafty to survive. Those who rebelled would be massacred. As a
young immigrant, he continued to live by his wits in the Greek ghetto of Manhattan. Underneath the façade of amiability was an abiding anger, a resentment
against those who seemed to belong. At Williams College this attitude hardened.
In order to make his way, he worked as a dishwasher and waiter. Because of his
lowly status, he was one of the few who weren't invited to join a fraternity. This
only served to intensify his antagonism toward privilege, good looks and those
commonly known as WASPs.

Disavowing the middle and upper class, "Gadge" eased into stage managing
and acting. Realizing he had no range beyond the rabble-rousing cabby in *Waiting for Lefty*, the insidious homosexual fight manager in *Golden Boy* and two-bit
gangsters in Hollywood B pictures, he gradually slipped into his director's chair.

His perception of a society hostile toward outsiders like himself made him
even more persistent and tenacious, determined to survive by any means. Concealing his true feelings, fixating on obtaining entrance without taking off his
mask, in possession of a driving will—all of these factors help to explain his con-
sistencies and inconsistencies. They also make clear the secret way he worked with
actors: mining the undercurrents he perceived beneath a character's facade; inducing a "confession," prompting sudden eruptions from someone like Brando or
Dean, reveling in some incredible disclosure. For Kazan, this was the significance
of what Stella Adler brought back from Paris: a license for true action—visually
striking, immediate, driven and surprising.

And so the puzzling Kazan moved on, sometimes identifying with the Group and missing the camaraderie, sometimes disassociating himself. He liked the idea of a league of outsiders who wouldn't assimilate, rebels with off-center characteristics who represented a buffer against a decidedly ungenerous world. He admired Clurman's stance: extolling the importance of theater, voicing the concerns of the common people, awakening and reassuring the masses, affording them the chance to see their dilemmas acted out. He identified with his fellow outsider Clifford Odets, the fearless romantic pounding away on his typewriter, grunting and groaning, intoning the actors' lines as he created them. The very same Kazan felt that the Group's cause was too simplistic, filling the audience with naive hope, blaming everything on the system rather than accepting reality. Ever conflicted, Kazan disliked the insular atmosphere, long rehearsal periods and endless talk. He would claim he was duped and misguided into affiliation with the radical fringe and Communism, taken in by the Group's activities. He would go on to justify his betrayal of Odets, Carnovsky, Phoebe Brand and others during his testimony for the House Committee on Un-American Activities. The Soviet Union was corrupt; he should have been told; not speaking out would have jeopardized his career (he would have been blacklisted, unable to work).

For a number of people his strategies and inconstancy continued to be troubling to say the least. Needless to say, for Kazan it was grist for the mill. It enabled him to secure directing jobs on Broadway working with insufferable but prestigious stars like Tallulah Bankhead where (in contrast with the Group ideal) everyone was unequal. He found himself engaged in vehicles that he couldn't possibly relate to like Thornton Wilder's *The Skin of Our Teeth*. The writing was bookish, like the summing up of a college text. It was light and frothy, with no opportunity to tap hidden behavior. Wilder couldn't abide that sort of thing.

The production, however, was a great success, bringing Kazan a step closer toward gaining enough cachet to pick and choose. For him, directing Wilder's play, struggling with a headstrong star and paying the price for notoriety were, as it turns out, invaluable—a priceless apprenticeship in reconciling opposites. As it happens, the experience prepared him for the major works of Tennessee Williams and Arthur Miller. It honed his facility in dealing with incorrigible personalities, made him a director of choice and brought into being some of the finest films and play productions of his time.

If you can reserve judgment, you can appreciate how expediently he moved up the ladder. In the thirties, the Group provided the stepping stones. In the early forties, it was the likes of Bankhead and Helen Hayes, as he threaded his way through the kind of star turns the Group supposedly abhorred and basked in the success of a series of Broadway hits that meant little or nothing to him artistically.

After serving overseas in the Far East during World War II, he was ready to call the shots. From all indications, the first thing he had in mind was bringing forth that "dangerous final intimacy" and "secret self" we've already noted. He no doubt recalled his radical days when the left-wing Theatre of Action became his own personal acting company. Following his lead, the youngsters would do anything he asked: "go to the limit" in terms of self-exposure as long as the material was within their range of experience.

At this same juncture, he also recalled his treks into the South on behalf of workers' issues, discovering an entirely new arena where the old and new came into conflict; where anything was possible—violence, poetry, humor. It was an exotic locale to Kazan, populated by dramatically eccentric women. The environment was unfamiliar and, therefore, provocative and perfectly suited to his driven, restless nature. Utilizing authentic locations would become a second component of Kazan's special directorial technique.

His restlessness and the chance to test his "intimacy" theory were both accommodated in 1944 when he accepted a film assignment and moved to Hollywood. Previously, while appearing in those few forgettable gangster movies, he had noted that the camera never lies. His limitations as a small, feisty, wiry figure could not be overcome through impersonation. Now however, as a director, provided with actors like Garfield with screen presence who, by nature, had the role within them, he could draw out any desired response. Once captured on film it was there forever. It didn't have to be repeated night after night as it did on stage. There was no need for vocal and physical projection or to sustain any of these emotional revelations. All that mattered was to bring the face and body to life, catch the fleeting moment any way he could and tap that special immediacy he'd found in his eager leftist students a decade before. As long as he had a cast with the right sensibilities, each one perfect for the part, his success with actors was relatively assured.

The rest was a matter of cinematic technique: stretching time during a critical moment from close-up to reaction shot; speeding time by omitting entrances and exits, exposition, chatter and any other extraneous stagy business; focusing only on the task at hand. The operative word was and always would be "action." It meant what the character wanted under stress. Sometimes "action" was openly expressed, sometimes indirectly through objects. Sometimes it was lying just beneath the surface and had to be coaxed or even jarred. Whatever the case, he could use any tactic necessary to gain the desired result and then take it all back.

Once he became established and proved his worth, he could add the component of authentic atmosphere and provocative locales. (In truth, this course of action wasn't laid out step by step but was part of an overall set of distinct possibilities.)

Needless to say, this whole approach had little meaning without a fitting catalyst. For Clurman the theme of the play and the mission were the be-all and end-all. For Strasberg it was an unqualified belief in the power of his theories of acting. For Kazan it was any material that struck a personal chord.

A Tree Grows in Brooklyn, his first feature film assignment, provided him with the perfect vehicle. The story centered on his abiding concern: the plight of the outsider. It also related to a current situation in his life.

Appropriately, the leading character was a complex dissembler who, despite his failures as a father, was charming and able to hold the love of his daughter. Kazan missed his own little girl and pictured his own wife in the same puritanical light as the fictional wife and mother. The setting was also familiar: a tenement, housing working class families of ethnic extraction. In this case, they were Irish.

Given carte blanche, Kazan cast according to his plan. For the central character, he remembered Jimmy Dunn who, as it happens, was the very embodiment of the role. He had great promise as an actor but was unable to find work because of a drinking problem. It was all there: Jimmy Dunn, Irish, a dissembler and failure but still charming; the guilt he felt due to his own self-betrayal could be clearly read on his face along with the stress and the desperate need to be liked. Without trying, Dunn was a touching figure, shot after shot, scene after scene.

For the daughter, Kazan chose Peggy Ann Garner. She too was made for the part. She wasn't pretty or cute, her face was drawn and pale. She had a certain light in her eyes and was extremely sensitive. Probing further, Kazan discovered that her mother had problems. In addition, Garner was highly anxious because her father was overseas engaged in active duty.

As shooting commenced, Kazan immediately applied his tactics. With his credo in mind that "you can only get out of them what's in them," he made certain he knew exactly what he was reaching for by, say, taking an actor for a walk, having lunch or dinner with him, probing into personal circumstances until secrets were revealed. For Peggy Ann Garner's pivotal scene in which she had to break down and cry, Kazan had no qualms about telling her that her father might not come back from the war. The camera caught the outburst of pain and fear as Garner was immediately instructed to enact the scene. As a result of Kazan's ploy, Garner couldn't stop crying long after shooting was over. She was inconsolable for the rest of the day. Kazan was a bit concerned. But more than that, he was proud of what she had been able to achieve.

As expected, his casting and working methods on *A Tree Grows in Brooklyn* became proof positive that he knew what he was doing. Dunn won an Oscar, Garner a special Academy Award. Although the setting and life style were sentimentalized due to the fashion of the time, it was an auspicious beginning. The compositions within the frame were apt, clear and potent; the revelations spontaneous, moving and true. He could move in and out of two media. He could improve. For plays it was a matter of scale, mood and tempo and coming to terms with a playwright who could supply him with a challenge that struck that same desired chord. With film, it was back to building a mosaic out of those priceless bits and pieces, expressing his own particular vision, and, ultimately, going on location where he could, at last, allow the atmosphere to permeate the entire undertaking and deeply affect the actors.

Learning more and more about the craft, he would find directors of photography who were masters at framing and the play of light, and then piece it all together as a unified whole. He would keep on demanding this kind of symmetry while remaining true to life and, whenever possible, seek out variations on the stories that struck a nerve.

His continuing success on both stage and screen would soon lead to the need for a gathering place for a pool of actors who were ready and willing to adopt his style of working. Correspondingly, his successes would attract a number of actors who were more than willing to work his way. But for the time being, his notion of a special locale or studio was just a pressing idea.

Among the movies he made prior to the formative phase of this studio was *Boomerang*, a neo-realistic look at civic corruption using nonactors and a handful of professionals. Shot in Stamford, Connecticut, about thirty miles from his home, he was finally able to utilize an actual environment. Once again given a free hand, he found suggestive realities inside the jails and on the streets, daytime and night. The only flaw was Dana Andrews, a serviceable Hollywood contract player, who was given the lead to help sell the picture. Still, it was distributed (slipped in amidst the usual potpourri of glossy features) and expressed Kazan's disillusionment with all governing institutions. To induce audiences to take a closer look at their supposedly normal towns and cities, he employed a documentary style. His specific aim was to bring people to the realization that disturbing things were happening behind these familiar patterns that passed for everyday life. He succeeded to some degree but was apparently still unfulfilled.

Gentleman's Agreement brought Kazan back to some of the old constraints and compromises. He could use Garfield and tap the pure-hearted honesty and bitterness underneath. He could hint at the premise that the average American is anti–Semitic. He could add to his prestige. But he couldn't push the script to the limit, couldn't bring the actors to any shattering moments of revelation. He had to use Gregory Peck in the lead because he was highly marketable, decent and beyond reproach. At best was the instant when Peck was called upon to suggest that he too was anti–Semitic. He had been trained briefly by Sandy Meisner who had decided while in the Group that actors should refrain from acting—to do no more or less than the situation required. Or as Meisner put it, "the reality of doing." What resulted was a matter of individual temperament and drive. (This is an oversimplification but seems apt in terms of Peck's performance in this film which was either unforced and highly believable or quite restrained, depending on one's point of view.)

The photography, processing, costumes, hair styling and sets were pure Hollywood, making the entire production look, in Kazan's view, like an illustration for Cosmopolitan magazine. The story-line was full of clichés. Dorothy McGuire, as Peck's fiancée, resided in a Manhattan home only a millionaire could afford. But no matter. Peck won an Oscar as the gentile writer pretending to be Jewish; Celest Holm won for Supporting Actress; and Kazan won his Oscar for directing. At this point in time, any project Kazan was associated with held the promise of some degree of realism, recognition and potential stardom for participants.

Nevertheless, his unspecified ideal continued to elude him. Given the perfect cast, the script or the locale was deficient. Some component or other always seemed to be missing from a completely satisfying whole.

For whatever reason—his impatience, his need to struggle, pursue and surmount a difficult challenge—he returned to Broadway and the stage. In 1947, in partnership with Harold Clurman, he began to zero in on the exact kind of directing assignment he longed for: a provocative dilemma that pulled no punches, encounters that generated what he himself so often had tried to conceal—the unexpected, destructive feelings and foolishness that embarrasses a person the most. The same over-the-edge outbursts he had fostered at his Theater of Action. The big scenes that went all the way, the ones like the producers of *Gentleman's Agreement* so assiduously tried to avoid.

In *All My Sons*, Kazan found not only the kind of material he'd been seeking but a playwright he could relate to as well. Arthur Miller had been inspired to write plays because of the Group Theater. Both men's lives had been shaped by the Depression, both aligned themselves politically to the Left, both had problems with their father's inhuman fixation on business and money making. Best of all was a moral issue that was met head-on. The central character didn't stop short for the sake of decorum or popular taste; he pursued the question of guilt to the bitter end. At stake was his love and admiration for his father pitted against the exposure of the business community and its profiteering and manufacture of faulty parts during the war which led to the death of loved ones. At stake was a point of no return and the upheaval of a family.

Another compelling factor was Miller's confirmation of ordinary human beings; the kind of people with whom Kazan had always been able to connect. All told, with this particular project Kazan was afforded three vital elements: a relevant play, his kind of writer, and his choice of the perfect "salt of the earth" actors like Ed Begley, Arthur Kennedy and Karl Malden.

By chance, prior to winning the Drama Critics prize for his direction of this Miller play, Kazan also produced Maxwell Anderson's *Truckline Cafe*. Directed by Harold Clurman, this short-lived venture was only distinguished by a brief turn by a young unknown by the name of Marlon Brando. The production was a step backwards and a step forwards. On the negative side, it convinced Kazan there was no place in his future plans for weakly structured, undistinguished scripts that didn't double back on his life. As for the step forward, it introduced him to intriguing possibilities through the work of one of his future "beginners" at a newly formed workshop. For one thing, Brando taught him that a person can possess emotions of terrifying intensity and a capacity for surprise that went even beyond his own expectations.

Through another act of chance and synchronicity, Tennessee Williams had recently seen *All My Sons* and was quite taken with it. He subsequently offered Kazan *A Streetcar Named Desire*. With this opportunity and under Williams' guidance, Kazan was to find the full extension of his particular approach. He could now incorporate his knowledge of the eccentric, extraordinary women of the South along with the volatile pull of its atmosphere. Whereas Miller's script was replete with ethical absolutes, Williams' work was morally ambivalent and startling. Williams' world consisted of characters who reflected his own psychic battleground: in admiration of those who could destroy him; full of self-doubts; fearful yet drawn to danger. With this work, Kazan could be challenged by a man who was even more captivated by moments of jeopardy.

On a personal note and to further illustrate this last point, I once had the unnerving experience of coming to Williams' aid. The occasion was the trial run of *Sweet Bird of Youth* in Coral Gables, Florida. In the dark of night, sporting a lime-green blouse, matching trousers and white slippers, he insisted on leaving the theater and sauntering up to four burly, self-styled rednecks. For some reason I felt obliged to accompany him. They began to taunt him despite my use of the "he's a famous playwright" ploy. Eventually, I convinced the foursome that he was a "show biz" personality appearing across the street who was trying out a new get-up just for fun. Grinning, still lingering, Williams was reluctant to part company as if courting a new, irresistible experience. In this same way, his fictional Blanche Dubois is attracted to the vulgar and crude Stanley Kowalski, a character who is dead set on destroying her and all she stands for.

But it's more than this, much more than Williams' vulnerability and perverse attraction to harm and his rendering of exotic southern locales that enlarged Kazan's vision. For the first time Kazan encountered characters who are insoluble. Stanley combines a sense of humor, a desire to bring affected people down a peg, a practical understanding of life, a need to protect the sanctity of his home and marriage, and a number of other good qualities to go along with a corrupt and animalistic nature.

And it's this wildness, this palette of strange colors and elements of mystery that took Kazan well past his Group encounters, placed a role like Stanley out of Garfield's grasp, and required the services of a new breed of actor like Brando. Trained by Stella Adler, Brando possessed the imagination, scorching power and unsettling presence that kept everyone in the project on their toes, never quite certain what he was going to do next.

As for the character of Blanche, Williams devised a perfect match for Stanley and a reflection of his own inner turbulence: intrepid while fearing betrayal, anarchy and the ravages of time; flirtatious, foolhardy and bold while suffering guilt over her sinful past; prim, sensitive, nostalgic, so fragile that the very thought of the fate of a gentle, cultured young man brings her to tears, then recalling how she offered herself to young soldiers. She courageously tells the truth about her former life. She also deviously entraps the gullible Mitch into a proposal of marriage, hiding the reality of her age and features under dim lighting and gauze and later defiantly lashes out at him. Then retreats once again, emitting an air of otherness.

For this new, psychologically raw kind of material, Kazan extended his directing style. The results electrified and intrigued audiences. Here we have Brando falling to his knees, wailing, half lost-child half wounded animal; Kim Hunter as his wife Stella, sensually descending the staircase in response, part nurturing soulmate, part wanton woman. Then there is Brando again, suddenly yanking the tablecloth, flinging the dishes after proclaiming himself a patriotic Polish-American. This primitive act totally disrupts the meal and any semblance of gentility and sets Blanche and Stella on edge. It could be said that Kazan intuitively understood what was needed, assembled those who had the talent to meet the challenge, pressed the right buttons and then stood well out of the way.

Kim Hunter and Marlon Brando in *A Streetcar Named Desire* **(1951, Warner Bros.) The opening in 1947 marked not only a landmark production under Kazan's direction but also coincided with the founding of Kazan's Actors Studio.**

As it turns out, this approach was just what Williams needed to bring this work to life. He relied on Kazan's restless dynamism to cut through his poetry and the characters' own deluded self-images. In essence, the leading characters were caught unawares, as they really were with all their flaws, and only actors who could literally surprise themselves could truly play them.

Into the bargain Kazan brought two other skills to bear. Through his life experiences and understanding of ensemble playing he was able to recreate the style and flavor of the French Quarter of New Orleans. And because he was adept at working with actresses of different backgrounds, he was successful in stimulating someone not conversant with Stanislavsky's techniques to the point where she could bring Blanche fully to life. Jessica Tandy, a graduate of the Ben Greet Academy in London, exuded the tone and refinement of a cultured woman ostensibly from the fictional Belle Reve. She also possessed great intelligence. Under Kazan's direction, she grew to relish Brando's unpredictability and turn it to her advantage. And as an unassuming and dedicated character actress, she accepted the given circumstances and mode of working and became an integral part of the whole.

Apart from all of the above, Kazan's involvement with this play reinforced his spiritual alliance with the outsider in American society. Williams was openly homosexual and, like Kazan, an outlaw and quirky rebel. The fault line Kazan was testing this time brushed against the straight culture of his day. With this association with Williams, he was pushing the parameters, ostensibly declaring that everyone had a shadow side. Life was a puzzle that couldn't be solved. Kazan, a man who had trained himself to conceal any show of pain, was now prodding for its public revelation no matter how bizarre.

At the same time it should be noted that, as ever, timing was an operative factor. Film noir, with its focus on the darker undercurrents of human behavior, and the growing interest in stories about abnormal psychology, phobias and complexes were featured everywhere on stage and screen. "Streetcar" was perceived in many quarters as part of this trend. It was a provocative theatrical experience, daringly up-to-date.

Moving from this venture to another landmark production, Kazan took on Miller's *Death of a Salesman*. By now there was a tacit understanding that serious theater worked on a deeper level. Whatever facet of life that was too difficult to face would be grappled with on stage through the playwright's voice and vision, the actors' willingness to invest in the struggle at hand, and, with someone like Kazan in charge, the director's connection with the material. As a result, and absolutely integral to the process, was the excitement that was then passed on to audiences. If they were shown their deepest anxieties, if they could confront something nameless but meaningful in the safety of their seats, some kind of closure could be attained and the circle would be complete.

With "Streetcar" as a point of reference, Miller took into account Williams' nonrealistic devices and the complexity of his characters as part of the evolving trend in theatrical experience. They inspired him to dig into his embattled central figure's psyche through memory. And Kazan was more than ready to meet this next challenge. He induced a memorable performance from Lee J. Cobb as Willy Loman who happened to be a member of the Group during its final years and emotionally, if not physically, perfect for the role. Once again, the playwright, director, cast and way of working formed a cohesive bond.

More specifically, Miller's play worked on many levels and Kazan's staging and encounters with his favored salt-of-the-earth players captured the poetic and psychological realism and the universal "tragedy of the common man." What's more, the springboard was as real and personal to Miller as Odets' struggles in his Bronx tenement house. Before the Depression, Miller's father was the owner of the Miltex Coat and Suit Company, responsible for the livelihood of countless workers, salespeople, clerks and an entire clan of immigrant relatives. With the Crash, Isadore Miller, the wealthy patron and successful businessman, joined the ranks of failed fathers who groped for some way to recover their lost dignity. America meant promise. Failure was unendurable. It was taken personally. It meant a life with no meaning or legacy to pass on.

Through Miller's imagination, his father and two salesmen—his cousin Manny and Manny's friend who, no matter how downtrodden, would talk about his inevitable triumphs—became one person: a single man trying to come up with some way to crown all his striving years, some victory, some way to redeem his lost self and his dream of continuity through his two sons. To follow the salesman's shifting thoughts as he tries to reconcile his failures and his present state—driving his battered car, fighting his failed eyesight, holing up in seedy hotel rooms, ready to end it all, unable to face his infidelities—required a fluid handling of time and place. Willy needed flashbacks and had to confront a disintegrating present as well. He needed some kind of playground in order to relive it all and finally come to terms.

And here Kazan's familiarity with the theatrical, his experiences at Yale and the open looseness of *Waiting for Lefty* along with the whimsical passage of time in Thornton Wilder's *Skin of Our Teeth*, came to the fore. The set he called for was indeed a kind of playground. When the action was in the present, the characters had to observe imaginary wall-lines. In scenes from the past, the characters stepped through the boundaries. A downstage area and spotlighting intimated the various locales of Willy's imaginings. Platforms and a backdrop suggested a cross section of Willy's fragile little house.

Moving well beyond naturalism, Willy is seen caught between two opposite poles: material success and the need for unconditional love. He had been taught that love and approval are withheld from those who fail. His struggle, literally and figuratively, is a matter of life and death.

Clearly, while owing a great deal to Odets, Miller's "Salesman" has traveled a long way from Garfield's Ralph Berger listening to his grandfather's hopeful dreams. Here there is no common theme the actors can subscribe to. Kazan had to steer his actors through an entirely new kind of fragmented progression—e.g., Willy returning unexpectedly, beginning to talk to himself ... the lighting cross-fading, shifting upstairs to his sons' reactions ... then slipping over to the forestage into the past when Willy and the boys were young and the car, house and appliances were fresh and new ... and then shifting further back into the past as Uncle Ben drifts out:

> BEN: I must make a train, William. Opportunities are tremendous. I have many enterprises. Principally diamond mines!

Thus with "Salesman" the old concept of the logical through-line had to be revised. Actors could no longer rely on cause and effect to see them through. It was a marked departure, yet met Kazan's basic need for challenging material that touched a chord. As in *All My Sons*, Kazan was reminded of his father, a rug salesman who, like Willy Loman, had high hopes for his two sons. The elder Kazan always played the merchant, selling himself in order to hawk his goods. Dealing with the elements in the play forced Kazan to come to grips with his parent, to realize how a misguided frantic man can barricade himself from the affection he needs, having no idea who he really is, pursuing the wrong dream.

Profiting from his work with Williams, Kazan was also able to see Willy as an unstable figure: ridiculous and tragic; evoking affection, concern, pity, love and all manner of responses in between. Moral ambiguity had by now become another hallmark of Kazan's approach to character. It also recalled one of Stanislavsky's earliest discoveries in looking for opposites: the good in an evil man, the strength in a frail man—whatever gives a person dimension, humanity and unpredictability. Even though it wasn't conscious on Kazan's part, his way of working now also recalls the inventiveness of Vakhtangov and Michael Chekhov to a much subtler degree.

From every angle things were dovetailing, including Kazan's evaluation of the Method. It was useless and maudlin for actors to make themselves pathetic and wallow in their own emotionality and pain. Rather, Kazan urged his cast to use humor, verve and a host of other tactics to rise above, conceal or contain their feelings while dealing with the given circumstances. Consistently with Kazan it was a matter of matching the character in the play with the emotional core of the individual actor and then focusing on the task at hand. As indicated, the contradictions within lumbering Lee J. Cobb's personality were already in place. Cobb was loving and hateful, anxious and highly pleased with himself, smug and full of doubt, guilty and arrogant. He was also fiercely competitive but withdrawn, suspicious but always asking for trust; boastful with a modest air, begging for acceptance no matter what harm he did to others. Cobb was Willy Loman. All he needed to do was focus on Willy's actions.

The results spoke for themselves. All in all, with the addition of "Salesman" to his repertoire, Kazan's reputation and position were secure. Predictably, however, plagued and fueled by the ambiguity in his own character, even though he had done a masterful job of mounting two monumental plays about two quintessential outsiders like himself, he was not satisfied. Despite all his misgivings, he began yearning for the kind of collective experience he had enjoyed a decade before. It was at this point that his notions of a gathering place began to take on more significance.

In the spring of 1947, he took a stroll in Central Park with his close friend Bobby Lewis (they had lived together and shared a dressing room for many years during their Group Theater days). Earlier, they had conceived of a popular-priced "Dollar Top Theater" so that people from all walks of life could attend socially relevant plays, just like the old days. But costs had skyrocketed since the war. And the need for some meaningful connection with their past and the current generation was still unmet.

Following Kazan's lead, a new idea was conceived. It wouldn't be a second coming of the Group; that was out of the question. There would be no manifestos, no auspicious beginnings. It would be more like a studio. Cheryl Crawford, their friend and fellow alumnus (who had just successfully produced *Brigadoon* on Broadway under Lewis' direction) was brought on board as business manager and the venture slipped quietly into being.

5

The Actors Studio: Phase One

In general, Kazan and Lewis decided to establish a laboratory where they could explore ideas and experiment with projects and acting techniques far from the pressures of commercial production. In this way they could exercise their franchise as artists while pursuing their outside interests and directing careers. The venture still necessitated a pool of talented professional actors. But they had to be dedicated: serious about being given an opportunity and a place to work on their craft in a way that was beneficial to themselves and compatible with the values of both of the artistic directors. And they had to be able to work collectively, sans the battles and radical preoccupations that often marked the Group experience.

For Kazan's part, he would still need to be in a position to select actors for his play and film projects—"genuine" people who would follow his lead as in the old Theater of Action days. Concurrently, he would once again be guiding and training a group of younger people whose work he was very familiar with. Effectively, he would be turning out a new generation of actors through a unique farm system—like baseball, calling up those who were needed and ready to play the game.

As for Bobby Lewis, he was chosen to partner because he possessed the exact qualities needed to balance the undertaking: simplicity, clarity and a strong sense of humor. Moreover, as an expert in style, he stressed the bolder, imaginative side of acting. With Lewis as a counterpart, the project naturally called for two groups. While Kazan took on the younger actors, Lewis would handle the seasoned veterans.

Soon interest became so high that the two leaders added a stipulation: participants would be dismissed if their work didn't measure up. But this posed no problem. By and large, everyone selected went along gladly. They coveted a place to get together and achieve self-renewal. They fully realized this particular kind of development was only possible within a serious, sympathetic atmosphere where they were appreciated and not regarded, as usual, as commercial types and commodities. They needed guidance from established directors who were once actors and had been in their shoes: teachers who could inspire them, challenge them and help them reach new levels. For a majority of the sixty-one original members, the Actors Studio was born out of need.

Yet, as ever in this continuing saga, the project was not fully embraced by all concerned. Clurman was miffed over the fact that he wasn't included. And he was still smarting over Kazan's recent decision to break off their production partnership. Also, many Group members still had an aversion to Kazan and his opportunistic tactics. Although Kazan considered the workshop as an extension of his collective experience of the 1930s, many from the old guard saw the Studio as a ploy, a thinly veiled source of actors for Kazan's private use which in no way reflected the old selfless vision of theater and life.

Another source of unease was the mention of Lee Strasberg. Since the late thirties, Strasberg had taken on directing assignments with little success. Discouraged, experiencing a lack of focus, Strasberg left New York in 1944 for Hollywood. Even though he had continually denounced the movie industry for its low standards and shallow commercialism and discredited Group members who gave in to its lure of money and fame, he accepted a three-year stint at 20th Century–Fox directing screen tests. During that same spring of 1947 he was back in New York teaching classes at the American Theater Wing and the Dramatic Workshop. Word had it that he was leaving his options open.

Kazan and Lewis felt he might be of use—given his acquired knowledge and voracious reading habits—as a lecturer in theater history. But it would be unwise to let him influence actors, especially the younger ones, in light of his temperament and fixation on emotional memory. The inclusion of Strasberg in some capacity thus became a possible issue.

Kazan's private reservations and ambivalence went deeper. On the positive side, Strasberg had been his boss, an archetypal figure who had pursued emotional truth in training and performance; a man who had introduced them all to some of Stanislavsky's basic tenets such as total concentration. He was one of the founders of the Group. His presence would validate the new Studio and link it directly to that heritage.

On the other hand, aside from the humiliation Kazan unjustly suffered during the run-through of *Gold Eagle Guy*, Kazan's ledger on Strasberg contained more debits than credits. As stage manager for Strasberg, it was his job to call out "Take a minute" before each scene. It was during these moments that Kazan noted how actors would compete to demonstrate how intensely emotional they could become to the detriment of the ensemble and the play. In directing love scenes, Strasberg demonstrated his own painful inhibitions, instructing partners to look away from each other; or he would separate them through the use of a post or door. These devices undermined the integrity of the characters and the scene. Through emotional memory the theatrical experience was further impaired as actors engaged in self-indulgence, self-love and, at times, a form of sleepwalking.

Strasberg's temper tantrums notwithstanding, Kazan resented Strasberg's domi-
nating, distanced posture as a judge, both in classes and during rehearsals. No one
was allowed to question his pronouncements. Joy was not in the offing or any
opportunity for flights of fantasy or humor. For Kazan, the inclusion of Strasberg
meant the loss of theater as something fancy free, a journey of the imagination
like painting and dance. A chance at wonder, a lightness of being.

As expected, Lewis insisted on vibrant theatricality as a necessity. Like Kazan,
his deep concern was that Strasberg would undercut the theatrical element in
favor of emotional self-indulgence. If you add Strasberg's regard for language as
external "decoration," as far as Lewis was concerned, the issue of Strasberg's inclusion was moot. As it stood during this formative stage, Lewis and Kazan were
more or less in agreement. Strasberg did not fit into their immediate plans.

But for some of those standing on the sidelines, the attitude was let's-wait-and-
see. Kazan had always protested too much. Kazan was a dissembler. Lewis was
admired. However, since he always played by the rules, he was bound to get caught
in the middle. It was only a matter of time. On paper, perhaps, these were auspicious
beginnings but those who knew better had been through auspicious beginnings before
and would not be taken in. What Kazan and Lewis envisioned in the spirit of the
moment and what would actually take place were, doubtless, worlds apart.

Sloughing off any misgivings, Kazan plunged ahead. He began working with
his "kids" like Julie Harris, Cloris Leachman and Nehemiah Persoff. He found
himself in a haven where, for the time being, he could let down his guard and
conduct the activities he envisioned with total abandon.

Kazan's Acting Sessions

From the start, Kazan outlined the parameters. He was forging a common
language so that he could direct actors, not coach them. Participants were not in
a school. They were in a lab, a place where they had to work hard to discover and
apply this vocabulary. (In point of fact, the "place" was several places as the early
Studio moved to a series of makeshift locales like the old Union Methodist Church
on West Forty-eighth Street and a dance studio on East Fifty-ninth Street before
settling in at the site generally associated with the Studio's name.)

As a matter of course Kazan stressed his major keynote, action—e.g., struggling, pursuing, moving around through and under, surmounting difficulties. The
questions repeatedly asked were, What do you want? What are you on stage for?
To get or achieve what? He wanted them alive, strong and dynamic. He didn't let
them explain or psychologize. In this emphasis on activity, emotions were trans-
ferred to objects, just the way Phoebe Brand, Morris Carnovsky and the others
worked when Clurman took charge. In Kazan's view, this way of working was
stage-worthy and cinematic. You could see things move from one hand to another,
see them break, see them embraced or thrown away. All energy was focused energy
in service to activation.

This use of objects (which is really a supplement to Stanislavsky's method of physical actions) is clearly illustrated in Kazan's direction of the film *Wild River*. The actress Lee Remick portrays a shy country girl who wishes to embrace Montgomery Clift's reserved and inarticulate government agent. The first opportunity arises when Clift awkwardly enters her modest little house, drenched from a soaking rain. Remick welcomes him in and searches for some way to make contact and ease his discomfort. Finally she settles on a towel. Despite his halfhearted protests, she closes the agonizing gap between them and rubs his wet hair. A character's reliance on tangibles as a means of release and communication is one of the signatures of a Kazan film.

Improvisation was another favored activation device, linked often to the very same use of objects. With his adrenaline constantly pumping, Kazan challenged and sparked the actors' sense of spontaneity and immediacy. For instance, he would toss a set of keys at one of them and tell the person to create a scene. The objects could transform into medals or fingernail files—anything, as long as they were dealt with as something vital.

To keep them in a state of readiness and stretch their imaginative capacities, he would switch tactics and omit all tangibles. Without notice, he would instruct them to become animals or a telephone book or a melting wax statue. At another point, he would call out three arbitrary movements and ask the actors to justify them: always focusing on the action, the dilemma, the situation that demanded a solution. Sometimes, he would call for an improv based on three words like "red, soup and line." Or he would give them a line of dialogue and have them act it out using twenty or so different actions—e.g., to belittle, to beg, to seduce, to gain sympathy, to frighten…

Always it was a character's driving objective that was paramount. He would not be satisfied until an actor could literally taste the need and fully "go for it." Often he would shout, "Get up! Do it!" as he impelled everyone to reach as far as they could go. No one was allowed to hold back because, as we've already seen, for Kazan this was the crux of drama. Revelations generated by irrepressible strivings were at the heart of it all.

To all who participated in these formative sessions, Kazan was affectionate, at ease and thereby able to put everyone else at ease. He was daring and induced them to be even more daring. He had a special freshness to his approach, a fervor. He knew how to make them come individually and collectively alive. They reveled in the fact that he called them glorious individualists. He rekindled something that many felt had been lost. They trusted him. As he got to know them and their limitations, they realized he would never push them beyond their capacities. For many, it was the best of times. After he relinquished the reins, it was never the same.

During this opening phase there was one significant addition: Anna Sokolow's movement seminars. Following Kazan's example (and willing participation due to his own background in dance), Sokolow incorporated "action" with various kinds of movements. For instance, she would ask her actor/dancers to walk while listening to a bird singing. Later on, she added appropriate music and eventually reached the point where she was able to stage a "total theater" exploration based on William Saroyan's short story "Elmer and Lily." Another dance/theater piece entitled *Rooms* examined the lives of people living in tiny quarters, struggling with loneliness in the big city.

In many ways Sokolow's work mirrored Helen Tamiris' approach during those special Group summers in the early 1930s. With Tamiris you were always someone else: "so-and-so doing such-and-such." And the focus was invariably on the "other"—e.g., with the palms of the hands close to each other but not touching, giving into the other's will … keeping your distance from others … observing another person and adapting their rhythm until you felt like someone else; observing in your mind's eye the character you are portraying until you sensed his or her inner rhythm and allowed it to take over and replace your own movement patterns. Tamiris is acknowledged as one of the five great pioneers in modern dance in America. Her focus was on the human condition and immediacy.

If you combine Kazan and Sokolow's sensibility with that of Bobby Lewis—whom everyone in the Group compared to Vakhtangov—it could be argued that the opening phase of the Studio was, in part, akin to the spirit of the Group's first phase and that of Suler and Stanislavsky in their First Studio as well.

The Distinctiveness of Lewis

Hearkening back to Bobby Lewis' portrayal of Mr. May in Odets' *Paradise Lost*, it's apparent that his interest in Vakhtangov-like fantastic realism never wavered since the time in the 1920s when he was fascinated by the stylistic turns of Jacob Ben Ami. In a pivotal scene in the Odets play, Lewis, as the weird little May, tries to interest Morris Carnovsky and Luther Adler in a scheme whereby their failing factory could fortuitously catch fire. The two owners could then simply collect the insurance money and be solvent again. In his characterization, Lewis whimsically dyed his hair red, combed it up at the sides in flame-like wisps, and wore a large black leather guard over his index finger to indicate some unfortunate mishap during one of his forays at arson. He added a bizarre accent, pronouncing his "v"s as "w"s; and also included a sickly-sweet smile and furtive movements, often cocking his head back and to one side and forming a spider-web with his fingers. These touches were typical of his singular approach to acting—inventive externals played with total conviction.

As a director, his experiments with style were encouraged by Clurman during the mid–1930s. Among Lewis' projects was a poetic play about a strike. Later on, he achieved his first artistic success when Clurman gave him carte blanche to turn a William Saroyan short play into a full production retitled *My Heart's in the Highlands*. Lewis set about augmenting the libretto and then unified all the elements—enchanting dialogue, music, movement, sound, color, sets, costumes, lighting—into a cohesive piece. Following Clurman's example, he pinpointed the theme: the agony of the artist's attempt to create while living in a hostile world.

More specifically, in tune with his own whimsical nature, Lewis' setting was a child's sketch of a poet's house and street framed by a huge stylized tree. Sustaining this antic tone, he asked the performer playing the escaped Shakespearean actor to crawl on his hands and knees and then atop a kitchen table, scribbling on a scrap of paper struggling to find a rhyme. In another scene, Lewis pictured a plant flowering as it was watered. To realize this effect, he directed the old Shakespearean poet to clamber upon his raised porch and summon one and all by blowing on his long medieval trumpet. In turn, the people gathering below formed a tree-like shape: a few in kneeling positions, others standing, the entire configuration leading up to a child held high on a tall man's shoulders; each person concealing a colorfully painted article of food. They all then revealed their offerings as the poet vibrated his trumpet like a tremulous watering can, the fruits seemingly growing out of the branches; the whole ensemble swaying slightly in the wind.

In its relatively short run during the 1939 Broadway season, audiences were touched by the effort and critics unanimously found it to be poignant, charming and indefinable. With this production, Bobby Lewis' belief that feelings could be fully aroused in theatergoers without asking the actors to do all the crying was, once again, validated.

As would be expected, his teaching reflected his unique directing style. He had begun refining his acting theories while running a small Group Theater school designed to train promising actors. Before long, he began speaking of the craft in the same terms as dress and conduct. Everything was a matter of appropriateness to the culture in question. A style of behavior that was suitable for one locale might be entirely unsuitable for another. Both would be perfectly natural and normal in their respective settings.

As for speech, while Strasberg had asserted that considerations like a New York accent were not acting problems, merely technical problems, Lewis was convinced that all considerations were integral to the whole. Lewis recalled Alfred Lunt, Pauline Lord and Laurette Taylor during the days when he was first exposed to Stanislavsky. They never seemed external. They were skilled at using language, controlling it and even distorting it, if necessary, as a means of communicating character. Feelings at the expense of diction befog and conceal the thought, essence and even the very plot of the play. The verse becomes altered by an actor's own rhythms and pauses. Stylistic demands such as characterization, text, tempo and the sentiments implicit in the playwright's language can only be met through vocal technique. Personal psychology, according to Lewis, has no place on the stage.

In practical terms, it was advantageous for the fledgling Studio to have someone like Lewis aboard, a flexible leader who had a proven record of adjusting to artistic and commercial demands as long as they were reasonable, a person adept at getting along with anyone as long as they were professional. He possessed just the kind of credentials and perspective the veteran actors needed.

As an actor in Hollywood in the early forties, Lewis went so far as to amiably portray a variety of peculiar characters, whatever was asked: a Nazi colonel with the unlikely name of Pirosh, a Japanese general, a German Officer in a supporting role to Lassie, a pharmacist (while working for Chaplin in *Monsieur Verdoux*) in a stodgy dark suit, with scholarly eyeglasses and a boring manner to match.

As a director, he could mount a commercial show with the best of them and switch back to more avant-garde, fanciful work like the poetic *Mexican Mural* featuring one of his favorite students, the luminous Mira Rostova; and the fantasy *Heavenly Express* with its star-filled sky looming over a gaggle of hoboes huddled around a fire. For *The Overland Kid*—a combination of hobo and child—Lewis had lured his old Group pal John Garfield back from Hollywood. This tall tale of God's special devotion to the tramp brotherhood took Lewis, Garfield and producer Cheryl Crawford back into their element—a collective ideal.

With *Brigadoon*, a musical based on another whimsical tale, it was more of the same, but this time he had a hit on his hands that was settling in for a long Broadway run. Here we have a confused young man looking for the perfect community. He eventually finds it in a fully populated two-hundred-year-old village in the Scottish Highlands. Since the community only comes alive on a special day every hundred years, the only solution is to follow the pure and lovely maiden into the mist as the village vanishes once again. In response, critics applauded Lewis for his restoration of theater to the purely imaginative and his "musician's feeling for rhythm and mood, and a theatrician's aptitude for emphasis."

To top it all off, in Tamara Daykarhanova's view (a noted former Moscow Art Theater actress who had employed Lewis as a master teacher), Lewis' approach to acting and theater was perfectly in line with Stanislavsky's precepts.

At the Studio Lewis felt it was his primary task to challenge the established actors, to induce them to go into unfamiliar territory while carrying out their assignments convincingly. Among the forty or so candidates he selected were Marlon Brando, Montgomery Clift, Karl Malden, Patricia Neal, Maureen Stapleton, Mildred Dunnock, Eli Wallach, Sidney Lumet and Tom Ewell.

Since he knew their work so well (Clift had studied with him at the time he was staging *Mexican Mural*; Lumet was the child in *My Heart's in the Highlands*, etc.), he could quickly determine which roles were best suited to stretch them in other directions. For instance, at the time, Tom Ewell was coasting along in the frothy Broadway comedy *John Loves Mary*. In the shelter of the workshop, Lewis gave him the part of slow-witted Lennie in the dark and naturalistic *Of Mice and Men*.

To move Brando far afield from the slovenly, animalistic Stanley Kowalski, he assigned him a sophisticated role from Robert Sherwood's *Reunion in Vienna*. As the Archduke Rudolph Maxmillian, Brando was forced to make a complete transformation replete with full uniform, sword, mustache and monocle, long cigarette holder and Hapsburg accent. Lewis also instructed Brando to incorporate recorded Vienna waltz music into the scene. In his portrayal before all assembled, Brando slowly circled the actress playing his intended, Elena. In the unpredictable way that was to become his trademark, he suddenly slapped his partner, grabbed her, kissed her passionately and murmured, "How long has it been since you were kissed like that?" The roar of approval from his Broadway colleagues spurred him on to sustain this light, comic tone throughout the scene.

In his effervescent manner, Lewis went on promoting the benefits of a wide range of styles counter to everyone's personality type. In every instance they were discouraged from working for emotion for its own sake or indulging in self-expression. The emphasis was always on intention in terms of their character's fears and desires within the special world of the play.

In response, his actors found Lewis to be fun to work with. To them he exuded a great deal of color and off-center panache and was "sweet ... kind, dear and patient" to boot. Like the characters he favored, he was characterized as larger than life.

On paper, the first season should have ended on a high note. Lewis was set to apply his principles to workshop performances of Chekhov's *The Sea Gull* featuring Montgomery Clift as Treplev the poet. Kazan was eager to culminate his sessions with an original full-scale project. He had been working closely with the author Bessie Breuer and had commissioned a number of made-to-order youthful roles to fulfill his students' expressive needs. However, as is often the case in this proliferating story, there was tension waiting in the wings. This time it revolved around a matter of integrity.

The linchpin was a musical Crawford had acquired for commercial production. It was called *Love Life* with Lewis slated to direct. When Kazan advised Lewis that the book and score needed major revisions, Lewis turned the project down. Soon after, Kazan accepted the assignment and instructed Crawford to notify Lewis of his decision. In response to Kazan's offhanded ploy, Lewis turned to their shared Studio guidelines. In the sessions three questions were stressed: what? why? how? Lewis knew full well what Kazan was up to and why. His motives, while not exemplary, were understandable. It was how Kazan went about securing the job and then placing Crawford, the producer, in the awkward position of messenger that Lewis found unacceptable. In Lewis' code of ethics, how a person comports himself was the basis for judging character. Lewis had put up with contradictions up to a point. What people professed and what they actually did were frequently never the same in the entertainment business. But this was a betrayal of friendship. Friends told you the truth immediately and directly.

Lewis went on to complete the "Sea Gull" project even though he had tendered his resignation. He had made Stanislavsky's interpretation of the text perfectly clear to the cast and resolved other questions of interpretation as well. His only regret as far as this, his first Studio production, was concerned was his failure to convince Montgomery Clift to play the lead. But the enigmatic Clift was ready for something more provocative. Lewis pointed out that the rebellious Meyerhold had played the role. Clift retorted that this wasn't turn of the century Russia. He needed to be part of something new, a different medium: opportunities that were his for the asking in Hollywood. *The Sea Gull* would have to go on without him.

In the aftermath, Cheryl Crawford found Lewis' direction of Chekhov's play "fragrant" with "incredible sweetness and truth." "You unfolded it," she wrote, "not slowly and grimly but with vitality and buoyancy." Her letter was touching but Lewis' mind was made up. As a result, the Studio never saw the likes of his brand of theatricality again.

Undaunted, Kazan pressed on. Juggling his direction of *Sundown Beach* with his outside commercial commitments, he added improvisations to the Studio project in an attempt to quickly bring the loosely knit scenes to life.

The setting was a small cafe off the Gulf Coast of Florida near a hospital for convalescing combat crews. The episodes focused on a number of young men suffering from a variety of psychiatric wounds and their effects on the girls who loved them.

Kazan kept adding new problems and changes, insisting that performance was like a little flame that had to be doused with kerosene to keep it from going out. He worked closely with Julie Harris, prompting her in different ways to give an affecting performance as the hillbilly girl, Ida Mae. He pushed the tension level of each and every scene as though something vital was at stake. For whatever reason, the production was booked outside the intimate confines of the Studio in venues like the Westport Country Playhouse in nearby Connecticut. Kazan envisioned the critical response as a test of his basic concept: engendering new talent through his own special techniques.

The reviews were mixed. The critics felt that the various story lines were not integrated. Their overall impression was that of breathlessness: running at top speed in order to go nowhere; violent physical interludes with no meaning; a series of high-strung self-conscious performances staged for their own sake. Some cast members claimed that without Kazan's protective presence—he was often absent during dress rehearsals and performances attending to other obligations—they became even more frenetic. Their protests, however, went unheeded.

Shortly after, Kazan decided that the Studio would never produce again. It would confine its activities and function solely as a workshop, a place where invited actors could work on whatever they pleased. Additionally, he concluded that he wasn't cut out to be a teacher for any sustained period of time. If his energy level was high, sessions profited. If his energy flagged, the level of work followed suit.

In the light of all that had happened, he made more decisions. He would try to find a substitute for Lewis and concentrate on his directing career, stop trying to be all things to all people. Given a provocative polished script and the right kind of seasoned actors—ones that didn't need reassurance and continual stimulation, people like Brando or Clift—he could continue to work his magic.

And this is where the equation began to change. As we've seen—more graphically with Brando during one of Lewis' sessions and hinted at in the exchange between Clift and Lewis—there was a different breed of individualist coming onto the scene: non-conformists who were not content to stay in New York, work on their craft at the new Studio and appear in plays. They were as restless as Kazan. As they began to make their mark on the silver screen and reach a wider audience, they were regarded as unique. Perhaps, in some ways, the ones in charge. Soon they became known as the prototype of the Studio actor even though they were only incidentally associated.

It may have been the need to simplify and explain things away, a habit left over from the war. World War II was, after all, the great unifying experience, the ultimate melting pot which pitted "our boys" against the Axis powers. In the same vein, there was a tendency to pigeonhole people in those days. You were classified by your religion, club, college, political party, etc. It gave everything the semblance of order and normalcy, putting things back in place. There was a new prosperity and a consumerism that would fulfill all needs. Everything was fine as long as no one rocked the boat. But there were undercurrents of doubt and anxiety beneath the post-war euphoria. Different stories were needed plus a new breed of actor to tell them. Resorting back to convention, that breed had to be given a name: Method actor.

In terms of the sources of doubt and anxiety, they stemmed from many things, problems cropping up that no one wanted to openly confront. Women didn't wish to relinquish their self-reliance and give their jobs back to returning servicemen in exchange for a well-equipped kitchen. The continued expansionist policies of the USSR, what lay behind what Sir Winston Churchill called the "Iron Curtain" and the threat of a nuclear doomsday were unnerving. The moral standards and taboos of the older generation that were being enforced were especially hollow to many. In turn, the powers that be were concerned about underlying desires. In this age of witch-hunts, threats of juvenile delinquency and a Kinsey Report that disclosed a 37 percent ratio of males indulging in at least one homosexual experience, greater efforts were made to insure that people conformed to traditional values and familiar types. There was an unstated fear of the marginal man or woman, ambivalence, talk of civil rights, people crossing the line, and enemies who were hard to define. Back on the other hand, there was the nagging question of finding one's true self in a country obsessed with conformity, where classroom teachers threatened to file acts of misconduct in a student's permanent record.

Because of this underlying ambiguity and the complexity of post-war life, the public needed these new prototypes. They needed Montgomery Clift and Marlon Brando as a way of glimpsing into those parts of themselves that were supposed to be kept under wraps and they needed to view their actions in the relative safety of the movie theater. Garfield had provided the romantic rebel hero for many, especially the poor and disenfranchised. But, as we've seen with the plays of Williams and Miller, it would now take actors with mercurial sensibilities to reflect the times and tell the tales. And they had to come from somewhere. Movie studies had to be supplied by an acting studio from New York according to the popular explanation. Needless to say, just like the ambiguity and complexity of the times, there was a lot more to the story than that.

6

The Enigma of Clift and Brando

Montgomery Clift

When the celebrated Hollywood director Howard Hawks interviewed Montgomery Clift for a leading role in his western *Red River*, he immediately liked Clift's attitude. Clift had never been in a movie, let alone ridden a horse. To make up for this deficiency and demonstrate his professionalism, Clift went to Arizona two weeks prior to shooting and worked with a real cowboy. He rode all day long, up hills and down steep places and through water. His work ethic and good looks notwithstanding, Hawks cast him for another reason. He had a quality that went beyond his trim figure, refined features and slightly cultured air. He chose Clift because he was different from any standard Hollywood type. He was nothing like John Wayne, Clark Gable, Gary Cooper and other movie heroes who approached everything in a straightforward way. Clift's special quality was impossible for a plainspoken man like Hawks to define but it was there all the same. And it was essential to play the enigmatic young Matthew Garth and reflect the tenor of the times.

Years later, the Italian movie star Marcello Mastroianni dubbed Clift the originator of the modern anti-hero. He spoke of Clift's restrained, inner tension and "ancient, melancholy eyes ... his presence so unobtrusively strong that it lingered." Others would refer to Clift in terms of the "fluidity of the self" and the essence of the contemporary male: a person who makes mistakes, gets hurt, is psychically bruised but never withdraws. A man who is always unnervingly present and real.

These attributes were all the more intriguing when you consider that Clift's roots were in the Midwest: the prairie country the pragmatist John Dewey described as the center, the area that held America together and gave it unity and stability. He represented possibilities for everyone, a chance for self-invention beyond wearing a conventional mask and assuming a fixed gender role. If Clift could be famous and provisional, if he could hail from Omaha, Nebraska, and still be released from society's prescriptions, movie audiences could imagine doing the same.

For aspiring actors this represented a new pattern. You could move from the conservative center to the East Coast, nurture your talent for reinvention and then light out for the West Coast for validation and success. All you had to do was find the right stepping stone. The word was out that there was a workshop in New York that could show you how to turn yourself into another Clift: open yet private; strong yet gentle; cool but not callous; independent but without conceit; dislocated yet completely engaged.

These suppositions—including Clift's rivalry with Brando, who also hailed from Omaha—helped create the myth that there was more to everyone than meets the eye. With enough grit, determination, sensitivity and a boost from Kazan's Studio, success was within reach. It was all just a matter of timing.

The actual elements that led to Hawks' *Red River* and beyond for Clift and the filming of "Streetcar" and beyond for Brando were far richer and more complex. And the Studio was closer to the periphery than the core.

For Clift, the path was oblique. The initial catalyst was an alleged birthright. His mother, a woman of regal bearing, was obsessed with gaining acceptance from aristocrats whom she believed to be her natural parents. Determined to raise her children in the elegant, princely manner they deserved and achieving this recognition, she eventually induced her husband to move and buy a capacious Tudor-style home in a wealthy Chicago suburb. From there she traveled to Bermuda and toured Europe with Monty and his brother and sister. Clift was tutored in the classical tradition, kept apart from those who attended school, and lived a privileged lifestyle.

With a weakness for Pouilly-Fumé and the finest caviar and as a master of etiquette, Clift was completely different from most children raised in the heartland. Because of his elitist lifestyle he became aloof and melancholic. He was the opposite of those first-generation Americans who hungered after community, a Russian aesthetic of theater, and a collective opportunity to teach others how to survive.

When his father went bankrupt and the family drifted to a small furnished room in Greenwich Village, Clift felt even more disoriented. His interest in acting was fueled solely from a need for self-definition to overcome his feelings of rootless alienation. A gifted mimic by the age of twelve, he mocked his elders and absorbed the marked differences of those who rode the subways and walked the streets. He studied them as avidly as he studied his books, which made him even more worldly. All of this, coupled with his cultured features—arched dark eyebrows, delicate nose and slender form—and refined manners led to modeling jobs as a teenager at his mother's instigation. He then went on to summer stock in the Berkshires of Massachusetts in a play that moved to Broadway.

While the Group was performing the plays of Odets, Clift found his mentors in Alfred Lunt and Lynn Fontanne, the glamorous husband and wife team who performed the type of stylish turns that distressed Strasberg and Clurman. Always the gentleman and apt mimic, Clift incorporated Lunt's gait and meticulous mannerisms in many of his sensitive-young-man portrayals on Broadway. This tribute to his mentor included Lunt's speech patterns—e.g., running words together quickly in mid-sentence and affecting extraneous pauses between others. It was Lunt who prompted Clift to seek out other venues, read more plays and broaden his range.

As a result Clift found himself in Bobby Lewis' class at Tamara Daykarhanova's School. By exhorting Clift to work in difficult areas, Lewis became the second influence on his outlook and technique.

The third influence was Mira Rostova. Russian by birth and a refugee from Nazi Germany, she eventually worked her way over to the United States. Because of her gifts as both a comic and serious actress, she was accepted into Lewis' class. She astounded Clift and everyone else with her ability to totally immerse herself into any given character. On stage, she possessed the same kind of radiance that Stanislavsky was so taken with a half century before. For example, in enacting the death scene from Margaret Kennedy's play *The Constant Nymph*, Lewis' student audience was so moved "they all went limp." Shortly after, with Clift in the cast, she portrayed a fake witch doctor in Lewis' production of *Mexican Mural* as a hilarious gadfly.

Under her influence, Clift came to realize that acting could have a richer dimension. Lunt indicated there were hidden meanings under a character's lines; Lewis emphasized the character's intention within the unique theatrical world; Rostova taught him about total involvement. Rostova, as companion and coach, stayed by his side for the rest of his career, keeping Clift on track searching for essences.

By the time he came to the Studio during that first year, Clift's qualities and approach had been shaped. Lewis kept trying to get him to deal with longer passages of dialogue; Clift preferred less talk and deeper introspection. Kazan felt that Clift was sexually ambivalent and should explore the feminine, fragile side of characters. Kazan looked for opposites, just as he strove to bring out the power in women to keep things percolating. When they finally worked together in the film *Wild River*, Kazan wanted him to work on his masculinity. Exactly what influence Kazan had on his technique is difficult to say.

The only definite Studio influence came from his rivalry with Brando during the brief time Clift was there. He was repelled by Brando's erratic impetuousness, his emotional exhibitionism and his lack of patience to think things through. He did, however, enjoy the unspoken contest, the way they measured each other. They were both complex, alert, and mysterious: you never quite knew what either was thinking or might do. In private, Clift would monitor himself in the mirror, watching his face register an entire range of attitudes and emotions. It was all part of the fascination of identity: being both extroverted and withdrawn, manic and serene, articulate and monosyllabic, assertive and shy. Exploring this same subversive freedom, he and Brando would continue to outdo each other. If you had to name the benefits Clift derived from the Studio, the presence of Brando would head a very short list.

Soon after he arrived in Hollywood, a few directorial suggestions from Howard Hawks put the finishing touches on his style. The film (*Red River*, 1948) hinged on the love/hate relationship between Matthew Garth and the cattleman Tom Dunson (John Wayne), Garth's intractable surrogate father. As though taking his cue from Kazan, Hawks counted on Clift's trim figure, refined features and aloof cultured ways to rankle Wayne (given Wayne's often overblown machismo). At the outset, the ploy seemed to work. Wayne poked fun at Clift's eastern arrogance, effete mannerisms and unwillingness to be "one of the boys." Misreading Hawks' intention and resenting the way Wayne was treating him, Clift not only rode like a cowboy, he tried to match Wayne's toughness as well. Hawks took Clift aside and told him that the object was to exploit what he had, not fake what he didn't have. Besides, taking Wayne on directly would never work. Wayne would simply overpower him and make him look silly. The key was in the mystery in Clift's eyes which the camera would convey. To illustrate, Hawks directed Clift to mask his feelings behind a tin coffee cup. While Clift was drinking, neither Wayne nor anyone else on the cattle drive would know whether Clift was smiling or upset or what-have-you. All they would see was Clift's gaze.

At that point Clift realized it was a different medium, more like his bedroom mirror than the stage. From that moment on, stillness and the look in his eyes would be one of the touchstones of Clift's film technique. During this particular project he added other little touches, like rubbing his forefinger against the bridge of his nose just to mock Wayne and gain his respect. These subtleties gave Clift a cocksure quality that Wayne understood only too well. It became Wayne's bluster against Clift's coolness that complemented their clash and underlying affection and propelled the story. Clift became convinced that the best movie acting is an accumulation of nuances like shaking ash from a cigarette when your character is preoccupied but supposedly listening.

As shooting progressed, Hawks revealed that Clift's eyes lit up for the camera. You could actually see him thinking as ideas crossed his mind. Other clues to the role of Matthew Garth came from Hawks' masculine code—e.g., "always let the girl do all the talking. If the man does a lot of talking he winds up playing the fool." This advice fit in perfectly with Clift's reluctance to recite speeches. Talk reduced the effectiveness of his natural detachment. Too much of it would kill the mystery.

The last thing he may have learned from Hawks was the fact that he projected a natural empathy for the weakness of others. As Garth, he is called upon to protect cowboys from Dunson's brutal ways, to foster male bonding through his softer individualism, conscience and quiet dignity. All of these attributes were amplified on the screen as part of his natural vulnerability.

Armed with the cinematographer's lens as his newfound mirror, and with

Rostova at his side, Clift was ready to take on a series of parts. Unwittingly he was sharpening his skills for the day, nine years later, when he and Brando would finally engage each other in a film called *The Young Lions*.

In the meantime, among the more notable of his roles was his portrayal of George Eastman, the young outsider and central character in *A Place in the Sun* (1951), hailed by Charlie Chaplin as the greatest movie ever made about America. Here we get an inkling of how material kept demanding the new contemporary approach, an unmasking of façades. In peeling away the veneer of the American dream, the camera draws the audience close to the subject and allows audiences to peer into George's private world. And, since the character seems to be an average person, ambiguous and somewhat inarticulate like many others, only someone with the right technique and attributes could fully realize his particular emotional journey leading to a capital offense. Only someone like Montgomery Clift.

In the film, George is placed in a variety of social settings. He must deal with conflicting desires and values, caught between loneliness and need, ambition and a fascination with beauty, power and wealth. He's a young man without formal education from a humble background of poverty and piety (his mother runs a religious mission). Traveling to some unnamed Midwestern city, he asks an uncle whom he has never met for a job in the family bathing suit factory. Constantly at a loss for something to say, somewhere to look, someone to meet, he sinks into a chair like a child who feels inadequate. In the factory though, starting at the bottom, he gets to wear a T-shirt and jeans on the assembly line. His youthful, lithe physique draws the attention of young women. He easily becomes the lover of a fellow worker, Alice Tripp (Shelley Winters) who is clinging, quite ordinary and socially inept.

Soon George finds he has a knack for rising above his station and is introduced to the glamorous world of his wealthy relations. In this setting he shifts his stance from awkwardness to a cool aloofness. Playing a solitary game of pool, he attracts the attention of the beautiful socialite Angela Vickers (Elizabeth Taylor). Using his appreciation of the power of eye contact and the natural chemistry between himself and Taylor, Clift plays many of their love scenes silently, allowing their deep gazes to express longing and unfulfilled desire. Tapping his background and talent for mimicry, he emulates the mannerisms of his superiors.

In a later moment, he switches modes again. He listens to a radio report, allowing his eyes to register an emerging plan to murder poor, hapless Alice. Alice, it seems, is pregnant and has demanded that George marry her. Later still, in a scene in a rowboat, Clift's eyes rake Alice's face. His frustration and smoldering anger are precise, immediate and expertly understated. Throughout the film in scene after scene, Clift aches with unvoiced longings and exudes a vague restlessness. He runs the gamut of escalating inner turmoil, culminating with restrained looks of pain and perplexity expressed in total stillness. The sum of George Eastman's life is captured nonverbally: a young man caught in a world he can't quite make out, looking past people into space, seeking some answer as he faces trial.

Montgomery Clift and Shelley Winters in *A Place in the Sun* **(1951, Paramount Pictures).**

The verdict and sentence of execution are carried out. The sin was one of omission, an accident, a crime that was only in his heart.

Most young actors of the time would have played what was obvious and on the surface. They didn't have his background or sensibility. As far as people knew, he was an interesting person from the heartland who was drawn to the Method. It had something to do with some studio in New York. Something different was going on in acting technique.

In subsequent movie roles, Clift continued to infuse each character he played with that same distinctive aura of mystery; a quality we'll note later intrigued James Dean and further blurred the link between the Studio, the Method and Clift and Brando as the new icons of the silver screen.

In his portrayal of Private Robert E. Prewitt in the film *From Here to Eternity* (1953), Clift added other subtleties. On the surface his character was a loner, a "hard-head." To give his acting more reality, he took boxing lessons and learned to play the bugle. As Clift saw the part, Prewitt was "a limited guy with an unlimited spirit." Acting with that unique active/withdrawn style of his, he avidly pursues a hostess at a club on the outskirts of the base in Pearl Harbor, jealously slouches and sulks and, later on, weighs her arguments as she pressures him to compromise his integrity. He also clowns around with his reckless pal Maggio (Frank Sinatra), alternately tries to nurture and protect him, recedes into his cool façade and springs back again, from outer to inner. He is always on some edge, never giving Prewitt the luxury of settling into a single groove. He is tough, masculine and unpredictable, as though defying anyone to explain away his craft or link him with any particular school or style.

With the costume drama *The Heiress*, Clift tapped his aristocratic background and insights in providing Henry James' Morris Townsend with a hint of moral corruption beneath a surface respectability. In *The Big Lift* he borrowed the just-one-of-the-guys persona of Kevin McCarthy, his old friend from Bobby Lewis' class at the Studio. Preparing for *I Confess*, he flew up to Canada, stayed at a monastery for a week and discussed the inner workings of a priest's mind with the monks. He went so far as to memorize the entire Latin mass. All of his work prompted Arthur Miller to remark that Clift's uniqueness stemmed from his cultural background. He was endowed with a rare combination of knowledge, thought and sensitivity that impelled him to seek out significance and meaning. Other writers simply dubbed him as "the poet of anxiety."

When, at long last, the chance arrived in 1957 to appear with Brando, he could no longer count his strikingly handsome face as an asset. His features had been marred as a result of an automobile accident. Undaunted, he accepted yet another challenge to play a character unlike himself. This time he was asked to play Noah Ackerman, a lonely inductee who, during World War II, is harassed by his fellow GIs because he is Jewish.

The screenplay charts a parallel story of another young man who is also unwittingly caught up in the war. He is German, a totally different physical type, from the opposing side. If you look deeper however, their backgrounds and sensibilities complement each other as they did in real life. They also contrast, even though many continued to lump the two stars and the way they worked together. A closer examination allows us to give this actor, who was to become an icon, his due.

Marlon Brando

On the surface, Clift was more European, subtle and aristocratic and Brando was more American, brash, impatient and direct. For this reason it was Brando who was generally regarded as the more blatant embodiment of the Actors Studio, the most conspicuously different, the one some prominent members of the Studio like Paul Newman began to imitate. Consequently, of the two, it was Brando who gained the most notoriety. Charlie Chaplin found him dangerous, a powerful presence of terrifying and awesome intensity. In the eyes of many young moviegoers, Clift's mercurial stillness was too obscure but Brando seemed to be giving them a strong message: a signal to reject their parents' values and strip away all illusions. They too could have contempt for authority because there was no law or power that could hold you back. The old solutions didn't work, being irresponsible was justified and so was insolence and being your own person even if it meant being alone. Brooding was cool. It was the order of the day.

These fans, however, were confusing Brando with his roles and reports of his private behavior. They were also confusing him with what was known as the Studio style. As we will continue to see, Brando was Brando. The publicity surrounding him was as misleading as the publicity surrounding Clift, his chief rival of the 1950s. Like any of the figures who have slipped in and out of the picture, there were influences, to be sure. But, by and large, his life and his perspective are chiefly his own.

Like Clift, Brando was born in Omaha, Nebraska. He was the third child of a prosperous father and, similarly, had a mother who had an effect on his frame of mind. The Brando line was long established, both parents descending from distinguished prairie stock; but in his case lineage was not a major factor. On the contrary, Brando's father was callous, had no interest whatsoever in propriety and spent long spells out of town pursuing a series of casual affairs. To cope, his mother—who unlike Clift's governing matriarch was protective and affectionate—became director of the Omaha Community Playhouse. As an amateur actress, she had appeared opposite a shy local boy by the name of Henry Fonda and always served as an emblem of culture and sensitivity for young Brando. However, when the Depression forced the family to relocate to a suburb of Chicago, she took to drinking in despair over her failed marriage and the loss of her artistic vocation.

In reaction to his family circumstances, Brando got into mischief, disrupted class and played the clown. The more irresponsible young "Bud" became, the more permissive his mother's response and the more his father tried to restrain him. In total frustration, Bud senior finally sent his son to his own former training ground, Shattuck Military Academy. And it was here that Brando began to toggle back and forth between taking part in plays as an avenue of escape and faking a variety of illnesses, continuing to "horse around" until he was expelled.

Unwilling to face life with his embattled parents, he followed his sister to New York. He had been impressed with the acting profession since the time his mother took him to meet her old chum Henry Fonda on a Hollywood set. Shortly after his sister Jocelyn was encouraged by Fonda to embark on a stage career, Brando decided to join her. If nothing else, pursuit of a similar career would afford him an outlet for his antic disposition and turbulent energy.

Like Clift, he loved to mimic people and "put on an act." He would constantly observe characters in Greenwich Village and copy their accents and eccentricities. Following his instincts, he relieved his feelings of anxiety and dislocation just the way his rival did, through playacting. The release came while slipping on a series of masks and becoming someone else. At parties he astonished people with his uncanny ability to change his voice and posture and affect the mannerisms of someone he had met or noticed only moments before. In this way his ready sense of humor continued to serve him as a handy avenue of escape.

Presently, as a matter of course, he enrolled at the Dramatic Workshop and studied with Stella Adler. With Adler there was no "horsing around" and, almost immediately, she acknowledged his singular qualities as an actor: a handsome face and athletic body, the perfect marriage of intuition and intelligence, the capacity for surprise, and the perceptiveness to instantly grasp a character's plight within the given circumstances of a play.

In a few years he would modify his impetuosity in favor of Clift's more subtle inventiveness, economy of gesture and graceful spontaneity. He did this for the same reason he grew to respect Cary Grant and Gerard Philipe: in admiration of the way they held back, never displaying their own pent-up feelings and personal concerns. Impersonation, control, irony—all of these devices became a means of self-protection for Brando against insecurities, over-sensitivity and a body that was always in motion about to explode. Soon after the time he began making films he was able to hold back 20 percent. But his struggle continued as he tried to balance urgency and honesty with refinement and his need to transform and live other lives.

Graciously, Stella Adler took no credit for bringing out Brando's natural gifts, nor for his formative training. As far as she was concerned, she taught him nothing. She merely opened the possibilities of realizing an author's vision through the imaginative use of his potent instrument. As she "opened the doors, Brando simply walked right through."

The first professional entryway she supplied 20-year-old Brando was an audition for John Van Druten's sentimental and nostalgic drama *I Remember Mama* (1944) and the part of Nels, the 15-year-old son. The critic of the *New York Journal-American* found his performance "charming."

"Charming Nels" would soon be forgotten as Brando began to release his awesome and sometimes terrifying emotional energy. Seeking a more appropriate venue for her star pupil, Adler tapped the upcoming Clurman/Kazan production of *Truckline Cafe* (1946) and easily secured a showcase for his talents from her two compatriots.

Set in a roadside diner, this Maxwell Anderson play concerns itself with the uncertainty of the post-war future. Brando played Sage McRae, a combat veteran who murders his faithless wife who strayed while Sage served overseas. Sage becomes a fugitive and pours out his story to a waitress just before giving himself up to the police. In the course of dealing with the part of battle-fatigued McRae, Brando lost weight, endured a grueling rehearsal schedule and battled Clurman over technique (reluctant to project his voice ostensibly because it seemed unnatural to him). Adding to the strain, Brando devised an enervating way to re-enter the deserted diner after McRae's failed attempt to drown himself in a nearby lake: he drenched himself in freezing-cold water.

Audiences found the results unnerving. Critic Pauline Kael was embarrassed and distraught, believing that Brando was actually having a seizure until she finally realized he was acting. His unbridled and unpredictable behavior invigorated the Broadway season. But to Brando, as a student of Adler, it was only a matter of sizing up the situation, letting it pass through his filtering system and attempting to serve the needs of the play. At this point his technique was raw and unrefined. He was just learning.

Following this same exploratory tack, he next portrayed Marchbanks, the fey young poet, in a Broadway revival of Shaw's *Candida* (1946). He appeared opposite Katherine Cornell, a major star cut from the same cloth as the Lunts, doing another of her stylized turns. But the public didn't perceive the pattern of Nels-to-McRae-to-Marchbanks as the way an actor learns his trade. They saw McRae as a tune-up for the auto-parts salesman in Williams' "Streetcar" (1947), the one whom the character of Blanche describes as a man "who eats like an animal, has an animal's habits, moves like one and talks like one. 1,000 years have passed him right by and there he is—Stanley Kowalski—survivor of the Stone Age!"

In preparation, having no inkling that this role and his inclusion in the newly formed Actors Studio would become linked, Brando jogged, worked out with weights, boxed, and labored over the concept of crass materialism. In fact, contrary to popular opinion, Brando felt the role was so far beyond his understanding, he doubted he could manage it. Kazan, however, kept persisting and lent him money to travel to Provincetown, Massachusetts, to read for Williams. Because Williams saw the potential in Brando for an intriguing ambiguity—e.g., Stanley is confused and baffled by Blanche, threatened and uncertain underneath his surface machismo—he immediately gave him the part. All told, it took Williams' writing, the repressive climate of the times, Brando's struggles once given the opportunity—not to mention Stella Adler's emphasis on the free use of the imagination and Bobby Lewis' insistence on Brando's stretching himself beyond his own inclinations—for this alleged prototypical Brando performance to come into being.

It should be pointed out that Brando also profited from a few of Kazan's "action" improvs at the Studio in which actors are given a secret objective to play. In one such encounter, Brando played a leading man who wanted a bit player to vacate a dressing room. After some haggling, Brando suddenly picked up the underling and carried him bodily out of the dressing room. In another improvised scene, Brando returned to his apartment where he had hidden some drugs. Finding Eli Wallach standing there, he cursed, using the crudest language imaginable (which was shocking at the time). He shoved Wallach and continued to curse at him until Wallach became so enraged he appeared ready to kill Brando. Afterwards, Brando smiled and apologized, reverting to his own soft-spoken gentleness. The coarse turbulence was there; it could be called upon if need be; it could just as quickly be disowned. Except by the media. The ripped T-shirt and Kowalski bellow ("Stella!—hey, Stella!") has been indelibly stamped on the public consciousness as the embodiment of the raw Studio actor.

It's also important to note once again that Kazan cast English-born and classically trained Jessica Tandy in the pivotal role of Blanche for strategic reasons. True to form, in pitting someone who liked to change line emphasis and physical actions to keep his performance alive against someone who was unsettled by this tactic he created a charged atmosphere. For her part, Tandy was "show-smart" enough to realize that—like opponents in a ring always on guard—the two of them would be compelled to sustain their performances at a peak level. In short, apart from everything else, the Brando phenomenon required a unique dynamic within a special set of circumstances.

Kim Hunter (who would soon be added to the roster of original Studio members) found the free license Kazan gave Brando exhilarating. As Stella, Stanley Kowalski's sensuous wife, she relished the sense of the unknown as she found herself yanked into Brando's ever-changing reality. The physicality of their relationship became palpable for the cast and audiences alike.

The irony of it all lies in the fact that not only was the performance subject to a great many factors including Brando's struggles to comprehend the role; all the while he detested his character and found Kowalski's brutal aggressiveness frightening. By investing Stanley with other traits, he somehow inadvertently made audiences root for him: showing disdain for Blanche's mannered aristocratic accent; seeing through her contrived gentility in order to obscure her checkered past and sexuality; becoming wary of her "magic" as a trick to take him in; taking pride in his "100 percent American" heritage and male bonding; protecting his privacy and his home. As a result, some critics thought that Stanley dominated so that he wouldn't be hurt, that he desperately needed tenderness and love. Others assumed that he did things like yanking the tablecloth and hurling plates and food on the dining room floor to get attention and respect; unsure, perhaps, of his manhood—then recovering, making jokes at Blanche's expense, interrogating her, trying to reclaim his life.

In giving Stanley a range of colors as he engaged in behavior that went against the grain, he also called upon his antic disposition and mimetic gifts, and it was probably all these shifting facets of Brando that made his performance subject to many interpretations.

In the aftermath of "Streetcar" he retreated to Europe. More intellectually curious than people gave him credit for, he sought anonymity and inspiration on the Left Bank of Paris. Conceivably he also tried to make up for his cultural deficiencies in his imagined contest with Montgomery Clift. Drawn to the cafe-society of the day, then in the throes of existentialism and New-wave cinema, he expanded his consciousness beyond his Midwest experiences, the Studio and the Broadway scene.

The philosophy of existentialism may be particularly apt in terms of Brando and Clift and this particular era. In a world in which all ideological structures were bankrupt in the face of such realities as Nazi Germany and witch hunts in the land of Democracy and the Bill of Rights, the only recourse was to start from zero and reinvent one's self. Unbounded transformation was the key. There is no documented proof, but artists and individualists of every stripe openly aligned themselves with this kind of ideology and Brando was no exception. At any rate, Brando's European experience affected his outlook and added to the paradox.

When he returned, he headed straight to Hollywood. Without hesitation he imbued his performance in *The Men* (1950) with the direct, unpolished European style of Italian neo-realism. Free of the outsized demands of the stage and the need to go through the entire arc of an experience over and over again, he began to cut back like Clift, working on one beat at a time. In film he found the subtlety he was looking for and was able to gauge the release of his explosive energy if and when it was needed.

For instance in this first film, employing this documentary style, Brando focused on Ken Wilocek's probable step-by-step handling of his disablement: a whole man, by turns angry, vulnerable and depressed; still charged with erotic power despite his sexual impotence; resorting to tantrums when overly frustrated but never giving in. He reacted to each task, encounter and precarious situation as Wilocek, never attempting to act or reach for more.

The following year when "Streetcar" was brought to the screen under Kazan's direction, Brando, like Clift before him, continued to use the medium to its full advantage. He capitalized on the boxed-in lighting areas, tight shots, etc., to fuel his frustrations as Stanley. He allowed the sexual chemistry between himself and Kim Hunter to take its own course. Trusting the close-ups, he slyly enjoyed his comic moments and slipped into moments of despair without concern for their dramatic impact. This time there were no misgivings on Brando's part and Kazan sat back and gave him carte blanche.

Working again with Kazan in *Viva Zapata* (1952) he further refined his skills. As the Mexican rebel leader Emiliano Zapata, a poor but honest man who leads a peasant revolt against a dictator, his style was even more predicated on the power of the camera to penetrate and reveal. Relying again on what he now termed Brando's magnetic screen presence, Kazan suggested that a young Mexican male in Zapata's position would never reveal his feelings. Doing so would be a sign of weakness, tip his hand and make him vulnerable to betrayal. Kazan let the camera linger as Brando experienced Zapata's thought processes (which was reminiscent of Clift's technique), kept his face impassive and held his irrepressible energy in check until key moments of anger and physical release.

Brando's next venture impelled him in the opposite direction as he took on the role of Mark Antony in the film version of *Julius Caesar*. Unlike "Zapata" he was immersed in a world in which language was everything. Needing help, he turned to John Gielgud, the celebrated Shakespearean actor who played Cassius. He soon found himself dealing with the text in a way Bobby Lewis would have heartily approved: learning about verbal relish, listening to the sounds and rhythms; picturing the flow of images; asking himself why the character uses so many words and why the punctuation falls as it does.

As he pressed on, he was forced to do what Clurman had urged him to do on stage in *Truckline Cafe*—project. Heightened language, argumentation and public speaking—especially in Antony's famous Forum speech—required space. Antony was under pressure to engage the attention of large crowds. Only momentarily was Brando allowed to combine techniques—e.g., turning away from the throng and smiling to himself and, in another solitary instant, discovering an idea as though the words were being freshly minted. Contrary to expectations, in take after take he was completely disciplined and spoke his lines at performance pitch. Gielgud found him enormously responsive and the movie critic of the *London Observer* thought him extremely versatile, a serious actor with an enviable range.

Still and all, many kept dismissing the scope of his efforts and simplistically identified him with parts like Johnny, the young biker in *The Wild One* (1953). But even in this film, with a script that bypassed the social issues it was supposed to confront, Brando still found nuances. As Johnny, after taking a beating from some enraged townspeople, he appears to be weeping in the shadows alongside his motorcycle. At other times, rolling his eyes, slurring his words, affecting a southern drawl, he suggests that it's all a put-on masking his inner self-doubt. Unfortunately the fan magazines chose to ignore these hints of vulnerability and confusion and continued to label him a rebel and a maverick.

Ignoring these misnomers, Brando looked for the kind of contest he had enjoyed filming "Streetcar" while Clift was engaged in *A Place in the Sun*. They were both up for an Academy Award and both voted for the other. Competing with himself and, apparently, Clift, Brando pressed on.

Among other things, *On the Waterfront* held the promise of recapturing the best elements of the old Group Theater on film. Kazan hinted at pure ensemble acting, a cast of characters with depth and conviction, a workers' drama of great social import—an artistic way to make a difference in the here and now. Brando accepted the challenge in spite of the fact that Kazan was directing not only an exposure of present day racketeering, he was also asking Brando to play the leading role of a dock worker who informs. Kazan himself had just testified against his friends and some of those very same predecessors from the Group. Once again there was that same old ambiguity: fervency, ideals, contradictions and mixed feelings operating at the same time.

It was filmed in Hoboken, on location in weather that was so cold, speaking became an effort that was highlighted with every breath. Events were being re-enacted that were still fresh in people's minds. Everywhere Brando turned, the energy was heightened. He was actually working with actors from the last days of the Group, like Lee J. Cobb and Karl Malden (an actor who always spurred him on during his stints in "Truckline" and "Streetcar"). There were also stimulating newcomers from the Studio like Eva Marie Saint and Rod Steiger. All in all, it was a company that thrived on immediacy, surprise and working off the moment on Kazan's terms. They all relished the opportunity to follow their unforced impulses, thrilled when the energy became self-generating leading to outcomes that felt inevitable instead of rehearsed. It all seemed to happen of its own volition, led by Brando who was given free rein.

Totally ready and fit to play Terry Malloy, Brando had the externals down pat almost immediately: copying a slight New Jersey accent, adapting the slouch and physicality of a boxer aching to step into a ring (acquired while "horsing around" during the run of "Streetcar" and working out at Stillman's Gym). He melded these trappings into Terry's slow-witted rhythm and easily-led persona.

Marlon Brando as Terry Malloy in *On the Waterfront* (1954, Columbia Pictures).

The effect is so seamless that all one notices is Brando's quicksilver shifts of thought and feeling, his eyes continuously seeking clues and answers.

Instantaneously, Brando expresses guilt and confusion over unwittingly luring a fellow dock worker, Joey Doyle, to his death at the instigation of John Friendly (Lee J. Cobb), the corrupt union boss who befriended him. The guilt and confusion deepens into torment as he learns that Joey is the brother of Edie, a sheltered convent girl with whom he has fallen in love. The toughness that is his shield turns to tenderness when he's with Edie and back to fear, pride and confusion, all unconsciously expressed as Brando goes through Terry's trials and ordeals. The emotional range widens as the stakes become higher and the decisions more complex. There are instances when the changes are so mercurial they are impossible to name but register all the same: shifting from sweetness to rage, callousness to shyness and then helpless despair. It all emanates from Brando's sensitivity to undercurrents beneath the lines, from impulses that are remarkably his and his alone.

To illustrate, there's the famous taxi scene. Charley (Rod Steiger), Terry's brother, has intercepted Terry to talk some sense into him and offer him a bribe. It seems that Charley is John Friendly's lawyer, hired to find loopholes in order to cheat the union's rank-and-file and maintain Friendly's dominance and control. If Charley doesn't protect Friendly's interests and obtain assurance from Terry that he will not testify in front of the Crime Commission about the murder of Joey Doyle, Charley has orders to kill him. When a frustrated Steiger pulls out a gun, most actors would have responded with anger given the following set of lines:

CHARLEY: Make up your mind before we get to River Street.
TERRY: Before we get to where?
CHARLEY: Take the job, Terry! No questions. Take it!
TERRY: Charley. Oh, Charley. Wow.
CHARLEY: Look, kid, I ... Look ...
                    [trying to recover his composure]
     How much do you weigh these days? When you weighed 168 pounds you
     were beautiful. That skunk we got you for a manager, he brought you along
     too fast.
TERRY: It was you, Charley. It was you. That night in the Garden you come
     down to my dressing room and said, "Kid, this ain't your night. We're goin'
     for the price on Wilson." My night? I coulda taken Wilson apart. So what
     happens? He gets the title shot in the ball park and what do I get? A one-
     way ticket to Palookaville. You was my brother, Charley. You shoulda looked
     out for me a little bit. I coulda had class. I coulda been a contender. I coulda
     been somebody instead of a bum ... which is what I am, let's face it.

Brando, left on his own, does the unexpected. He gently pushes the gun away, shaking his head, comforting his brother. He expresses his sorrow over whatever has brought Charley to this sorry pass. Then, as a lament for lost innocence and forgotten dreams, he recounts the time his brother first led him astray. He does so with a sweet sadness that embodies one of those moments of inspiration that Stanislavsky prized: an unexpected disclosure of some facet of life's hidden agenda.

As another example, in an earlier incident (his first private encounter with Edie) Brando picks up the white glove his acting partner (Eva Marie Saint) inadvertently dropped. He hangs onto the glove, tries to slip his hand inside it, wearing it throughout the scene as if unconsciously trying to make some physical contact with a kind of decency he has never known. In so doing he exhibits a Garfield-like chagrin in the company of a sheltered young lady who knew him in grade school and witnessed his disruptive, socially unacceptable behavior. And in a later scene when he takes Edie to a seedy neighborhood bar and restaurant and delivers lines like "Do to him before he does it to you" and "Everybody's got a racket; down here it's every man for himself," he imperceptibly seeks comfort and forgiveness. In extreme close-up you can sense him hearing the imaginary voice of the priest who has become his conscience and imploring Edie at the same time.

And all the while, his power and physicality are at the ready: running for his life, sprinting down an alley with Edie in tow, smashing his hand through a window; telling the priest (Malden) to go to hell while coiled to spring at anyone who comes through the bar doors; boxing expertly, slamming his fist into Friendly's midsection and then, in the climactic scene, after being beaten to a pulp by Friendly's henchmen, holding his broken ribs, swaying, slipping and regaining his balance, threading his way up a steep gangway, his eyes rolling back in their sockets, on the verge of passing out.

It is little wonder that in endowing Terry with multiple shadings and affording audiences everywhere a down-to-earth journey to redemption, Brando was awarded an Academy Award. Kazan would always claim that his performance was the greatest achievement by an actor on stage or screen. The film also garnered awards for best picture, best director for Kazan, best actress (Eva Marie Saint), best story and screenplay (Bud Schulberg), best cinematography (Boris Kaufman), and in 1998 the American Film Institute ranked it among the top ten in its list of the best movies ever made.

With his zest for character acting, Brando would carry on, lose his way, briefly get his second wind and then lose his way again. It all depended on the gauge he used in choosing his projects and his level of involvement. To play Sakini in *The Teahouse of the August Moon* (1956), he studied Japanese, altered the look of his eyes, nose and cheekbones, worked long and hard to perfect an Okinawan accent in English and adopted a whimsical tone. All to no avail. The rest of the cast and the direction were adequate at best, the material providing only a change of pace.

By securing a difficult role in *The Young Lions* and appearing in the same film with Montgomery Clift, he found himself back on track. The two had continued to intrigue one another, gone to each other's movies hoping the work wouldn't be as good as it should be and discovering it was even better. They competed in the same way fine actors competed like, say, Lawrence Olivier and John Gielgud. If they could somehow keep the rivalry going, they could use each other as a yardstick of achievement and growth.

With this project, their respective characters never actually meet except tangentially at the climax. But there was a contest all the same, hinging on character acting and the ability to gain sympathy. Originally, Brando's task was to portray an athletic German ski instructor, Christian Diestl, who quickly transforms into an ardent Nazi soldier. In the spirit of competition with Clift's Noah Ackerman, Brando pressured author Irwin Shaw to alter the part. Gradually, through Brando's stratagems, Diestl becomes blond, handsome, well-mannered, soft-spoken with a cultured German accent, and charming. He also becomes idealistic and thoughtful. Speaking his revised dialogue as if reaching for just the right turn of phrase, he suggests that the Nazis stand for something hopeful. He justifies his rise in the ranks as the only means to go beyond one's station in European society and pleads that he is not political. Shortly after his promotion to lieutenant, he courts a French girl in occupied Paris and convinces her that German soldiers are not all insensitive.

Unlike Brando, Clift accepted the given circumstances and immersed himself in the role. Finding a springboard in a portrait of the novelist Franz Kafka, he distended his ears with putty and altered the shape of his nose. To give Ackerman the prescribed hint of frailty, he lost well over ten pounds (he was already underweight due to complications from his accident) and changed his walk by bouncing slightly on his toes. In his love scenes with the Christian girl from Vermont (Hope Lange), he gazed into her eyes with that patented look of wonder. Then, to counter the delicate vulnerability and decent honesty, he added another dimension. He imbued his character with a hidden toughness when pushed to the limit by anti–Semitic fellow GIs, fearlessly boxing a bully twice his size.

All told, try as he might, Brando lost the sympathy vote. At the end, his character becomes totally disoriented, shambling aimlessly in retreat through foreign territory. He registers his dismay and disgust as he stumbles upon a concentration camp. In his only encounter with Clift, he raises his hands. At a distance, Clift and his companion mistake Diestl's gesture for a threat. Mortally wounded, Brando attempts to turn his death scene into a bizarre crucifixion, rolling down a hill with barbed wire tangled in his hair. However, after Clift's protests, Brando's effort to graft on a Christ-like image in a final plea for compassion was rejected.

When all is said and done, the final results don't afford us a fair basis for comparison. In the first place, the rules for the competition were never laid down. What's more, in Brando's case, the author's intentions weren't served by his gratuitous tactics; he clearly needed a firm directorial hand. As for Clift, his work came to life only when in the presence of Hope Lange, a sensitive actress in her own right. There wasn't much he could do when given Dean Martin, the nightclub singer and former straight man for Jerry Lewis, to work with as his gentile "service pal." Deep preparation, a talent for resonant characterization and a quicksilver sensibility can't make up for weaknesses in other areas, including the scenes that rehash anti-Semitic clichés. Given the collaborative nature of the process, one or two actors, no matter how gifted and challenged by one another, can only go so far.

And anything at any time can go awry. For Clift it was his health. Frail, in pain or under the effect of painkilling drugs, no longer possessing the stamina he once had, he found his options limited. His shoulders hunched and pinched, his speech parched and hesitant, he became like an ailing dancer with only a few steps left in his repertoire. In his cameo appearance in *Judgment at Nuremburg* he was relegated to distorted hand gestures. Arthur Miller wrote a part for him in *The*

Misfits comprised of brief, intense encounters. In one of the scenes, he lies on Marilyn Monroe's lap like a sickly younger brother and grieves for his lost past. He did eventually work with Kazan in *Wild River*, but was too fragile and indecisive to fully carry out the leading role of an embattled representative of the TVA, struggling with issues of love, bullying townspeople, and a mandate to single-handedly clear people off the land to make way for the dam.

Brando too would go on but, without Clift as a gauge, or a director like Kazan and the coherency of a project like "Waterfront," he began to flounder. In part, he succumbed to the Odets syndrome of money and celebrity, losing the edge he once had while taking on roles that challenged him. In former times he wanted people to argue with him so that he could weigh his options and keep that extraordinary motor of his in check or, alternately, release its irrepressible energy. But with the power of stardom and no overriding frame of reference, he resorted to biding his time and or "horsing around." He did a camp exaggeration of Fletcher Christian in *Mutiny on the Bounty* as a self-centered charmer. Wickedly making fun of an upper-class Englishman in the cast, he wore a preposterously large silk dressing gown, topped by a matching night cap and nonchalantly sucked on an enormous clay pipe. Lowering his eyes in disdain, he relished each of his outrageous quips. He indulged himself in the movie version of the musical *Guys and Dolls*, taking singing and dancing lessons for the part of Sky Masterson, accomplishing little more than rendering an amiable impression of "a man who will do anything for a bet." It could be argued that in playing an emotionally crippled misogynist in *Last Tango in Paris* (1972), Brando again took risks: improvising, exploring the psychology of his own myth as a self-pitying, self-dramatizing clown who has traded too long on his good looks. But Brando dismissed his work with the Italian director Bernardo Bertolucci, claiming that he didn't understand what he was doing except acting out Bertolucci's own emotional problems.

Fortunately he did come upon one significant challenge. In his audition for the role of Vito Corleone in *The Godfather* (1972), Brando appears to have taken a cue from Bobby Lewis. He invested the character with an outer façade first, beginning by placing cotton inside his cheeks. Next, tapping his gift for mimicry, he shifted his voice from his chest to his throat emitting the strangled whisper of real-life gangster Frank Costello. Then he added a shrug that was both defiant and apologetic, floating his hands helplessly up to the ceiling.

After winning the part, he gave the character other dimensions: gently showing affection for his family; craving acceptance from the ruling class; thoughtfully making decisions in a moral vacuum—e.g., bringing the force of "justice" to bear against a crooked policeman, traitors from other families, drug pushers and a venal movie producer. The explosive physicality was missing but the old familiar obscurity was intact. The characterization was enhanced by cinematographer Gordon Willis' selective use of light which cast deep shadows over Brando's eyes, making him that much more a Sicilian peasant operating mysteriously in the shadows of American life.

With this portrayal, Brando momentarily regained his touch and was honored

The home of the Actors Studio (NYC).

with another Academy Award. Clift quietly appeared a few more times, weakened and passed away.

In the final analysis, although both actors were affected by each other and a variety of people and experiences, they were unique, going their own distinctive way. Even so, when they were in their prime many tried to follow in their wake. Thousands of hopefuls auditioned at the Studio seeking the secrets of their success, the patronage of Kazan and an exclusive haven that, ostensibly, would put them in the same league.

The handful who were accepted found their shelter. By the spring of 1955, a two-story Greek Revival building (a former church over 100 years old) situated just west of the theater district on 44th St. was purchased. Now and then, some were able to join forces with Kazan. Others found promising projects and a members-only networking process as well.

No one discovered Brando's or Clift's secrets. Instead they found a guru and a singular way of doing things. They found something that may at times have seemed comparable. But in truth it was something else.

7

Inside Strasberg's Studio

Depending on your point of view, Strasberg took over by chance, default or design. Kazan tried to replace Bobby Lewis. Because of his growing outside commitments and disenchantment with teaching, he also tried to find a replacement for himself as a mentor. Within a period of three years, the list of substitute instructors included Josh Logan (the noted Broadway director who was conversant with Stanislavsky's techniques); Sandy Meisner from the old Group Theater days and the artistic director of the Neighborhood Playhouse; David Pressman, Meisner's assistant; and Martin Ritt and Daniel Mann, theater directors involved with the fledgling television industry. These people, in turn, brought in actors and actresses they had worked with and admired like Eva Marie Saint, Rod Steiger, Richard Boone and Jo Van Fleet.

In the meantime, Lee Strasberg was in flux. Bristling from the chagrin of directing screen tests in Hollywood, he attempted to revive his career as a stage director in New York. He taught acting classes at the American Theater Wing and Erwin Piscator's Dramatic Workshop. In 1949 he became an adjunct at the Studio as well. Disgruntled over the fact that he wasn't consulted about the formation of the Studio, he continued to explore his options.

His directorial efforts were greeted with mixed reviews. His last two ventures were critical and commercial failures, especially his staging of Ibsen's *Peer Gynt* which was considered "earthbound" and lacking in essential lyricism.

As a theorist on the subject of realism and naturalism, he received a much more positive response. Because he was so articulate on how an actor could approach the works of playwrights like Williams and Miller, he was invited by John Gassner, Sterling Professor of Playwriting at Yale and editor of *Producing a Play*, to submit an essay for the new revised edition. (Gassner's text was the principal sourcebook on practical matters at that time.)

Under the aegis of "modern training," Strasberg provided a distillation of Boleslavsky and Ouspenskaya's ideas plus his own abiding views. In essence he posited a choice between two opposing techniques: inner versus a reliance on skill and externals. The external choice was unsuited for fundamental tasks. One way of working was, therefore, "true and the other false. One is right and the other is wrong; the better is the one which is truer."

Basing his argument on Hamlet's advice to the players, Strasberg reminded the reader that the purpose of theater was to "hold as 'twere the mirror up to nature." He further proposed that in this particular speech Shakespeare divided the world of the stage into two parts: acting that captures the essence of truth versus acting for effect. Restating his case, Strasberg claimed that it was purely a matter of values: acting for outward show or acting from inner conviction.

Continuing on, Strasberg skipped to a reference to Baron (a pupil of Molière) who allegedly spoke but didn't declaim and always listened to his fellow actors. From there Strasberg moved his argument forward to 18th century English acting and suggested that David Garrick reflected the simplicity of individualism and the depth of personalized emotions. Next, Strasberg alluded to Stanislavsky who supposedly delved into the creative process seeking the key to this same kind of response. The answer, according to Strasberg, was the stimulation of subconscious emotional resources. The concentration on emotional undercurrents gave acting its "modern emphasis. The use of affective and sense memory was the discovery of Constantin Stanislavsky and the cornerstone of the modern method." Strasberg ends his argument with a notation from Boleslavsky's lectures in the 1920s: everything centers on "the knowledge and practical living through of all soul states."

Having established his premise, Strasberg proceeded to give a few hints about what actors could do to achieve these deep states of being. One clue was derived from an Ouspenskaya concentration exercise in which you take a match box, examine it carefully for three minutes, put it aside and see what details you can recall— size, shape, printing, colors, size of the letters, etc. Other clues are under the heading of work on one's self: starting with the way you really are; making things alive for yourself; responding naturally to stimuli instead of pretending, and so on.

In an addendum, Strasberg referred to a performance of *King Lear* that greatly displeased him. The actors had no inner motivation, didn't "plumb the depths of human despair and feeling," and neglected to ask themselves "What has to happen to make it necessary for me to do this?"

Taken as a whole, the essay was a campaign for his singular approach, an uncompromising point of view which, under the circumstances, began to appear more attractive to Kazan. After three years of interim teachers, contrasting techniques and the shifting of acting units back and forth, there was no cohesion at the Studio. The work was unfocused. There was no commitment by any of the instructors whose primary interests lay outside the workshop.

By the year 1951 Strasberg had no outside interests to speak of. And his reputation as a seasoned theorist was steadily growing. More importantly, he possessed the single-mindedness to consolidate all the comings and goings and provide the place with a certain uniformity. In a word, by this point Kazan needed to establish order. Order meant continuity. Strasberg was a significant link to the Group, a founder.

Despite his misgivings, Kazan continued to rationalize. Strasberg was essentially a teacher. His rehearsals with the Group were opportunities to "take a minute" in order to apply his acting techniques. Strasberg's suggestion that his role be limited to moderator at Studio sessions ostensibly caused Kazan to make a final decision. By the opening of the fifth season (1951-1952), Kazan handed the reins to his former boss and gave him the title of Artistic Director.

Soon after taking control, Strasberg went beyond his initial function. He discredited Kazan's "superficial" emphasis on action and dispensed with the amiability that had permeated the atmosphere. He brooked no contradictions. As he had indicated in his essay, there was only one true way.

He also made a tacit demand for retribution. Somehow the Studio would make up for the way the Group had treated him. No longer a younger man among equals, he made certain that no Stella Adlers would confront him, no Clifford Odets would answer him back, no commune would decide to curtail his activities. He had earned the right to regain his sole authority.

One burning question remained. What was his Method? Moreover, what could members expect if they brought their work to him and had to weather his allegedly harsh judgments of their personal strengths and weaknesses? If you took away the cordiality of Kazan, Lewis and the others, if you deleted the clarity of action and style or, say, Sandy Meisner's reality of doing, what was Strasberg after in its stead? By what standard did he supposedly test an actor's true worth? The answer wasn't easy to come by. In fact Strasberg often told members at the outset not to look for a clear-cut method.

Another change took place. The standards for admission became extraordinarily high. You now had to audition and as few as two applicants were accepted each year. To make matters more complicated, no one knew exactly what or how to prepare. A number of people like Dustin Hoffman had taken Strasberg's classes and had an advantage, but even they had to try out several times before gaining entry.[5]

To eliminate some of this confusion, it might help to catch up with Strasberg in his role as an acting coach in the 1950s. And then examine the catch-as-catch-can nature of his sessions inside the Studio.

The Private Classes

As one might guess, the primary work hinted at in Strasberg's essay is based on sensory exercises: getting in touch with sensations and feelings. In this approach, the actor must live in the moment, from the very center of his or her being, responding to imaginary stimuli as if they were real. As a musician plays on an instrument, an actor plays on himself. He is his own instrument. To play well, you must strengthen your imagination and make yourself so sensitive that any key you press will elicit a full and truthful response. If not, the moment can't be realized and the Method is of no avail.

For example, in one typical exercise the actress Vivica Lindfors was working with her own imaginary shoes and stockings, taking them off and putting them on. If she were working properly she would have created the objects through the memory of the actual sensations—experienced the shape and texture of the shoes, the arch support, the silky stretch of the nylons as she unraveled them and tugged with her fingertips. When Strasberg asked what happened to the stockings, Lindfors confessed that they disappeared. She was unable to stay focused. She would need to continue working on her concentration.

Under Strasberg's wary eye nothing could be simulated or faked. When you enacted these sense memory exercises in his private classes and were using a needle and thread you were not pretending. You were actually sewing. It just so happened that the needle and thread weren't physically there. The choice of stimuli was up to you. You could recreate a morning drink, recapturing the feel of the cup or glass, its shape and weight and the smell and taste of the liquid. Once you mastered the basics, you could advance by going through a graduated sequence like applying makeup or shaving, trying to alleviate a pain, dealing with extremes of snow or rain or working on the recreation of a favorite place.

To deepen the exercise you were told to recreate objects that had some special significance for you such as a childhood toy or a keepsake.

If tension became a factor due to the strain of working in front of your classmates or anxiety over Strasberg's critique, there was a solution. You sat in a chair and sequentially relaxed areas associated with mental stress: the temples, muscles of the jaw and neck, places around the mouth that were conditioned by external pressures. The rigidity of the chair was the obstacle to overcome. It represented the demands of the stage and the resistance of personal defense mechanisms. When you were able to open your throat freely and emit a deep rich sound from your chest, the problem was solved. Your concentration and emotional release mechanisms were no longer blocked. A creative state had been attained and you could carry on.

If the instrument was still blocked, Strasberg employed a song and dance exercise to liberate the impulses. On the first pass you were instructed to sing one note at a time of some well-known song. On the second pass you were to sing each note in short, impulsive bursts, breaking the pattern by creating a succession of rhythms and vocal inflections of your own regardless of melody, key, tempo or appropriate movement. In doing the exercise, nervous tics and trembling would course through one's body. Tears or laughter would well up. All that had been repressed would come bursting forth: a range of unexpected colors revealing your true expressive nature.

As would be expected, among Strasberg's other devices were a set of Ouspenskaya exercises. To free students from the restraints of language and dialogue they were told to speak in gibberish and make nonsense sounds to gain greater emotional openness. Likewise, there were animal exercises to release untapped elements percolating beneath the surface. Strasberg seemed keenly aware that in everyday life emotion operated as a tentative rush forward and a hasty retreat. People cloaked their feelings and kept emotional outbursts at a well-controlled remove. That tendency had to be eliminated in order for the illimitability of his Method to prevail.

Put simply, in these classes the overall goal was a state of public solitude. Strasberg often asserted that Stanislavsky's system was based on the actor behaving as he would in private while appearing in full view of the audience.

Following this tack, the work would progress to the point where students brought in familiar objects from home. The object was to sensorially create an environment in which you felt securely alone. Then, to test this accomplishment, you were asked to engage in an activity that would normally cease if someone entered the room, like childishly skipping about while sweeping the floor.

Once you became adept at all manner of private sensory work, you were advised to go deeper. This meant testing the limits of relaxation and concentration by engaging in the controversial emotional memory exercise. Guided by Strasberg, you related what you saw, heard, smelled (and so forth) in the present tense. You re-experienced the sensations that were present during a significant event that caused great joy, fear, sadness, anger, etc.

Contending that the Method was boundless, the next step was to integrate the sensory work with scene work. Physical objects, memories, sensations, objects, previous events, the imaginative substitution of someone who was, for example, particularly hateful, the presence and qualities of a scene partner—anything you could strongly identify with was utilized to cause any given circumstances to come alive for you personally.

Then, and only then—armed with sufficient positive feedback from Strasberg—would his students audition for the Studio. Coupled with a number of acting credits, this background gave them a fighting chance to get past the first audition into the finals. From that point the hope was to be accepted for life, do something notable during one of the sessions, impress Kazan who might be present, or some influential member, or someone from the director's pool like Frank Corsaro. From there the dream was to advance through a progression of highly realistic roles, in plays and, hopefully, films. And if you didn't make it through the first audition, you might succeed next year. Or the next. Or a few years down the road.

Those were the general expectations in the heyday of the 1950s. In truth, the precise qualities Strasberg, Cheryl Crawford (acting as administrator once again as in the Group Theater days) and Kazan were looking for at the finals—no matter what your background—were always impossible to define. Three abstract priorities were set down: professional status, an instrument of sufficient depth and pliability, a willingness to make a personal commitment and sustain high standards. The best we can do to make these criteria more tangible is to quote Strasberg directly: "The thing we look for, and if we're lucky we'll find one after hundreds of auditions, is a kind of chemical something, an awareness, a sensitivity, some kind of innate quality. I don't know how to describe it. Let's just say a highly unique, interesting personality."

Once admitted, you were no longer treated as an aspirant or a student paying tuition who could expect certain considerations. The stakes were now much higher. As indicated, you found yourself in uncharted territory; the man in charge was not just a moderator, a teacher or the person in charge. He was a carryover from his days with the Group, his experiences since that time and his struggles to champion himself, his precepts and his Studio. Who he was also depended on the situation and his own volatile and veiled nature. The excerpts that follow were taken from transcripts of acting sessions during the 1950s and 1960s and from personal observations.[6] They represent a time when the activities of this closed society were of great interest and Lee Strasberg was in his prime.

*The Elusive Leader**

Predictably, one operative element was Strasberg's assertive/defensive tone:

> My suggestions have always been fed by those principles that derive from Stanislavsky. But I never do anything because anybody else said so. Things that I pass on to you are things that I've tried. Whatever it is I say has sometime or other worked. If the thing isn't happening it's probably because it's not being tried properly.

And here he is again, deflecting from the acting problem at hand, still wary, still on guard:

> I flatter myself that I have as much knowledge of theater as any theater person. This knowledge is not theoretical, talking to myself, and for myself, but it is simply the sum total of the experiences which I've had, and been able to define that experience and share it with you so that you don't have to take the same many years to find the things I have.

In all probability he was answering critics who were trying to turn Studio members against him. In the 1950s especially, he may have had accusations such as the following on his mind:

> The Actors Studio has inflated the importance of the actor's calling at the expense of the author's. The Studio actor has been unable to make the essential imaginative leap into another's life. ... One must conclude that the Actors Studio, instead of being a temple of high theatrical ideals, reflects the most pernicious qualities of our theatre: the fear of risk and the desire for quick easy success by playing according to type.
>
> There is too much emphasis on self-analysis. ... The Method has neglected the principal means of communication.

*Strasberg's commentary is excerpted from Actors Studio tape recordings of Strasberg's critiques and discussions over a period of 11 years (1956–1966). Wisconsin Center for Theater Research. The University of Wisconsin.

> The audience wants sheer theatrical bravura. They want entertainment not Method actors. Let us forget the Method and concentrate on the techniques of stagecraft and audience excitement.

Even Daniel Mann, the professional director who taught at the Studio before Strasberg's reign, went on record to say that those under Strasberg's influence could peel an imaginary orange and feel the juice running out, but were incapable of performing a simple direct action like walking up to another actor and saying hello.

In rebuttal to these kinds of remarks, Strasberg would continue to make his case:

> Why defend the Actors Studio or Lee Strasberg when no defense is necessary. All they have to do is look at the results. They speak for themselves. Our work has led to truthful, exciting experiences that is most of the time not there on the stage. Our actors bring a kind of excitement and inner belief that the audience can share with. The reason why everybody is talking about the Actors Studio work and so on, is because the work has received acclaim. Not from us but from the public. ...
>
> Problems are not only your own but are the problems that all actors in the theater have felt there is no solution to, that is where we bring hope. ... By making use of what all the great actors of the past have said and done, we will be able to help not just ourselves, but the very actors who are arguing against us.

In defending his principles for all assembled, Strasberg called upon the same arguments he used in his essay in Gassner's book:

> Great actors used affective memory unconsciously. We are joining in the great tradition of acting. When Edmund Kean in *Hamlet* picked up the skull of Yorick, he cried because he always thought of his uncle who first introduced him to Shakespeare and taught him to act. Tears would always come to his eyes. The ancient Greek actor Polis brought on the ashes of his own deceased son when he delivered Electra's funeral oration....

At other times he invoked the spirit of Eleanora Duse, using her as a quasi-patron saint to validate his cause:

> Duse on stage was terrifying. There was a sense of revealing the innermost parts of herself. The essential thing the actor reveals at the moment for the audience is his own emotion. ... Her work had meaning and reality and conviction greater than any in the entire history of the theater. It will take the next one hundred years to deal with her accomplishments.

This apprehensive stance manifested itself in other ways. He had a tendency to let his thoughts wander, to go off on a tangent so as to maintain his inscrutability and keep anyone from pinning him down. As an example, to alleviate an actress's feelings of self-consciousness, he advised her to recreate some difficult and highly personal activity and follow it through. A moment later he began to change his mind:

Do something simpler, like re-enact something you do when you get up in the morning. But if you have difficulty in that area, that's fine. Then we make the thing a little easier for you. Take for instance the thing of getting up or some other thing. Bring it all together and see whether you can do these things fully. But I would prefer that you don't do that. I would prefer that you do the other thing. That you really do that. Well, maybe it isn't necessary for everybody. It has value for some people.

Because there was no opportunity to question his judgments or confer in private, dealing with his remoteness could be difficult. And even though he contended that the Studio was a place to experiment and "fall on your face," in practice more than a few were reluctant to show their work for fear of Strasberg's notorious temper. This led to even further complications. Some members—especially females—viewed him as a substitute father figure: the one who is cold and aloof, the one who intimidates you but, at the same time, you try to please seeking any sign of approval no matter how slight. As a result, there were times when it was hard to tell whether Strasberg was meting out punishment as a parental figure or issuing a critique:

> In your work there is an effort to solve scenes for some kind of ego self-gratification. You are lazy. You are undisciplined.
>   You make yourself act confused when you are not confused. You have built an image of yourself that you're confused. Well, you're not. There's nothing confused about you. You're just shying away. Telling yourself things.
>
> ACTRESS: I'm just terribly nervous whenever I work here, Lee.
> STRASBERG: Then why the hell do you come here?

In the next exchange the parental figure is more tolerant, like an elder trying to pacify a child:

> ACTRESS: I'm scared, Lee, I am not a singer.
> STRASBERG: It's okay, darling, you're standing self-consciously. Try to relax.
>   This is good for you ... You see, it's not that difficult. You're still alive.
> ACTRESS: I don't understand how it works?
> STRASBERG: Darling, nothing here can be understood. You have to do it.

The statement "nothing can be understood" was part of his same stratagem. He was unpredictable, even to his former students. He might defend himself, circle around and back, attack, support or withdraw at a moment's notice. It's been reported that once, after an actress exposed her innermost feelings during a love scene, Strasberg asked her to do it again as kabuki, the highly stylized popular drama of Japan. All assembled were surprised to hear Strasberg give an uncharacteristic "external" directive and to view the equally surprising results as the actress's work was infused with a sudden clarity and ease.

In a sense, the sporadic and haphazard nature of the work is intricately connected to Strasberg's personality and differing interpersonal responses. A member might bring in an exercise for Strasberg's perusal as infrequently as once a year. Moreover, because of varying needs and levels of ability (the woman performing kabuki may have had an extensive background as a dancer), each of the twice-weekly two-hour sessions featured highly dissimilar presentations. During one session an actress indulged herself by gradually stripping off her clothing save for a pair of tights and walked around aimlessly talking to herself. She later revealed that she wanted to free her inhibitions. The alternate exploration consisted of a casually dressed male busying himself with mundane tasks like making a bed, fluffing up pillows, etc., while, in some offhand way, carrying on a conversation over the phone. Only those who had seen the actor work some six months before, dressed in more flamboyant garb, still unable to put aside his flair for musical comedy, could appreciate his attempt at being mundane. Similarly only those who had witnessed the topless actress rigidly performing a two-character scene a year previously, were able to fully understand the motives behind her brash striptease. And only the individual members themselves could reveal their personal view of "Lee" and when and why they presented work for his approval.

Nevertheless it's not all as unfathomable as it seems. If you can sift through Strasberg's idiosyncratic responses, you can find a pattern that, for the most part, is an extension of his take on Stanislavky's system during his days with the Group, his private classes and his vision of the craft while working with the chosen few.

The Sessions and the Way

Every Tuesday and Friday morning from eleven until one, October to June, Strasberg's clinic took place. The intention was to give members (alone or in pairs) the opportunity to solve certain problems and or actualize their potential. It was work in progress, conducted in private because, as he reiterated over and over, "every creative artist requires a studio where he can practice his scales, try new colors and test himself away from the unsympathetic eye of the public, exploring the personal process of creation." Idealistically speaking, the sessions embodied each member's "artistic mission to search for the true expression of reality on stage."

The ritual was repeated in exactly the same way to evoke a sense of stability and permanence. Approximately twenty minutes before 11:00 AM anyone scheduled first would walk up the stairs to the little theater and start their preparation. They would, for instance, go onto the playing area, get out a deck of cards and start smoking a cigarette. Sometimes playing solitaire, then flipping the cards one at a time into a hat, then beginning to pace, they would impel themselves into a desired state of being.

A few minutes before the appointed hour, the members in the common room below were given the signal to begin filing in. They would then climb the short flight of stairs and occupy the limited rows of bleachers or wend their way up an additional narrow set of steps, choose from the dozen or so chairs and peer down as the preparation continued. All the while the actor or actors remained completely oblivious of those taking their seats. At that point Strasberg would enter, sit in the front row in the director's chair, consult a white card and announce the first offering. At that point the house lights were turned off. Spotlights from the tiny church balcony above flooded the playing area. The preparation segued into the scene or exercise until some signal of completion. The house lights then came up, at which point the actor or actors announced the intention.

Presently Strasberg would ask, "Okay, what would you say?" Observers attempted to come up with insightful remarks like "The behavior was too general ... the inner life didn't really take over ... the atmosphere was good, really established but the situation wasn't dealt with ... I didn't really believe the coffee was there but I liked the way you gave yourself permission to take your time ... "

When the comments ran their course, Strasberg would take over. Oftentimes he would ignore the preceding remarks unless someone had said something unusually pithy such as "I didn't see what your problem was. We all confront failure every day. You know this character very well. It's you." In that case, prompted by a remark he considered apt, Strasberg might very well use that statement as a springboard for his critique based on the actors' relative success in bypassing commercial pressures and external professional demands and attaining self-actualization:

> External stage techniques are matters of superficial skill which only take a little time and practice and don't take talent. They are not a sign of anything. They are not acting problems. They can be worked on outside ... Here there is no acting. There is only work for yourself. The actor is not here to deliver.

The succeeding edited samples indicate the range and scope of these "acting problems" and Strasberg's remedies.

On this occasion Strasberg discloses that the outpouring of emotion is not the be-all and end-all. The actress Anne Bancroft has just finished pushing her emotionality to extremes, responding fully to each and every stimulus:

> You are more vivid than necessary. You are hiding beneath the need to fight for expression. You don't sit at ease on the stage because you have this basic sense that you yourself don't amount to anything. You think that when you don't do anything you are nothing. You have a problem with tension which is relieved by trying to get a sense of yourself.

Anticipation is a similar problem. Although the actor has read the script and knows what is going to happen, Strasberg asserts that the character has no right to know. If anyone can predict the actor's next move, he is not operating from the center of his being. The work is calculated. It falls into mechanics, another occupational hazard that comes from trying to please and relying on what has worked before. The only solution is to play each moment freshly as it comes along:

> The character hasn't read the play, the play is about him. He does have a right to know everything that has led to this point, the previous circumstances and

everything that is going on now. Therefore, what we always advise is, what would be going on here, what would you really be doing if this scene never happened?"

In this next instance Strasberg is pleased. The problem has been overcome. The two Studio members fully experienced each moment of a scene from the light comedy *Desk Set* disregarding prescribed comic bits of business, pace, tempo, and style and tone of the dialogue:

> Always start where you are. Accept the natural level of your own response patterns. You will always be logical and believable.

A greater difficulty arises when an actress is caught between the demands of the script—especially when the character's attributes are clearly described—and Strasberg's insistence on finding the character within. Here Strasberg is chiding an actress for resorting to imitation:

> How can I paint? How can an artist work unless he is willing to use his own feelings? I have to have the skill and technique to make my feelings apparent. But I can only work out of my personal attitude. How else can I work? When you go up there on the stage it is with the idea that you will give your life to this character. There is no life in her. There is only the sequence of behavior that the author gives you but the life is your life. That's what you give. You give it to her.

Carrying on, Strasberg points out that meeting someone else's specifications cannot achieve anything original and artistically worthwhile.

In another example he is more specific, calling the process a "fusion"—e.g., after determining the character's behavioral patterns, you then elicit those elements from yourself:

> To play a girl who is physically attractive, use your body in a way that would cause you to believe in your own attractiveness. Confidently use certain sensual aspects of your personality, then you will naturally behave in a manner appropriate to the character. ... You don't go personal enough. You give us a general and abstract picture of yourself. But you must be true and real to those things in yourself so that you fuse the living human being with the abstract one. I want to see your legs and I want to see your body in this way. Your work lacked the particular quality of a girl who feels herself to be attractive. You have to permit yourself to use this side of yourself so that you become more personally involved. You need confidence, faith and then somehow the body naturally becomes more attractive.

In Strasberg's idiom no character is larger than one's self. "All one has to do is live simply and believably how you would be inside that character." During one session, he pushed this prescription further, instructing the actress to stop intellectualizing and bring the character of Hamlet's mother Gertrude down to her own level:

We have to arouse the necessary behavior in this scene by extending our imagination so we can find out why she acts the way she does. In order for you to be able to respond emotionally when Hamlet starts to speak, you must know about whatever experience Gertrude had that led to her quick second marriage. Maybe she's too sexy. I don't know. People think of all kinds of things. Not in the head but in terms of experience, of the things that have happened to them. If you think about this situation that way, you can then have at your disposal experiences, not thoughts and ideas, but actual experiences of your own. When these experiences come into your work and stimulate you, exploration has taken place.

Sometimes the directive to find the character within is met with some resistance. Shelley Winters didn't feel at all capable of playing the female lead in Tennessee Williams' *Sweet Bird of Youth*. But Strasberg pressed on:

WINTERS: My image of myself is a weak lady, not a dragon lady like Tennessee's character. I'm more comfortable playing victims. I feel ashamed to reveal nasty aspects of myself.
STRASBERG: Look, darling, you always make things hard for yourself. You've got more of the character inside you than you think.
WINTERS: My psychiatrist says I am not the character.
STRASBERG: Your psychiatrist doesn't know as much as I do. Don't tell yourself in advance that you can't do it. You can play this bitch very easily. You tell yourself in advance that you can't do it and that's why you can't.

An alternative is a sensory adjustment to one's personal reality, thus still bypassing any struggle to be someone totally different. If the character is timid and shy, for example, you might treat pieces of furniture like strange and foreign objects. These kinds of "do-able" incentives were offered as options, effective in some cases and, at times, producing no discernible affect at all. Or a participant might have felt her tack was working until receiving a negation from Strasberg. In a scene from *Tender Is the Night*, an actress decided to stimulate mental instability by inducing a throbbing headache. In that way she assumed that she would attain the proper fusion with the character due to her inability to think straight. Strasberg told her that she misunderstood the symptoms of irrational behavior and needed to find a better stimulant.

Another time he suggested a change of attitude as the key to mental instability. A belief in the logic of the illogical behavior would do the trick. All told, he claimed the number of keys was infinite. It all depended on what triggered the appropriate behavior.

Inevitably, however, even though Strasberg had stated that "one can have brilliant theoretic, literary, critical or philosophical concepts of a play and not be able to create reality on stage," Studio actors continued to bring up the issue of a playwright's concepts, words, imagery and stage directions. In this example he had to convince an actress who had just presented a scene from Chekhov's *The Bear* not to be subservient to Chekhov but, rather, to run with her own feelings:

The expression of a role is never really satisfied just by doing the things indicated in the script. There is in you deeper and stronger expression or, as you said, you couldn't emote as you do at home. There is no way of getting at these things in ourselves except by going with it. You don't know where the river will carry you except by jumping in and finding out. There is no other way to be an explorer. It is the purpose of technique to incite, to arouse that kind of reality which the human being already has to begin with. You should certainly at least be able to bring that onto the stage.

He once advised Estelle Parsons that feelings were all: The "emotional experience washes the words. Sing it, to get away from words at a logical level. Don't interfere with yourself."

To Paul Newman working on the character of Petruchio in *The Taming of the Shrew*, he repeated the same dictum:

Don't rush to the words. Once you use only the lines, you're stuck to the lines. Don't be held by the words. It's the events, the situation. The actor then is embarked on the use of himself. Use the physical logic. You can't do much of anything with the words.

At one time he assured Steve McQueen—who was mumbling and having difficulty with phrasing and projection—that when you're acting properly, attention to language and speech doesn't come into play. It was only the "actual work that counts. Natural, believable and never forced."

Apparently the message had to be constantly reiterated: the text was the outer layer; the subtext—what lies beneath—was the source of life and truth. The written words only provided hints. Since "the purpose of all plays is to reveal human experience," the quest was always to find the "implicit behavioral factors." Inner thoughts and feelings were, by definition, underneath the dialogue as one of the prime generators. Other primary generators were anything an actor immediately sees, hears, feels and touches (and or an imaginative substitution) and what he or she gains from working with others who are working in a similar way.

To illustrate the concept of words as hints and behavioral imperatives, on one occasion Strasberg took a line from Williams' *Summer and Smoke*—"We are weak, but sometimes find the strength to look truth in the face"—and turned it into a need for a previous incident. He advised the actress that, in order to motivate those words (which were based on a past decision to break out of her nervous breakdown and face reality), she had to create the experience. She had to go through an improvisation, cause something appropriate to happen and then draw on it while doing the scene.

As for the subtext, one of the most striking examples of finding the generating force beneath the lines can be illustrated by an improvisation by Anne Bancroft and Viveca Lindfors. They were exploring some way around a scene from Strindberg's *The Stranger*. Bancroft, especially, had difficulty finding a provocative stimulus while sitting in silence. What were her true feelings toward her vociferous sister? What were her desires? What was really going on? They had tried improvising on their own but to no avail. This time Strasberg, in an unprecedented move, resorted to side coaching:

Bancroft remains silent as Lindfors unleashes a torrent of harsh words. The talkative sister goes on as her counterpart holds her ground.

"Don't anticipate," Strasberg says. "Don't anticipate, it depletes the work. Don't try to make it happen."

Strasberg turns to Lindfors. "Play the first part on the basis of the cold. Come in for the hot chocolate. Put in your own words if you want or go on with your own sequence of thought before you come to the next words."

Lindfors continues to goad and challenge Bancroft. Still repressed, Bancroft begins to bristle. Presently, she emits a series of grunts, growls, moans and wheezes. Suddenly, without warning, Bancroft strikes Lindfors. Stunned, Lindfors strikes her back. The melee proliferates. By the time the improvisation is resolved, Lindfors is black and blue.

Strasberg seems pleased with the surprising results. The members are also surprised and pleased. The moment becomes part of Studio lore; another revelation of the power of the unconscious. This kind of concentration and courage is hailed as the epitome of the work. You do what you do completely with no concern for onlookers. Actors, like doctors, have a license to do things that everyday people are not licensed to do. They make love publicly, they go mad, they die. All the fuss about the Studio comes from critics who feel uncomfortable with the full realization of the actor's calling. As for the audience, the exact opposite is true. It's the very reason they go to plays and films—to come in contact with volatile situations and discover what actually happens, to discover the truth.

At the Studio in the 1950s, the struggle with underlying feelings and their release was justified not only by the vogue in psychoanalysis reflected in movies and plays on Broadway. It was magnified by the life just outside the door where, as Strasberg always reminded the membership, the pressures were relentless.

In Strasberg's parlance, an actor who couldn't liberate his or her own deep feelings was talentless. They had cut off the primary means of expression. That pronouncement was tantamount to failure. Admission to the Studio had been a mistake. The only hope was to remove the block. As a teacher/therapist, Strasberg could alleviate the problem and restore the actor's expressive potential.

During this one particular session, the actor was seated, his arms dangling at his sides, his eyes closed almost as if he were slipping into a trance. Strasberg was on his feet, circling by him. He reminded the seated young man that emotion can not be stimulated directly. "If you anticipate the result, you choke the emotion." Minutes passed as the actor was prompted to become even more deeply relaxed.

"Tell me where you are, what you see and touch," said Strasberg.

The actor complied, returning in his mind to an event which moved him deeply, speaking in the present tense. "I'm in a house."

Strasberg turned to his audience. "Notice the wonderful resonance induced by relaxation."

"I'm in a room," the actor said, continuing.

"I don't know what a room is," said Strasberg. "I don't want the words."

"It's dark brown. There's a lamp by the couch. It's brass ... There's a musty odor."

"I don't know what musty means."

The actor went on, reaching for the exact sensory details, beginning to respond, gradually allowing his emotions to pour out as Strasberg receded into the background. The words began to lose their clarity leaving only the feelings. The treatment was successful.

Facets of psychoanalysis imperceptibly went hand in hand with the ritual. Inhibiting blocks were sometimes referred to as tricks of self-deception. Anxiety on the part of many participants was heightened in the belief that Strasberg possessed X-ray vision and could see through them. He wouldn't tolerate mannerisms (letting their hands flutter, then pausing, groping for words as a habitual set, etc.); or claim they could only play inept, retiring victims; or disown unpleasant parts of their personality. He often resorted to the vernacular of the analyst as these excerpts from his judgments of three actresses indicate:

> In some of your recent work there has been an unconscious effort to solve scenes for some kind of emotional ego self-gratification ... You want to be treated as a sincere person and you're unconsciously unwilling to treat yourself as an actress.

> You make yourself act confused when you are not confused. You have built an image of yourself that you're confused terribly. Well, you're not. There's nothing confused about you. In a way, by shying away from finding the solution you encourage yourself to feel, "I guess I must be that way, I don't know," and so on. And after a while you begin to believe it.

> The reason you refuse to carry out the tasks relate to your insecurity, your self-consciousness which comes from how you think you look and how you think you impress people. You wonder and become scared that perhaps we see the feelings you have and misinterpret them. I could see you thinking, "It's hard to speak, I'm getting scared, I'm not sure I can make it."

At times, as the probings continued, Strasberg would reassure the membership of their necessity within the parameters of the work:

> These exercises do involve revelation which has a scary quality for the actor.... Because the actor can't know in advance how it will turn out, what he might learn about himself during it or what feelings it might arouse. ... It can rip through the actor's defenses and release tensions that have built up over years. ... The person can relive a moment and not be able to stop it. ... When you know the people, it may not be dangerous, especially when done in the sequence of the work.

However, as he indicated more than once, aspects of "the work" weren't confined to experimentation in the shelter of the workshop. His evasive/aggressive stance behind the scenes was designed to have an impact. Word was out that he was fostering the compulsive behavior being exhibited on stage and screen. And it wasn't just the outsider-critics who were unsettled. Former insiders like Bobby Lewis were making their reservations known in print:

> In the role that he has given himself, Strasberg assumes the power of the minder of souls and prober into the unconscious. He doesn't realize one of the dangers of the use of his emotional memory exercise is the blindness—to say nothing of deafness and paralysis in general—that happens when the actor hangs onto the emotion, making it impossible for him to fulfill the author's ideas and relate to the activity going on in the scene. This is pathology, not art.

Lewis' concern over the promotion of pathology was echoed by others—insiders and outsiders—whose objections took on the same tone: "The Method actor is only occupied with work which more closely resembles psychotherapy. These marked Freudian overtones foster a preoccupation with the abnormal. A bias of this kind can reduce every characterization to a neurotic."

One of the insiders who helped fuel the controversy was a mercurial young man who was receiving great notoriety and purported to be a product of the Studio. In an interview in *The New York Times* he declared that acting is "the most logical way for people's neuroses to manifest themselves in this great need we all have to express ourselves. An actor's course is set even before he's out of the cradle." He went on to attribute the key to the release of this neurotic energy to the Studio's special way of "working from the inside out."

This notion of linking acting with troubled personalities soon crossed the line of make-believe. According to some, a force was pervading the standards of the culture, a flight from tradition and personal responsibility advanced by stars like this young man in his early twenties. He and others like him had been seen on live twice-weekly shows like the Kraft Television Theater. In one typical drama called "A Long Time till Dawn" this so-called Method actor played an incorrigible youngster who alternately beats up an older man who befriends him, springs forward to attack his parole officer, retreats to his home in New Jersey and flops around on his bed altering his mood constantly, and later shoots a pistol out an open window. No director was listed. The other actors seemed to say their lines and keep out of his way.

Because of these shows, media attention and many of the elements of Strasberg's work, the Studio, distressing behavior and role models for rebellious youth became all mixed up. No one was either able or willing to distinguish between actors who had problems and thrived on aspects of the Method and those who simply possessed acting gifts and applied anything that was of use.[7]

As in the case of Brando and Clift, the new tales of neurosis, fame, the Actors Studio and the effect on the youth of the country were a poor substitute for the realities of the Studio and the individuality of the life in question.

8

The Case of James Dean

By the time Strasberg took over the Studio, James Dean had already been captivated by the screen performances of his idols Clift and Brando. After moving to New York, he began following them along the street. He even resorted to calling Clift on the phone, trying to get the secrets to his style. Noting Dean's "Wild One" getup at a party, Brando took him aside, noted the obvious homage, asked him if he "realized he was sick" and gave him the name of an analyst.

Granted, Dean's fascination with Brando and Clift was obsessive but it was also motivated by a desire to succeed. The issue here centers on the differences between a struggle for identity and an aim to improve at one's craft.

As we've noted, Brando and Clift used acting to escape from themselves, to try on different masks, live through other lives and, in so doing also meet the demands of their profession. When the task was completed the mask came off. With Dean there was no awareness of a mask. Brando "horsed around," loved to mimic and put people on. James Dean was often unable to detach himself from his whims and his needs. Trying to impress Brando by wearing an outfit from *The Wild One* was mixed up with a search for himself.

Moreover, his behavior was consistent with the adolescent sensibility of his day. *The Catcher in the Rye* had been on the New York Times best-seller list for months. The fictional account of Holden Caulfield's miseries and ecstasies as an adolescent rebel who delights in being a little crazy was a trendy notion for thousands of young men, even though few had the courage to put it into practice. It was "cool" in the early 1950s to be confused, engaging in all kinds of unconventional behavior and discrediting every aspect of a phony society by following your own impulses and mood swings.

Here, for instance, is an example of Holden's mind-set: "Everybody stood right under the roof of the carousel so they wouldn't get soaked but I stuck around. I didn't care. I felt so damn happy all of a sudden the way old Phoebe kept going around and around. I was damn near bawling."

And, in the final chapter, when the psychoanalyst asks Holden if he's ever going to apply himself, Holden finds the question utterly stupid: "I mean how do you know what you're going to do till you do it?"

From Holden's voice we can move to the unease that marked this period and attribute it to the hollow emptiness of the Eisenhower years. Those who were "calling the shots" took themselves very seriously. In turn, America took itself and its conventions very seriously including its post-war materialism and taboos. It wasn't until after the mid–50's that Nichols and May broke new ground with their satirical TV sketches on such forbidden subjects as adultery, sex, homosexuality and U.S. blunders and policies. Outbreaks of delinquency were suppressed. Rule infractions or unbecoming behavior would go on your permanent record. Obedience was still a habit. The shooting war in Korea had reinforced the wartime myths of compliance for the good of society. The Cold War generated the inquisitions of anti–Communist witch-hunts. The undercurrent of fear was amplified by the possibility of nuclear doomsday, attack from outer space, job loss if you're suspected of being an upstart, and so on and so forth.

Subcultures were either nonexistent or undefined. If you were a moody Midwestern farm boy and had talent, your only recourse was to become an artist of some kind. Acting fit into that category. Actors were supposed to be different than other people, not conventional or well-behaved. The best ones, like the best artists, were said to be disruptive, on the side of the devil. In Greenwich Village, a character like Holden could find a niche.

In other words, in terms of his day and age, what James Dean sought after could be regarded as a combination of self-expression related to the stories about Clift and Brando and their films, and the plays running on the Great White Way. Are we simply speaking of a gifted person who had a little trouble growing up? Was this a case of a young man going through an understandable identity crisis who came along at the right moment with the perfect qualities to embody the anxieties of youth? Or was he really a quintessential product of the Studio, a fusion of acting and neurosis?

Like Kazan's view of action, it all depends on who he was, what he actually wanted and how he went about trying to get it. In Dean's case the operative word is who. And any explanation of this third alleged Studio prototype requires a return to that same zone of transition that spawned Brando and Clift: the heartland.

The salient factor here was his mother. A warm, gregarious farmer's daughter, she taught him to think imaginatively and to entertain the grandest ambitions and dreams. She read poetry to him, played to him on the piano, built him a toy theater and sent him to class to learn to dance. It was said that she was overprotective. The key factor was her death at the age of twenty-nine when Dean was only nine. Acting, adolescent trends, hero worship and the Studio may have remained in the remote background were it not for the psychological affect of this tragedy.

He felt deserted. Living with his aunt and uncle in the small agricultural town of Fairmount, Indiana, he suffered from grief and moods of withdrawal. He also had irrational outbursts of anger. His insecurity extended to a vulnerability to rejection and a set of defense mechanisms to cover up his loneliness. He later told actor Dennis Hopper that when his mother died he kept asking, "Mother, why did you leave me?" He transposed it to, "Mother, I hate you, I'll show you, I'll be somebody." This misplaced energy was then released through play-acting and the need to create and share his feelings.

In sum, as generating factors we can pencil-in a self-image of a lost orphan (he was estranged from his father) and loner. As a result he was aggressive but directionless, longing for affection yet thrusting it away, sometimes using petulance and a surly manner as a buffer, giggling at other times as another kind of release, ambiguous and curious about everything.

Another key factor is psycho/physical, from his early dance training to his athletic prowess in track, baseball and basketball while attending high school. In fact it was Dean's physical expressiveness that first attracted Kazan (who was always interested in dance and movement). Kazan called this attribute "body-acting, a natural faculty that can't be taught." One critic described Dean as an "American farm boy with the eyes of an injured animal and the innocent grace of a captive panther." The director Nicholas Ray went so far as to suggest that he was more of a dancer than an actor, his body so graphic that every mood shift and nuance of feeling was instantly physicalized through some telling gesture, change of rhythm or position, contraction or release. Dean studied new modern dance techniques in New York with his friend, the singer/musical-comedy star Eartha Kitt, as a way of enlarging his movement vocabulary—writhing, twisting, undulating, flopping, working off-center well beyond the staid conventions of ballet and traditional forms.

A facet of the psycho/physical—along with his androgynously beautiful lost-boy features—was his short-sighted stare. He was so nearsighted that he couldn't fully make out what was happening around him. When not wearing glasses he was forced to fall back on himself, create his own universe and make others enter his world and adjust to his rhythm. In this way his outlook was even more self-centered, relating to external reality when his glasses were on and transposing it by literally "taking it all in" when his glasses were removed.

The third quality that he brought with him to New York was his burning ambition. After making his mark in the drama class and debating society in high school, he became determined to prove something; perhaps, as he confided, as a way of dealing with his anger over his mother's death; perhaps out of sheer, restless desire. At any rate, not only did he absorb the performances of Brando and Clift on the screen, he devoured people, consuming all they knew and their mannerisms—anything he could use and possibly assimilate as grist for the mill. He studied Clift's fractured, dislocated quality, the unique way he reduced lines down to their barest minimum, the way he implied more than he said. Unable to get Clift to divulge the exact means no matter how many times he called, not realizing that Clift regarded him as a jerk, he switched to Brando. But the best he could do was watch the movie *The Men* over and over, taking in Brando's raw emotional intensity, mulling over his preparation (spending four weeks actually living as an inmate in the paraplegic ward of a military hospital), noting the way his moods changed without warning, echoing Dean's own way of being in the world.

He took everything in, but still had no technique. It was no different than when he studied Theater Arts at U.C.L.A.: just a kid from the Midwest, living near his father but having little to do with him, taking conventional parts in conventional plays. As his roommate recalls, it was all a matter of needing a creative outlet, never able to sit still, constructing pieces of sculpture, drawing and making cartoons.

Finally, it was James Whitmore, a movie actor who was part of Kazan's original contingent at the Studio, who introduced him to a more appealing means of release. During a series of informal sessions, Whitmore stressed the Kazan credo: immediacy and focused energy in pursuit of some compelling goal. Through Whitmore he discovered that he was in the wrong place if he wanted to develop and capitalize on this way of working. He would have to go to New York. New York was a haven for nonconformity. As a pastor of the Wesleyan Church back home in Indiana always told him, "Conformity is cowardice. Live deeply and experience all you can."

He loved innocence and wonder; he needed experience and technique. They gave you perspective but they also inhibited your exuberance and unpredictability. It was another struggle, like coming to terms with himself and latching onto Clift and Brando's secrets. It was another dilemma he couldn't resolve.

As an aspiring professional in Manhattan all of these factors and traits came into play. Some appreciated his undisciplined sense of immediacy; some found him intolerable and either fired him or refused to work with him again. In the play *See the Jaguar*, Dean played Wally, a feeble minded teenage hillbilly who, in one scene is captured and dragged offstage. Completely taken with his own impulses, Dean fought back instead of following the blocking and allowing himself to be dragged offstage. His acting partner stomped on Dean's bare foot. It was the only way he could force him to stop. Shortly thereafter, the play closed.

He was more successful performing a sensuous dance with scissors as Bachir, a thieving, blackmailing African boy in a stage adaptation of André Gide's *The Immoralist*. But again his quirks and inconsistencies were a problem. He left the cast but not before a few critics singled him out as an actor with promise.

Looking for a haven, he recalled Whitman and the Studio. By chance he ran into an actress close to his own age (in her early twenties) by the name of Christine White who was auditioning. Dean badgered her until she finally relented and agreed to let him "ballet" a scene she had made up, set on a beach in Cape Hatteras, North Carolina. On a whim, he choreographed everything. He staged the scene on a quilt and incorporated grand Shakespearean gestures and arm movements. They performed the scene over and over for friends and anyone who would offer them tips on how to make the short piece effective.

When the time came to present the scene for the Studio judges, Dean refused to wear glasses. Short-sightedly he stumbled on, unable to find the middle of the playing area. He kept groping for Chris White who had plunked herself down center stage as planned. The mishap unsettled them both. Fueled by the tension, they discarded everything they had rehearsed and just played it by ear. As it happens, Strasberg viewed their accidental interplay as simple, unforced, natural behavior and accepted them both as members.

Still choreographing and fond of the theatrical, it wasn't long before Dean decided on his first offering for his new colleagues. Remembering how the pastor back home showed him home movies of bullfighting in Mexico, Dean chose a passage from Barnaby Conrad's novel *Matador*. In Dean's eyes it would be challenging and fulfill his need for fresh and intriguing experiences.

After a great deal of practice, Dean appeared during one of the sessions replete with cape, brocaded vest and hat. Keeping his back to Strasberg and the audience, he assumed the postures of a matador and deftly executed a series of muleta passes with an imaginary bull. In response, Strasberg severely chastised him in front of the membership. Needless to say, Dean was devastated. There was no way he could have known that Strasberg dealt only with certain kinds of explorations. None of this had been spelled out. And even if it had, it would have stifled his whimsical nature.

On the other side of the fence, what Dean displayed was taken as style for its own sake. It had nothing to do with the naturalness Strasberg had perceived in this raw young talent. He was hiding behind a set of meaningless flourishes. He was playacting. He was avoiding growth and true exploration. He was wasting his and everyone else's time.

Still depressed over the episode, Dean confided to his roommate: "I don't know what's inside me or what happens when I act. But if I let him dissect me like a rabbit in a lab, I won't be able to produce again. That man has no right to tear me down like that. You keep knocking a guy down and you take the guts away from him. And what's an actor without guts?"

In so many words Dean kept repeating the same litany, trying to come to terms with people like Strasberg who wielded power: "Whatever's inside me making me what I am is like film. It only works in the dark. Tear it all open and let in the light and you kill it."

Having been humiliated in front of what he supposed were the best of his profession, he was left immobile and began to withdraw. Never again would he submit to Strasberg's critiques. At the suggestion of director Frank Corsaro, he drifted back into the Studio from time to time, still sullen, slouching in his seat, taking in a session or two. On occasion, he took part as a bit player in a workshop project, petulant, hanging around the edges to everyone's annoyance.

What Dean needed at this point was a mentor/director who would work through him. Someone in New York who valued his powers of intuition. Someone who, up to this point, didn't seem to exist. However, by some stroke of luck, Kazan began taking notice of him. He disliked Dean's disheveled appearance, his ill-mannered selfishness and his expressions of hurt and anger. But underneath he found something of value: "If they've got the shine and shiver of life, a certain wildness, a genuineness, I grab them. That's precious ... the smell of it, the sound of it, the leap of it."

To be sure, with Kazan the "grabbing" wasn't out of any altruistic motive. He needed someone with the perfect looks and personality to play Cal in the film adaptation of Steinbeck's allegory *East of Eden*. As we've noted, Kazan wasn't interested in anyone who could play the part. He wanted people who were the part: "Jimmy was it. He was it. He was vengeful, he had a sense of aloneness and he was suspicious. And he had a grudge against fathers."

In the story, Cal has a love/hate relationship with his father, desperately failing time and again to please him. Moreover, it was the old familiar theme of the outsider, the rebel, the one who doesn't belong. As ever, Kazan was working with a script that touched a personal chord, assembling a cast that would, through natural chemistry and his prodding, generate the desired results. Kazan the misfit had tried in vain to please his own father. As a consequence he despised puritanism—this is right, that is wrong—believing that right and wrong were mixed up. As for James Dean, like Cal he couldn't handle any kind of rejection. Nor could he take judgments that he was abnormal and intrinsically bad. After receiving the part, Dean stopped off in a section of L.A. to see his father. Kazan noted the tension. They could barely look at each other. It seemed that everywhere Kazan turned, the pieces fell into place.

Off the set, the perceptive and sensitive Julie Harris—Dean's costar who played Abra, the love of Cal's life—immediately felt a deep fondness for her acting partner. She loved his unpredictability and the way he would say and do things to throw her off-guard. His antics kept things alive and made everything an adventure. In turn, when his moods shifted, she comforted him. Never before or since would she enjoy such a deep professional rapport.

In contrast, Raymond Massey, the consummate Canadian professional who played Cal's self-righteous father Adam, took an immediate dislike to Dean and his undisciplined, callow ways. And there was the matter of the two brothers. To generate their prescribed relationship, Kazan arranged to have Dean and Richard Davolos share accommodations. They intuitively helped each other out and competed for attention. The locations were authentic, especially the exteriors. It was easy to accept that it was truly Salinas, California, and thereabouts circa 1918. At every turn, Kazan was primed for success.

True to form, most of the time Dean's impulses were fresh and appropriate for the shot and the circumstances. For instance, tapping his own yearning and anger—still anxious over his own identity—Dean fretfully trails after Jo Van Fleet (who may be Cal's real mother), hands in his pockets, scuffing his feet and, after she slips out of sight, suddenly hurls a stone at her bawdy house. In another early scene he furtively follows his brother Aaron and Abra, darting in and out of the leafy shadows, snapping twigs, prompting Abra to say, "He's scary. He looks at you sort of like an animal." Dean's physicalizations in both scenes are so vivid that even in long shots he looks like an awkward, lost child. Left to his own devices, Dean is as inventive as Brando, flopping down, lying in a furrow, peering up at the rows of beans he has planted to impress his father, watching them grow.

Julie Harris and James Dean in *East of Eden* (1955, Warner Bros.).

As was his custom, to spur things on Kazan would whisper instructions in an actor's ear, something the others weren't to know—a gambit Dean was familiar with from the improvs he did back in L.A. with James Whitmore. In one such happening, Kazan exploited the animosity between Raymond Massey and Dean telling Dean to write obscenities in the bible and show them to Massey. Immediately, Kazan shot the scene as Massey's Adam compels Cal to repent for his willful behavior. Dean added mumbled obscenities under his breath, "just for the fun of it" in Julie Harris' view. Massey's outrage struck the right note, Dean's mischievous glee played right into Kazan's hands.

The only problems were the few scenes Dean couldn't get right off the bat. With no technique to speak of, Dean relied on his intuition. When that failed, he needed Kazan's help. During one take, the script calls for Cal to shove blocks of ice down a chute in a jealous rage over Abra's displays of affection for Aaron. At first Dean was at a loss and couldn't summon up the strength or the anger. Resorting to one of his tricks, Kazan made derogatory remarks about Dean's feeble acting ability. Incensed, Dean picked up the ice and hurled the chunks down to the ground below.

A melding of styles with James Dean (center) flanked by the folk singer/actor Burl Ives (far left) as the sheriff, Canadian actor Raymond Massey (far right) as Dean's father Adam and actor Albert Dekker in the background all participating in one film.

There are sequences where no one had an inkling what Dean would do until the last moment. Examples are the shot where he flings Aaron into his mother's den of iniquity; and another time when he clings to Raymond Massey, desperately trying to offer his disapproving father a sum of money for a birthday present, choking with tears, straining to embrace him. Then, he stumbles out of the house into the darkness. At times, Dean's actions were purely instinctive and unrepeatable.

In terms of the issue of method and neurosis, questions can certainly be raised apropos of Dean's performance in this film. Are his fitful gropings for affection from Jo Van Fleet as his mother an attempt to cathart his own personal angst? When he utters lines that his wildness and sinful ways are an inheritance and a reflection on her, is he acting? One of his roommates observed that watching his performance was as close as anyone could come to knowing his hidden self. His former high school drama coach noticed the same "funny little laugh which ripples with the slightest provocation, the quick, jerky springy walks, and the sudden change from frivolity to gloom" that he displayed as a young man. But again, is this acting?

Therapists have pointed out that those who have suffered in childhood want their hurts healed; but getting lost in these experiences and being overwhelmed by them is a sign of instability. So is the chronic desire for support and approval: gaining a false sense of love by exhibiting and acting out personal pain. And so is the lack of objectivity and inability to separate yourself from your work.

But, for the sake of argument we could also ask, Does any of this really matter? And does the artistic end justify the means? In Dean's case the only certainty is the result, not only in the mid–1950s when the movie was released but for decades afterwards. And not only in the United States but throughout the world. On screen Dean was perceived as the original teenager, the first to transcend the vapid Hollywood clichés and reveal to young people who they really were: awkward, inarticulate, volatile; repressed and filled with a hidden rejection of the materialistic values they had been brought up with; angry, insolent yet innocent. For this age group he was a rallying point against disenchantment, non-belonging and discontent.

In *Rebel Without a Cause* (which was made soon afterwards) Dean's work had an even greater impact. The role coincided with a new concern in America with social problems and the growing awareness that children had certain rights. That parents should show some sensitivity instead of either dismissing their youngsters as potential adults who had to first go through annoying phases, or as possessions who had to be molded and subjugated.

In both films Dean's acting style sent teenagers the message that impulse and intuition were preferable to conformity; that playfulness and wild mood swings were openly expressive of their own contradictions, uncertainties and enthusiasms. Dean's confrontations with his unyielding father in *East of Eden* dramatized the gap between generations and revealed a son who rightfully questions his father's values and the consequences—you became an outcast. But, as an actor in that day and age, you became a success. You fulfilled a need. And as far as neurosis, the Method or Dean's own special way of working went, who cared?

Along these same lines, in *Rebel Without a Cause* the indulgence toward Dean's needs and ways continued. This time the director was Nicholas Ray, an assistant to Kazan in *A Tree Grows in Brooklyn* with ties to his good friend Clifford Odets and the Group. For Ray, Dean's insecurity bordered on an almost pathological vulnerability. Somehow, imperceptibly, a point had been reached where some film directors had to know an actor intimately in order to realize what buttons to push and which ones to let alone. Ray learned that both Dean and his character Jim Stark were seeking an escape from the surrounding world. He discovered that Dean needed reassurance and tolerance and decided to involve him in every stage of production including the freedom to prepare in any way he saw fit, offer suggestions and improvise. He was also allowed to ad-lib many of his lines.

This was not done out of condescension on Ray's part. The script was loosely structured, subject to continual adaptation. Ray himself was temperamentally an anarchist who liked to live dangerously and see how far he could go. It didn't phase him in the least to realize that Dean was peculiarly restless and impatient, sensitive to the shortness of life and looking for novelty in order to experience all he could. It was something Ray could easily relate to and use for the part along with everything else, like Dean's suppressed anger that was always close to a violent flashpoint. There was also Dean's desire to belong and a fear of belonging— again just like Jim Start—plus a wild eagerness coupled with a habitual mistrust.

However, his performance wasn't all generated from self-reality. Out of his natural curiosity and with a nod to what he'd heard about Brando's way of preparing, Dean consulted with actor Frank Mazzola who had been involved with gangs. From Mazzola, Dean became familiar with delinquent personalities, speech patterns and modes of movement and dress. He visited gang hangouts and went to club meetings. He took it all in and incorporated it.

By this point it was understood that Dean was more or less on his own. His responses would be pure and naked. He would direct himself. All Ray had to do was point the way and give Dean enough leeway.

In the structure, Jim Stark, a high school student and misfit, tries in a 24 hour period to meet a series of unusual challenges—e.g., dealing with familial dysfunction, peer rejection, a knife fight provoked by a leather-jacketed gang led by Buzz, which, in turn, leads to a high speed "chickie run" as both cars hurtle toward the edge of a cliff. Then there is the aftermath of Buzz's death, the pathetic needs of Plato (a youngster who idolizes Stark), and a search for a haven with his new found love who—like Jim—finds herself lost and alienated.

The results of Dean's creative freedom are apparent from the outset. During the opening credits he lurches down the street drunk, then lies down to examine a toy wind-up monkey, making a blanket for it out of scraps of paper, curling himself up and squeezing the toy monkey protectively against his body as the police sirens approach. In the next shot he giggles while being searched in the police station, standing in a drunken daze with his arms outstretched, imitating the sound of the sirens.

Unwilling to fake anything, and with the indulgence of Ray, Dean "psyched himself up" before shooting the next sequence in which he was required to vent his anger by pounding his fist on the police counselor's desk. Dean proceeded to hole up in his dressing room, drinking red wine, listening to a recording of Wagner's *Ride of the Valkyries* over and over until he was ready. On the first take, releasing his pent-up emotions, he pounded the desk so hard he bruised his hand and required medical attention.

Many moments required no thought or preparation: reaching into the refrigerator after returning at night from the "chickie run," plucking out a bottle of milk and rolling the cold bottle against his forehead; grabbing the older and much heavier actor who plays his father (Jim Backus) by the lapels of his dressing gown, lifting him up and hurling him across the room while guiding Backus' fall at the same time; meeting Judy (Natalie Wood) outside her garage, moving restlessly around her in an uneasy dance, attracted to her yet reticent, nearly kissing her, nearly embracing her, barely slipping away; responding to Plato's killing, making dazed movements around Plato's body like a wounded animal.

The critical response to "Rebel" was enthusiastic and the impact, as noted, had even greater immediacy than "Eden." Through his immersion in the part, Dean personified a mythic journey for a new generation, a fresh way to come of age. The *Times Educational Supplement* praised the disclosures of anguish, bursts of joie de vivre and confidence. It also praised the questioning demand for honesty, truth and direct behavior along with the painful awareness that none of this was possible.

In *Sight and Sound* the English critic Derek Prouse defined the singularity of Dean's portrayal in greater detail:

> The eyes withdrawn and undeceived; the inflections at once relaxed and bitter in denial of all expectation; the awkward grace of youth and the moments of eruptive conviction that somewhere, something is hideously wrong outside himself. He drifts, recoiling on the one hand from the cruelties of other adolescents, and on the other from the stifling claims of his parents. He captures the conflict in all its multiple evasions, sudden giggling release of tension and agonized deadlock, and achieves a genuinely poetic account of a modern misfit.

Doubtless Dean had no notion that his intuitive responses to this sketchy material would evoke such a response. It was also surprising that Dennis Hopper, who had a minor role in "Rebel" as one of Buzz's gang, would look upon Dean as a mentor, begging for his secrets just as Dean had implored Clift to reveal his. It's even more ironic in light of the fact that Hopper was a student in Strasberg's private classes but sought the true inside information from Dean—an actor who had no conscious system; a person whom Strasberg had severely criticized in their only encounter.

What Hopper was taught was this: You never think about the lines in terms of emphasis or inflection. You don't act like you're smoking a cigarette, you smoke it and never think about what it looks like; you play the moment your way and make it your own. Most of the things you do are not written on the page. They're invented. Before you go on you clear your mind, making certain you have no idea what is going to happen and then you inform the director that you're ready. It doesn't matter what behavior you find yourself doing as long as the audience can see your eyes and believe you.

Dean also told Hopper that he had Clift in his left hand saying, "Please forgive me," Brando in his clenched right hand saying, "Go to hell," and himself somewhere in the middle. What to make of this statement is anyone's guess.

But this is where Dean's way of working became problematic once again, just as it did when he was first starting out in New York. In *Giant* he worked with George Stevens, the acclaimed director who worked so well with Montgomery Clift in *A Place in the Sun*. With Stevens, Clift was the consummate professional, in service to the character, the script and the demands of the project at hand. Clift had no need to be indulged. Dean was unaware of this or the fact that, unlike Kazan and Ray, Stevens never worked through his actors but insisted that they work through him. Dean's refusal to play any scene exactly as rehearsed (attempting to sustain his adrenaline and avoid the predictable) disrupted Steven's demand for continuity. It undermined his preparations for each take and gave him the extra burden of re-shooting and breaking scenes down into too many bits and pieces which might not match during editing. Dean's caught-in-the-raw style also disturbed actors like Rock Hudson who took a controlled, external approach to acting, executing an action exactly as told. Hudson also resented the time Dean wasted and the probability that Dean was stealing every scene in which he appeared.

In this, his third and final film, all the pluses and minuses of what he had to offer came into focus. The production was filmed on location in Texas in the heat, boredom and expanse of an endless cattle ranch. Dean played the supporting role of Jett Rink, a young cowhand and surly outsider who represented the rags-to-riches anti-hero of an American fairytale, the one about the fact that money doesn't buy respect, love or happiness and the fault is not in our stars but in ourselves. On the plus side, Dean managed to strike up a friendship with Elizabeth Taylor who played Leslie, the spirited wife of Brick Benedict (Hudson), co-owner of the half-million acre ranch along with his sister Luz. Relying on that relationship (just as he had with Julie Harris in "Eden"), Dean was able to draw on his attraction to Taylor along with a touch of jealousy. At one point when they were alone together, he unconsciously slipped into what became known as the crucifixion shot, laying a rifle across the back of his shoulders, holding onto it from end to end and dropping his head.

Calling on his natural love of movement, he displayed the lock-hipped high-heeled stagger of a wrangler. He also added his own wry little smirks, grunts and giggles to the vocabulary of a young man who, as an outlander, resorts to talking to himself. Other physicalizations included lurking on the edge of the frame; leaning on a verandah; tinkering with a car, sullen, muttering, and scuffing about in embarrassment; striding, pacing the boundaries of a parcel of land, taking big giant steps like a kid lost in some secret game; shrieking, flinging his arms in the air, drinking in a shower of oil, releasing all the suppressed energy in his body and leaping into a broken-down truck. Within the tight latitude Stevens afforded him, he was able to do subtle things as well, like toying with Rock Hudson as he did with Raymond Massey: twisting a lariat, pretending to be contemplating an offer to relinquish the parcel Luz had bequeathed him for a cash settlement, fashioning a trick knot, tipping the brim of his cowboy hat, then letting his sly little smirk slip out.

As for the disagreement about his ability to play anyone beyond his own psychology and age, to portray the middle-aged Jett Rink, he wore a mustache, grayed his hair, cut it so that it receded at the temples and brushed it back. Some found it to be a remarkable transformation. Other critics felt that except for the Texas twang, it was still 24-year-old James Dean. For the big scene in which he was supposed to be totally inebriated, his physicalization was as loose and shambling as his speech. The words were almost incomprehensible. It required at least one retake if not more.

But there would be no next time. On September 30, 1955, he slipped behind the wheel of his new Porsche Spider convertible with a male companion and set off down a lonely straightaway. Imperceptibly, another car drifted out in front of him from a deserted crossroad. Dean swerved to avoid it as he had been taught as a novice race car driver, but there was no leeway. His companion and the other driver sustained injuries. Dean lost his life.

Over the decades, he became an icon and a role model who changed the way teenagers behaved. Countless young actors assumed his technique was the mysterious Method and tried to emulate his style, linking it with Brando and the Studio.

Dennis Hopper, still claiming Dean as his mentor, directed and played a feature role in the 1969 cult classic *Easy Rider*, a film that launched Jack Nicholson's career. But Hopper was part of the drug culture and the filming process was in such chaos that it drove the screenwriter Terry Southern to distraction. Here we have no line at all between acting and self-indulgence: those who pretend to smoke marijuana and those who actually inhale; acting as an art or craft and acting as some sort of whimsical release—unbridled narcissism with no regard for form or a semi-documentary new departure in filmmaking.

Obviously none of Hopper's dealings on this or any other film can be ascribed to Dean just as Dean's way of doing things can't be directly attributed to the Studio or Brando and Clift. His strokes of inspiration were as singular and resonant as Clift's moments of stillness or Brando's acts of tenderness and rage. Julie Harris likened him to a comet, something special that came from nowhere, emitted a unique special glow and then was seen no more. He had his own magic, his own way of being, she felt. A noted artist who knew him and sculpted a bust of his features felt he was incomparable. He was not at all like Brando. Brando had a certain heft and weight; Dean was as light as dance.

Nonetheless, the popular notion of the 1950s continued on. Clift, Brando, Dean, the Method and the Studio were all one and the same. Cast from the same mold. Actors of this caliber were a world apart from movie stars. They were serious, they had depth.

When, in this same time frame, Marilyn Monroe's name became linked with the Method, the notions about the Studio became blurred. Inside the Studio, members were puzzled and dismayed by Strasberg's patronage of Monroe, knowing full well how he felt about the movie business and lightweight Hollywood fare. Something was amiss.

To appreciate how far things had begun to veer off course, we can examine the nature of Monroe's acting career and compare it to the artistic development of Julie Harris. Harris was there at the Studio's beginnings. She studied with Kazan and, as we've just noted, worked under him and with James Dean, encountered Strasberg and continued on. Her background and philosophy represent a counterbalance to the cautionary tale of Norma Jean.

9

"Marilyn" and Julie Harris: Celebrity, Instability and Art

Marilyn Monroe

In some theories of human development there is a focus on the evolving self which, in order to mature, goes through stages. At each of these turning points, there is a crisis: the old self clings to the known, uncertain about the new. After each of these key experiences and a letting go, the individual looks back at the old self—the one that was afraid of the dark, or leery of leaving home, or marriage, etc. That self is no longer internal, subjective. Subject has become object. If, on the other hand, the individual persists in clinging to past fears or childhood ways, he or she becomes embedded. Such was the case with Marilyn Monroe.

Understandably, writers have compared her with James Dean and concluded that they were both suffering from the same syndrome: an unhappy childhood from which there was no escape. In actuality Dean was the more stable of the two. He *could* let go. He had fun playing the Frankenstein monster in high school. In college he portrayed Malcolm in *Macbeth,* the effeminate Arab boy Off Broadway, a youthful and middle-aged Texas wrangler and so on and so forth. He could forget himself for a while and still have a self to come back to. In this sense he was self-reliant.

True, there were those times when his lack of technique failed him, like the shoot on a rooftop in *East of Eden* when Kazan had to ply him with a bottle of Chianti to get him in the proper mood. During those moments he did rely on someone older and wiser. But, given his choice, he preferred to be in charge, giving advice, having others look up to him as in "Rebel." Granted, he was subject to mood swings and bouts of anger and depression over his mother's death. In comparison to the former Norma Jean Baker, however, his orphanhood was not subject; it was object. Compared to Marilyn, he was able to stand on his own. In

121

the year 1990 Paul Gassenheimer, the Dutch graphic artist, designed a poster depicting a steel-eyed James Dean astride a Harley Davidson motorcycle confidently tooling along. Seated behind him, her arms around his waist, eyes shut, her soft lips parting as if in some protective dream is Marilyn Monroe. Dean is in charge, headed in some new direction. Monroe is passively hanging on.

Unfortunately, as John Strasberg (Lee Strasberg's son) pointed out after Monroe came to live with his family, she couldn't evolve. She was always a child and never had enough ego to fight back or stand her ground. Kazan described her as "an eager young woman" with a "thin skin and a soul that hungered for acceptance by people she might look up to." With no sense of self-worth, she was forced to seek validation from others. In terms of acting and characterization she had to stay close to home. It would be too threatening to transform. She might get lost in a part and not be able to return. Whatever fragile identity she possessed had to be pacified and embellished. And this is where Strasberg and the Studio came in.[8]

The cliché under Strasberg's regime was "use yourself, your past, your pain." The painful past that Monroe offered Strasberg in order to "enhance her natural talent" included a haunting moment when, as a very young child in her home-town of L.A., she was told she was just going for a ride and then abandoned at an orphanage. She screamed and protested that it was all a mistake. But she had no father. She was led to believe that she was illegitimate, the product of sin. She was worthless. And her mother could never come to her aid; she was a paranoid schizophrenic who had tried to smother her in her crib when she was an infant.

And there was the fundamentalist church her foster family attended. Under the sect's rule she was once told that Jesus would not forgive her for forgetting to turn the red side of her cape to white. In the ceremony, red stood for sin, white for salvation. The other girls had followed their cue. They were on the side of the angels. Norma Jean was bad.

More indiscretions followed. The list of painful memories mounted. The question that needs to be answered is this: Should someone with her background and temperament be subjected to Strasberg's Method, especially in light of its use of traumas from the past?

In Kazan's view the answer was clearly "no." Kazan had observed that the more naive and self-doubting the student, the more Strasberg would abuse his power. The more famous and successful the student, the headier his enjoyment. As Kazan saw it, the perfect victim-devotee to feed Strasberg's vanity was Marilyn Monroe. But Kazan was in no position to interfere.

She was twenty-nine when she came under Strasberg's influence in 1955, almost at the exact time Dean lost his life at the age of twenty-four. She left Hollywood to acquire the inspiration and schooling she assumed Dean and Brando and Clift had received. She came east to fill a professional void. The circumstances surrounding her decision were whimsical to say the least.

She had begun absenting herself from movies until her business partner could renegotiate her contract with 20th Century–Fox. Her long-term goal was to make her own independent pictures which would afford her decent roles, personal dignity and the chance to overcome her reputation as a dimwitted sex symbol who couldn't act. In response, the then powerful Hollywood columnists supported the status quo of the motion picture industry. At every opportunity they discredited her plan as a misguided ploy. Everything written about her was condescending. The cynicism and codes of purity and virtue of the Hollywood system were beyond her grasp.

She persisted in her goal: obtaining recognition from her profession and enduring acceptance (even though she had learned that nothing could last). But she needed a vehicle, an idealized mentor and a link outside of her accustomed world that offered her comfort and support . For these reasons Marilyn Monroe was ripe for a provocative change.

An affair with Kazan afforded her a different view of the Hollywood scene, a connection with Marlon Brando's director—the acclaimed winner of prestigious awards on Broadway and in film and the founder of the Actors Studio. At an L.A. social gathering, Cheryl Crawford, the Studio's administrator, told her she could profit from Studio training. It was suggested that her former coach had only shown her how to display results: how to look sweet, demure, puzzled, thoughtful, aloof, alluring, etc. She recalled the handful of drama classes she had taken with Michael Chekhov. She had been amazed at the way he could transform himself in seconds without changing into a costume or putting on makeup or even getting out of his chair (like the time he transformed into King Lear). Even though she had skipped sessions and arrived late, he had hinted that Hollywood was misusing her. It was another prod from another influence that had roots in another time and place.

The final catalyst was her introduction to Arthur Miller via Kazan. She was awed by his dignity and the fact that he was a Pulitzer Prize winning playwright from New York, not like movie people at all. By 1955 she was engaged to Miller. Doubtless, she now envisioned Chekhov, Kazan, Miller's plays, Cheryl Crawford's advice and Miller's support as an arrow pointing to Strasberg's door. If she could receive a badge from this high priest validating her as a real actress, she could recreate herself and carry out her quest which was, by this stage, all mixed up with father figures, anxieties and a combination of naiveté, power and fame. When Strasberg agreed to take her under his wing, the question of therapy's place in the performing arts finally came to a head.

It began when Monroe attended Strasberg's classes and was given private lessons in his apartment as well. Arthur Miller was advised by Montgomery Clift— someone Miller respected for his astute grasp of acting and its problems—that Strasberg was a charlatan. Because Monroe needed to idealize someone beyond all human weakness, and even though (according to Miller) she was incapable of judging people and had no common sense, Miller stood back.

Elaborating on his own misgivings, Kazan was convinced that Monroe was Strasberg's "ticket to the big time." Strasberg therefore made himself indispensable to her, turning her against all other authority figures and influences (except for his wife Paula, a Studio member and acting coach). He was a crutch for "Miss

Monroe," the only means by which she could deepen her confidence. When he worked with her privately, he assured her that one day, if she continued to work with him, she would be able to conquer Lady Macbeth's great scenes. He could take her where she wanted to go. He would give her special attention because she had "tragic" potential. Through him and him alone could she ever attain the station in life she desperately coveted.

Presently, Monroe began to sit in on Studio sessions, hiding in the background wearing dark clothing and no makeup. Strasberg had informed her that she didn't have to audition; as soon as she was ready she could present her work and become a member—any time she wished.

His unprecedented preferential treatment created a great stir. Everyone at the Studio felt that had she been Norma Jean Baker or some unknown contract player from Tinseltown, Strasberg wouldn't have given her the time of day. Supposedly Studio people were special, carefully chosen for their potential. Furthermore, as we've noted, Strasberg claimed artistic work had to be done in private, far from the press and commercial pressures. Publicity of any kind would taint explorations and distract people from their true purpose. Marilyn Monroe's presence attracted great publicity. Strasberg basked in its reflection. Some distraught members claimed that their leader often confused disturbed personalities with talent. But nothing they could say or do made the slightest difference. They couldn't vent their disapproval on Monroe. She was humble, defenseless and in awe of their seriousness and gifts. And they were never able to confront the man in charge.

Undaunted, Strasberg kept reassuring her, telling her that she could play Grushenka in *The Brothers Karamazov* and would make a splendid Cordelia in *King Lear*. Echoing her growing dependence, Monroe would call up her friends and say things like, "Let me tell you what Lee said today ... Oh no, I think Lee would disapprove. I mustn't feel this way." It was said that she tried desperately to please him. It was also said that there was another subtle side of the coin. Monroe's seductive wiles included the ability to convince someone that he was the only person who could save her. And back the ball would bounce to Strasberg, assuring her that she had raw talent that he was shaping and providing with new remarkable form.

In his private classes, he eased her into the sense memory exercises and suggested roles and behaviors close to her own age and or experience—e.g., Molly Bloom's monologue in James Joyce's *Ulysses*, Lorna in *Golden Boy*, Holly Golightly in *Breakfast at Tiffany's*.

Presently a big moment was slated: Marilyn's presentation at a Studio session of the opening scene from Eugene O'Neill's *Anna Christie* with Maureen Stapleton as her partner. The play is set in a flophouse/saloon on the New York waterfront of a bygone era, patterned after a place O'Neill knew full well, which attracted the dregs of society. Monroe was to play the title character, Anna, a prostitute with a touch of poetry in her speech and a deep feeling for the sea. As the story unfolds, she is drawn to a swaggering stoker but is caught between this rough suitor and her father's wishes that she lead a different life. It wasn't the character or the circumstances that worried Monroe. It was clearly within the scope of her experience. The problem was in the lines. Arthur Miller helped her all he could, explaining the meaning, the syntax, etc., but nothing could relieve her fear of memorization. Stapleton suggested that she leave the script on the table in case she did indeed "go up." The presentation was canceled again and again because of last-minute "nerves."

Finally, in February of 1956, both partners girded themselves with coffee laced with Jack Daniels whiskey and the scene went on with Miss Monroe sans makeup wearing a plain dress. Miss Stapleton held herself back in concern for Monroe and was subsequently criticized by some of the members. For her part, for the first time ever Monroe got through the scene quietly without dropping a line. No one except Strasberg commented on her effort. He declared that she was luminous and exuded a wistful yearning that set her apart. She radiated despite the fact that she wore no makeup. He praised her courage in appearing before such a formidable assembly. He went on, claiming that her delicate tremulousness was phenomenal. She was better than most of the great actresses of his time which included the likes of Jeanne Eagels, Pauline Lord and Laurette Taylor.

Objectively speaking, after being afforded a great deal of latitude, she may very well have surpassed her limitations. She may have resigned herself to the situation and said her lines with complete honesty. According to actress Brett Somers who was watching closely, "She chose simple actions. She accomplished them. She played the moment. She was there." On balance, apparently there was more to Marilyn than met the eye, even though she couldn't summon up the anger and near-violent anguish the role required.

Still under contract, Monroe returned to the screen, ready to apply her new-found technique. The opportunity was the filming of William Inge's comic play *Bus Stop* (1956). The character of Cherie (another saloon girl with a checkered past) required no deciphering on the part of Miller, no aid at all. The part was tailor made. She had already proven herself time and again as a comedienne, rue-fully poking fun at herself as a dumb sex kitten, sharing the joke with movie audiences with her own inimitable sense of timing. But, according to Strasberg, it was now her task to find fresh ways to apply his training and insights. And since Strasberg himself couldn't be spared to oversee, she would have to work through his proxy, his wife Paula. Paula would be in daily contact with her husband on the phone. In effect, as Monroe's hired coach and companion, Paula became a medium speaking for Lee.

As Paula began to accompany Monroe, another tack was added to Strasberg's pursuit of the limelight and to continue to assure his pupil that she had associated herself with a teacher of great renown. Paula began to spread the word about her husband's influence. According to Arthur Miller, Paula continuously weaved triumphant tales about herself and her legendary husband and passed them on, making statements like, "Our people are now all over the world." It mattered not if the famous person in question sat in on only one or two of Strasberg's classes, committed herself to training over a period of years, spent a moment in passing or donated a sum of money. It reached a point where Paula Strasberg referred to the celebrated Jean Louis as "one of our best dress designers."

Under this reminder that she was aligned with one of the most preeminent theatrical institutions in the world, Marilyn kept trying to please Paula and Lee. For Monroe, her obedience continued to hold the promise of praise and recognition as a legitimate actress. The price was conflict and tension for everyone else. Paula stationed herself directly behind the director, signaling to her student whether or not to demand a retake. No director with integrity would normally allow an acting coach to undermine his authority in this way. But Marilyn was a highly bankable star. In deference to Paula, realizing that Marilyn had held up projects by coming to work late or calling in sick, the director would re-shoot the scene.

In Kazan's opinion, something else was at work here. Through Monroe, Strasberg now had power and revenge over producers who had hired him years earlier to make screen tests and then fired him. With Paula as his agent, he was the one who could cause delays, appear for conferences and work out solutions that bore his approval, then confer with Monroe and give her permission to proceed. As a director himself, Strasberg would never have tolerated this kind of interference. As a guide to a famous movie star, his views of professionalism had obviously changed.

It's ironic that Josh Logan was the first to suffer this dubious arrangement. Not only was he a successful director of films, plays and musicals, he had studied the techniques of Stanislavsky firsthand and was one of the acting instructors at the Studio before Strasberg took over. During one of the scenes in question, Monroe wanted the tail of her saloon-girl costume ripped off so that she could respond to something real and use the mockery of her attire to vent her anger. Logan did not see the point. In phone calls to Miller she protested that she couldn't pretend to do something that she didn't believe. She also complained that Logan thought that ripping off the costume piece would be "vulgar" as well as inappropriate and a waste of time.

If you examine her performance you can get an inkling of what Logan meant. Her approach doesn't quite match the material or Logan's lighthearted tone. Don Murray who plays Bo, her suitor who won't take no for an answer, works in a broad one-dimensional musical-comedy style, mugging, bragging, hollering, indicating for all to see that he is your typical young and brash cowboy who knows nothing of city ways. Everyone else in the cast works the same way. Hope Lange is the stock nice pretty girl. Every character is immediately recognizable as a type. Monroe is caught somewhere between the musical *Lil' Abner* and Tennessee Williams. She affects a generic hillbilly accent and the wide-eyed delivery of the sweet tramp with the heart of gold. But she also flops around, taking Bo's interruption of her beauty sleep literally, using it as one of Strasberg's sensory keys, dragging her feet, straining to keep her eyes open in scene after scene. When Don Murray or any of the other actors refers to their aspirations or some past event, it's only a line delivered with energy. When Monroe speaks of her feelings or

Marilyn Monroe and Arthur O'Connell in *Bus Stop* (1956, 20th Century–Fox).

Kim Stanley posing as *The Goddess*, Paddy Chayfsky's study of Marilyn Monroe's troubled life (1958, Columbia Pictures).

experiences, it becomes a private moment about seeking "direction" and making it in Hollywood. Recalling the boyfriends that she's had since she was twelve and the man who wanted to marry her when she was fourteen, the close-ups reveal Marilyn Monroe doubtless remembering the actual occurrences. When she speaks of her desire for someone to respect her, a man she can look up to, someone who has a real regard for her "apart from that loving stuff," it's personal and autobiographical. So are her blushes on the verge of tears when Don Murray says, "I want you just the way you are and I don't care how you got that way."

In her next film, *The Prince and the Showgirl* (1957) on location in London, the pattern continued. This time the director (who also played the leading role of the prince) was the legendary British actor Laurence Olivier. This time one of Strasberg's coveted goals—to hold his own on the shores of the U.K. with its haughty "external" approach—was conceivably within reach through the work of Monroe.

However, Olivier had conceived the project as a lark, taking Monroe at face value in order to juxtapose their social and cultural types: a courtship between a pompous monarch and a dizzy American showgirl. It was high comedy. It was trivial. The Method had no application here. Besides, Olivier had no patience with acting systems. To him it was a matter of common sense—the proper nose putty, costume, vocal inflection, imitation of life, etc.

Unfortunately for Olivier, Paula and Lee insisted on deepening Monroe's role. Paula insisted that Monroe must not perform one of her usual turns; it would be demeaning to her talent. Olivier resented Paula's advice. He regarded her presence and "inane suggestions" as a threat to the spirit and aim of his film. But the more he attempted to assert himself, the worse things became.

Arthur Miller tried to see the situation from his wife's point of view, wanting Olivier to be an actor-escort who would think only of safeguarding her. She idealized Olivier and thought of him as a great and serious artist from the world-renowned British stage. By not living up to her image, by resenting Paula's coaching, he was betraying her.

Miller also viewed his wife as someone who could only live on a safe, carefree plane. Anything that compromised that illusion caused her to turn against herself, unable to sleep, needing pills or drugs to reach a facsimile of that forgetful state. The way Miller tells it, Monroe was constantly distracted by all the "pseudo–Stanislavskian imagery," continually forced to intellectualize, searching for some magical key Paula or Lee would sanction. During this routine, Paula would call Lee about problems on the day's shoot, get Lee's advice, act as a surrogate mother, keeper of the pills and chief facilitator. And when, after Paula advised Olivier that his performance was artificial and she was summarily dismissed, she used her hold on Monroe to become reinstated.

Oddly enough, the results of all this agitation are not reflected in the finished product. Monroe wears a revealing white dress, speaks in her usual girlish breathy voice and appears to be at ease as herself doing Marilyn Monroe. Some devotees of Strasberg's teaching point to the superiority of Monroe's use of sensory stimuli such as picking away at a buffet in comparison to Olivier's bluster in the background over the phone. Arguably, if Olivier hadn't been so miffed he might have seemed equally at ease. As is often the case with Strasberg's technique, in the wrong hands and under the wrong conditions it becomes a hindrance to the process rather than an aid.

The subject as far as Monroe was concerned remained moot when, a year or so later, she worked with the famed Billy Wilder, a focused and resourceful director who brooked no interference. The film was *Some Like It Hot*. Marilyn was to do one of her patented self-parodies as Sugar Kane. The farcical dialogue had to be precise, the duration of the exchanges timed, the rhythm and the tone just so; otherwise the whole fabric would unravel. Joe E. Brown was doing a takeoff on himself. Tony Curtis did an impression of Cary Grant. Jack Lemmon and Tony Curtis did a send-up of themselves as women. It was all tongue in cheek, full of ironic contradictions. Curtis and Lemmon assume Monroe's character is loose and wanton but she's quite sweet. Toying with Monroe's sincerity, Curtis (now playing a man) pretends to be naive and innocent in order to garner some kisses. Lemmon decides he's better off as a woman as he enjoys both Monroe's sisterly concern and Joe E. Brown's money, love and protection. Each and every actor/character relishes the interplay and shares the fun and games with the screen audience. There is nothing much Paula or Lee Strasberg could do.

Nevertheless, Paula managed to disrupt the flow, telling Monroe to insist on take after take until it felt right and came from Monroe's own impulses rather than the execution of Wilder's direction. Monroe kept flubbing her lines, even the simplest ones. She frequently answered the nine o'clock call at four in the afternoon, constantly exhausting the talents around her. Between her personal problems and Paula's interjections, a director's vision and desired way of working was again compromised.

Fortunately the results on the screen were totally positive. Her bewilderment, goofy sweetness and perfect rendering of a flawed dim-witted angel made this portrayal of facets of herself her finest on film. It's difficult to see where the Method and Paula Strasberg's judgment as to Monroe's most truthful moments come into play. It's easy to see how her natural comedic gifts and sense of timing helped make this movie a classic of its genre.

On her final effort, *The Misfits (1960)*, she was brought deeper into her troubled life. Arthur Miller was on location acting mainly in his capacity as screenwriter. Just before the failure of their marriage, he had written the part of Roslyn as a gift to lift her spirits. At the outset, the character is as homeless as the horses who run wild in the canyons and far reaches of Nevada. But she recognizes in these free creatures "life's sacredness and a meaning for existence." In Miller's mind, the part was rife with the dignity his wife longed for. By living through the sequences, Miller felt Marilyn could gain faith and confidence and, with luck, believe in the possibility of a home for herself.

Pressing forward with the project, Miller's hopes now centered on John Huston. Here was one of the world's most celebrated directors, a winner of prestigious awards. Secondly, there was the cast to see Marilyn through: Clark Gable, the famous movie star and an older legendary figure to look up to; Montgomery Clift from the original ranks of the Studio; Eli Wallach, a stalwart from the Studio's present roster; Thelma Ritter, a character actress who always seemed genuine; and Kevin McCarthy, one of Bobby Lewis' discoveries, a good friend of Clift and another person listed on the Studio's rolls.

There were, however, the inevitable highs and lows. The first problem was fueled by her incompatible relationship with Huston. After praising her for her comic performance in *Some Like It Hot,* he put her on her mettle. As a film director, Huston relied on the resilience of the actors. Having been a fighter himself, he had no patience with those who needed coddling or avoided the task at hand by tinkering with such things as keys to motivation. He supplied the overview, the actor did the work, he evaluated the result. In dealing with Paula, he made a mockery of listening to her suggestions, overdoing it, telling her how right she was and how profound, ostensibly hoping she would get the point and stay out of the way.

The rift between Monroe's needs and Huston's expectations widened over the issue of language. Following Strasberg's teachings, Monroe assumed words were, more often than not, a hurdle that could be skirted in favor of freshness of feeling. The big problem was that Huston was also a writer. It was Miller's script, imagery and use of language that caught Huston's interest in the first place. Monroe's paraphrasing and omissions brought her directly in conflict with Huston who refused to accept any of her revisions. They not only subverted the screenplay; they also disrupted the work of her fellow actors who had learned their lines exactly as written.

Her acting problems were exacerbated by some of the emotional demands of the script, chiefly the requirement of falling in love with Gable. Paula and Lee Strasberg had taught her to search for substitutions and powerful objects and stimuli. But Monroe had difficulty finding ways to make herself respond passionately to Gable or any man for that matter under her present circumstances. As a result there was Gable, who was convinced that film acting was all in the eyes, being masculine and straightforward, supposedly falling in love with Monroe who, in turn, was only able to look up to him as a dependable older man. In limiting herself to feelings she could relate to, her best moments came when reciting the most autobiographical of her lines: "We're all dying, aren't we? All the husbands and the wives. Every minute ... I hate to fight with anybody. When you win you lose ... The trouble is I always wind up where I started."

When Thelma Ritter suggests that her life couldn't have been all bad, she had her mother, Monroe replies, "How do you have somebody who disappears all the time?" When Monroe runs out of the cabin, suffering from another mood shift, drunk, barefoot, clinging to a tree and spots Gable coming after her, she says, "You're worried about me. How sweet."

When she couldn't relate to the dialogue or given circumstances her difficulties continued. In the sequence revolving around Roslyn's divorce proceedings, she protested, "I can't memorize this. It's not the way it was."

There are breaks now and then when she's relieved of all this introspection. At one point she's given the opportunity to listen to Montgomery Clift as he lies on her lap and recounts the time he was slighted by his stepfather. Using a technique almost the opposite of Monroe's, Clift portrays an illiterate cowboy who enters a rodeo competition, a part far removed from his own background and personality. His head is bandaged from a bull's kick and a bad fall but he doesn't focus on this sensory detail. More like an actor influenced by Alfred Lunt and Bobby Lewis, he lets the dialogue carry him, flawlessly executing his lines for a full five minutes as Monroe emits encouraging murmurs and sighs. And, like an actor coached by Mira Rostova, he seizes the moment as the failed ranch-hand who finds himself under the stars with a beautiful girl willing to listen to his misfortunes. He circumvents his own personal pain and chronic illness. For the time being he is the character: a heedless young man, buoyed by cheap whiskey, adrenaline and the imaginary situation. For the time being Marilyn Monroe is free to simply listen. The joy of their joint escape is almost palpable.

Unfortunately, this joy is short-lived. Her subsequent bouts of depression threaten to close down the film. Paula intercedes; Huston will have none of it and refuses to speak to her. Strasberg is summoned. In Miller's version, Strasberg is uninterested in Monroe's mental state, only in Paula's needs: "Paula has to be respected. She has worked with the greatest stars."

Despite all of the obstacles, shooting on *The Misfits* was somehow completed. In the fall of 1960, she returned to New York. Living in Arthur Miller's apartment, she made one last foray into Lee Strasberg's world playing yet another semi-courtesan (Blanche Dubois) for his private class. But she was uninterested in participating further or struggling with the demands of the stage and moved back to Hollywood.

After her apparent suicide over a year later, Strasberg gave the eulogy. He talked of her wistful radiance and her childish naiveté. It's been suggested that his model of psychiatric crisis as a spur was perilous. She was already rootless and fearful of happiness. His focus on her past—considering her deeply trouble childhood a useful tragic reservoir—and the psychiatric sessions he prescribed doubtless made her feel even more adrift.

In any event and whatever the judgments about his procedures, his attraction to celebrity became more apparent. In an interview in a Los Angeles paper he claimed that movie stars who drew upon their personalities were unconsciously using the Method. This kind of statement, plus the fact that Marilyn Monroe left him well over 10 percent of her estate (which was worth millions), led Kazan to assume that Strasberg was parlaying the use of "a modest girl of modest talent" into a great deal of media coverage, fortune and fame as a maker of stars.

Perhaps this isn't entirely true. Perhaps Strasberg was conflicted. All that is certain is that the episodes with Monroe and Paula and Lee Strasberg clouded the differences between therapy, celebrity and the craft of acting to a great extent. In the wake of these actions, certain Studio members continued to feel dismayed, unable to comprehend how "Lee" could switch back and forth between discrediting the movie business and extolling the virtues of dedication; juggling a daunting admission policy and serious acting on the stage and stardom and Hollywood.

It may have helped if they had conferred with one of their own, someone who had taken part in the workshop's beginning phases. Someone approximately the same age as Monroe who worked successfully in both mediums and, at the same time, balanced the filaments of reason and passion that connect a life to art.

Julie Harris

She is barefoot and slender, her eyes aglow, her hair cropped short. She wears a rumpled pair of shorts and a worn workshirt open at the neck as if she'd torn off the top three buttons out of spite. Rolling up her sleeves, she moves about the kitchen of a weathered Georgia bungalow like a restless tomboy. You would assume that her speech would be coarse, her words clipped, her vocabulary limited to bits of slang. But her voice has a melodious power and resonance. Like a gifted musician, her pitch and rhythm change in time with the sometimes-plain sometimes-poetic musings of a motherless 12 year old who is painfully coming of age. Even her southern accent sounds melodic and modulated. At the same time she is totally in the moment: spontaneous yet in control, lost yet possessing some inner compass that keeps pulling her back on track. What is working here is a special kind of duality. The character is truly 12 years old but the actress is older, in her twenties. When she cries, the tears are genuine. It seems she is so crestfallen she will never recover, but somehow she does and is off on another tack, unpredictable, with a sense of humor bubbling beneath the surface ready to strike when least expected.

Fusing the internal and external, making full contact with the imagery in her mind's eye as well as with people, sensations and things—always present, always sensitively aware and at the ready—she is the force that drives the action. The play is *The Member of the Wedding*. It was staged in New York in 1950; the screen version with the identical cast premiered in 1952. The author is Carson McCullers. The leading character's name is Frankie. The actress is Julie Harris.

To further illustrate the emotional, verbal and physical demands in sustaining this role, imagine Frankie playing cards in that rustic kitchen, hot and sweaty, her opponents an earthy but wise and loving nanny (Ethel Waters) and a pixilated 7-year-old cousin (Brandon DeWilde). Frankie plops on a kitchen chair, head thrown back, dreaming about her older brother's impending marriage. She says things like, "They were the two most beautiful people I ever saw. My heart feels them going away while I'm stuck here by myself." Bernice (the nanny) chides her, telling her she doesn't have her mind on the game. Instantly, Frankie fixes her gaze on the wooden table, then on her hand of cards and draws and discards as if she were playing for high stakes. She scours the rest of the deck for the jacks and queens. The second John Henry (her little cousin) admits that he absconded with them, Harris springs up shouting, "I am sick unto death! I wish I could light out and never see this town again. I wish I was somebody else except me." The scene keeps alternating from Frankie's wistful yearnings, to direct confrontations, to fervent outbursts, to long monologues and then to tomboyish antics. As the action continues, Harris sticks her head in the sink, confronts a gaggle of older girls— hopeful that she's been elected to their club, disheartened to learn she wasn't even considered, flying into a rage as she chases them off screaming, "What are you doing in my yard?" And then she wistfully murmurs, "Why didn't you elect me?"

After crying, then calling out, "I could shoot every one with a pistol!" and then whimpering that she doesn't want to be one of those leftover people, she throws her head back laughing, teasing Bernice about her glass eye. Next she tries out a new name for herself and couples it with her brother's name and his bride to be, resonating the sounds, almost tasting them: "Jane ... Jasmine ... Janice, Jarvis and Jasmine ... F. Jasmine Adams." The rhythms and awkward groping for connection go on as she circles after John Henry, breaks into a pirate song, tries to dig a splinter out of her foot with a kitchen knife, hobbles around, flings the knife at Bernice, tells a tall tale about going to Hollywood, and slips into another poetic fantasy about the coming wedding.

In subsequent scenes the scope of her behavior pattern widens. She philosophizes about moths and the irony of fate, spins in her pajamas showing John Henry how the world turns, and suddenly makes a decision to join her brother and bride. She no longer wants to think about herself and remain an "I person." "I love the two of them so much," she cries out, "because they are the *we* of me." Carrying on, wearing a pretty dress in the light of day, bicycling down the street, bubbling with happiness, she informs a neighbor of her delirious plans.

In viewing this performance, there is the uncanny sense that the actress is playing the role and the role is playing her. Strasberg spoke of fusion but Julie Harris gives it an entirely different spin. In her lexicon it means everything including teamwork, text, style and character, voice and movement, the author's intention and communication with the audience. From her standpoint it's better to go back to "what they originally wanted at the Studio" and proceed from there.

As a result she exuded a unique versatility and power that won her great critical acclaim and a record five Tony awards for best actress. Her particular outlook enabled her to envision herself as a femme fatale in the first Studio offering (Kazan's production of *Sundown Beach*) and then run a gamut of roles including, Frankie, the gracious and benevolent Abra who nurtures James Dean in *East of Eden,* Joan of Arc in the Broadway production of *The Lark,* a variety of distinguished parts on television and in films, an affable Emily Dickinson confiding to the audience in her one-woman touring show *The Belle of Amherst,* and a witty, sensible retiree dealing intrepidly with old age in *The Gin Game.* Through Julie Harris' background and sensibility we can see how it's possible to be on the Studio roster, set aside some of Strasberg's preoccupations while retaining a deep emotional sensitivity and the attributes of a complete artist.

She was raised in Grosse Point, Michigan, a fashionable suburb of Detroit. Except for modern dance and ballet lessons at a summer camp in Colorado, she was completely untrained. Her ear for stage speech can be partly ascribed to her mother and father who had good voices and mainly attributed to the host of plays they took young Julie to in Detroit that, in effect, made theater integral to her upbringing. She saw all the great stars: the Lunts, Maurice Evans, Paul Muni, Louis Calhern in *Life with Father*, etc. When Eva LeGallienne took her under her wing in New York at her American Repertory Theater, Harris found herself surrounded by notable and accomplished actors who performed in every style. She learned stage speech and stage presence as a matter of course, instilled in her the way someone with musical gifts acquires appreciation and understanding by listening to and playing with the finest soloists.

When LeGallienne recommended her to Kazan as a pure talent, Harris was eager to learn how to deepen her experiences as an actress. Considering herself a slow learner, she wanted to take it all in while, at the same time, refusing to be a disciple, sitting at a master's feet saying, "Yes, master." And, "Tell me, tell me." When she stepped out on the stage she felt she was totally on her own and had to know what she was doing in terms of what worked for her. By this simple logic, unlike Marilyn Monroe, she had to find out for herself.

From Kazan she learned that acting is "wanting"—to get from here to there with all your fiber. She also learned it wasn't easy. Even when you feel immersed in the given circumstances, it's no guarantee. You still might lose your drive and concentration. You still might suddenly "break." To illustrate, there's a story she likes to tell about an improv in one of Kazan's early Studio classes. Her partner was James Whitmore (the one who introduced James Dean to Kazan's approach in L.A.). Kazan whispered to her that for some reason she had to pawn something and couldn't leave the shop without the money. All Whitmore was told was that he was a pawnbroker. In preparation Harris imagined that she needed an abortion and had traveled to a part of the city where no one knew her. There she would pawn her ring and come away with the necessary cash. Set and determined, she made her entrance. Whitmore immediately looked up and said, "Hi, Julie." Harris turned toward Kazan and asked, "How did he know my name?" Kazan informed her that the improv was over. "You broke," he said. "You broke."

Anna Sokolow, the dance teacher during these early years, reinforced Harris' belief in devotion and discipline. She also taught her the importance of the previous circumstances. When working on a dance/theater piece based on Strindberg's *Miss Julie*, Harris was thrown off guard when Sokolow questioned her entrance. "I've been in the wings," Harris answered. "I've just come from the wings." When Sokolow pressed, Harris realized that Sokolow was referring to her character. "She's been dancing outside in the woods with the servants," said Harris. "It's a midsummer night." Sokolow replied, "I didn't see it." "Oh," said Harris. "I have to bring it on with me. I haven't just been in the wings. I've been somewhere. I'm coming from there."

What this continues to tell us is that actors in the same mold as Brando and Clift take what they need and create their own method. To some degree, the same applied to James Dean. Harris took lessons and criticism from everywhere. She listened closely to talks given by a variety of prominent theater figures like playwright Thornton Wilder, stage designer Robert Edmond Jones, Moss Hart, Charlie Chaplin, Richard Rogers, Aaron Copland, Leonard Bernstein and critic Stark Young.

When she first encountered Strasberg, she assumed she would continue to learn from improvisations, the rehearsed "wonderful performances" of others and her own efforts. However, as we've seen, that wasn't his procedure. When she presented a scene she was criticized for her tendency to impersonate. Accepting his appraisal as part of an ongoing challenge, she decided to become more deeply immersed.

Playing Laura, she enacted the gentleman caller scene from Williams' *Glass Menagerie*. When Joe (her acting partner) picked her up to dance, she uttered her line, "No, I can't," as he proceeded to swing her around. Her foot accidentally got caught on the legs of a table, sending the little glass unicorn crashing to the floor. When she saw it break, she disengaged from the action, gingerly picked up the pieces and began to cry. She then went on with the scene, her partner at a loss because she couldn't stop sobbing.

In the discussion that followed, Strasberg told her that her work was brilliant, as if she knew exactly what she was doing. She confessed that "it just happened" and wanted to know how she could do it again. That's what she now felt she was in the theater for—to reproduce those moments night after night. That was her job, to keep it all alive and spontaneously moving. The way she puts it is, "You as the instrument have to know what's going on while the character doesn't know."

However, "knowing what's going on" (recreating happy accidents at will) remained as elusive as ever. She performed again for Strasberg, this time as a dying mother in *Peer Gynt*. She got carried away, really felt ill, but Strasberg took her efforts apart step by step. His critique left her unsettled, as feverish as the sick, old mother. But she made the best of it. She transposed the experience into a maxim: acting was a matter of life and death. Something was at stake, something vital could be lost or gained. This amplification of Kazan's "wanting" made her even more aware of the amount of concentration, power, passion, imaginative belief and control it took to disarm an audience. Otherwise, she felt, they'll shrug it off calling it "just a play" or "just a movie."

Deepening her philosophy of acting and theater, she thought of Chekhov. When a character says, "Why do you wear black?" and the actress answers, "I'm in mourning for my life," the moment is funny but the pain is still there. Both the humor and the struggle had to be communicated to the audience. No teacher could show her how to attain that. She would have to rely on her own intuition and resources. And be grateful for a director like Kazan "who showed you that he loved you" and created an atmosphere of trust so that you could reach for whatever inspired you, explore and take chances. For Harris, that kind of benevolent presence was firmly in the tradition and made inspiration that much more possible. As previously indicated (during the filming of *East of Eden*), Kazan drew out her bubbling love of life, a glint in her eye and an instinct to nurture James Dean.

This filtering process was ongoing, incorporating anything of value. When Strasberg once mentioned that in moments of anguish Duse's cheeks would flush and in moments of joy she would blush, Harris nodded in agreement. But she never got caught up in his "sensory thing" or arguments about externals and the superiority of the Method. Heat, for instance, was something that might affect you within the given circumstances but working for it was only an exercise. It all depends. During *The Gin Game*, for example, Harris was directed to swat imaginary insects. When a member of the audience wrote her a note asking her if her flicking hand movements indicated haunting disturbances from her past life, she eliminated the insects from the scene.

She also took no notice of Strasberg's preference for feeling over language. She empathized with writers and took their words and poetry to heart. During a conversation Tennessee Williams' name might pop up. She would recall how sad he was and, like a victim, placed himself in danger. Expressing how much she missed him, she might—in the spur of the moment—recite some lines from his play *Night of the Iguana*:

> How calmly does the orange branch observe the sky without a cry, without a prayer. It's no betrayal of despair sometime when night obscures the tree, the zenith of its life shall be gone past forever. From thence a second history will commence, a chronicle no longer gold, a chronicle of mist and mold, loosening its stem, plummeting to earth and then...

The recitation would continue, the melodious voice modulating, articulating words and phrases, reflecting her empathy through the final line: "Oh, courage, could you not select a second place to dwell, not only in that golden tree but in the frightened heart of me?"

Before long, technique faded into the background. The only question was, Why do you want to do it? Why do you want to be a storyteller? "Storyteller" incorporates it all: a deep understanding of the oral tradition and literary heritage, imagination and interpretive gifts and much more. The word implies an appreciation of music, song and dance and the ability to play a musical instrument. It suggests the ability to play all manner of characters as she recalls an actor from the Moscow Art Theater who continued to play the role of a young man although he was thirty years too old for the part. Her definition also includes those who have had no training, spent no time analyzing technique and still are brilliant storytelling actors. "They just do it."

By the early 1960s, appearing as young June in June Havoc's self-portrait of her Depression era experience *Marathon '33*, Harris just "did it." She worked hard to perfect her dance routines and fell into the heightened vaudeville style of the 1930s. As one of the dazed finalists of the dance marathon, she instinctively began to daydream. According to the rules you had to keep moving 24 hours a day, except for twelve minutes out of every hour when you were allowed to sit down or eat. It was three AM during the scene in question, a juncture when partners took turns sleeping on each other—e.g., you drag your partner across the floor and then he

Julie Harris as the vaudevillian Baby June in *Marathon '33* **(1963). Photograph courtesy of June Havoc.**

drags you. But you had to keep moving. You were under the watchful eye of Joe Don Baker (an imposing figure well over a foot taller than Ms. Harris) who was ready and willing to disqualify you. As the piano player tinkled the keys in the background, Harris remembers leading Lee Allan (her partner) and then glancing up at a spotlight hovering above her downstage center and imagining a Tintoretto painting of Christ appearing before Pontius Pilate. In her mind's eye, Christ began to transform into a slender column of white. No one asked her to daydream, no one knew what she was doing. As with all her special moments, it just happened.

In recalling her different experiences at the Studio, she used the word "they." "That's what they wanted at the time." It was her way of expressing her individuality, like taking part in *Marathon '33* and then moving on. In short, Harris's brand of independence can be placed at one end of a sliding scale; while Monroe and those in the workshop who suffered from her kind of co-dependence can be placed at the other. "They"—the ambitious ones who lived by the rules and bent them at the same time—operated somewhere in-between.

10

Testing the Waters

At times from the early 1950s until the year 1962, the Studio resembled a house of games. The doors were open, the doors were closed. People entered, people left. Players·clustered together, broke apart, regrouped, ventured out and circled back. Some changed postures and switched sides; some refused to play at all. It was a private workshop; it was a hothouse and launching pad for new projects; it was apart from worldly concerns; it was a trendy celebrity watering hole—it was all of the above.

For many active members there was only one raison d'être: the possibility of working together in productions. From the very beginning people were chosen for their individuality, charm and potential to succeed in the market. Kazan's declaration after the demise of *Sundown Beach* was unrealistic. Few were willing to content themselves with exploratory work. As a rule most actors will go to any lengths to engage an audience. One member by the name of Fred Sadoff went so far as to translate J.D. Salinger's novel *The Catcher in the Rye* into a full-length play, played the lead, cast, directed, set and lit the entire piece for the edification of his colleagues and invited guests. This effort was even more telling when you consider the risks. Salinger zealously guarded the rights to his work and, doubtless, would have stepped in had he known what Sadoff was up to.

Strasberg allowed these experiments to take place, maintaining that there was a marked difference between running a workshop and "putting on a show." It didn't matter whether the actors' explorations were good or bad as long as they were confined to the Studio.

Consistent with this policy, playwriting and directing units were set up. But there was a catch. It didn't matter what was accomplished as long as "name" writers and directors were involved. And it didn't matter if they resigned as long as others with similar credentials took their place. And it was this prestigious activity that, ironically, led full circle to the irresistible urge to "put on a show."

Authors of fiction like Norman Mailer, James Baldwin and John Updike passed through the portals but had difficulty with the demands of the playwriting form. Working playwrights like Israel Horovitz, Robert Anderson, Terrence McNally, Edward Albee, Arthur Kopit, Jack Gelber and Lorraine Hansberry also took part. Among the directors who came and went were Gene Frankel, John Stix and Alan Schneider. Among the directors who stayed on were Jack Garfein and Frank Corsaro, with Corsaro ultimately taking on the mantle of "Lee's man" (otherwise known as the one who truly understood Strasberg's precepts and intentions and would insure that they were upheld).

Briefly, the writers and directors were to develop their craft by regarding the actors as creative collaborators. Through the actors' intuitive insights and use of the Method, scenes and short plays could be enriched. In similar fashion, treating the writer's lines like the tip of an iceberg, considering the main elements to be lying below, the director could stimulate the actors and probe for "the life."

As we shall soon see, the only one who would fully utilize these guidelines was Corsaro through his work with the actor/playwright Michael Gazzo. Others, especially writers, were leery of the actors' contributions to their text. Some felt that the idiosyncratic behavior of Studio members clashed with literary values, dramatic clarity and their original aims. Playwrights like Edward Albee had unshakable ideas as to how their characters should look and behave and how their lines should be delivered.

To illustrate how far apart the writers and actors were at times, on one occasion, after the actors gave a reading of a new work, the playwrights in attendance quickly dismissed the author's work, faulting every aspect of the writing. Corsaro asked for a short recess and, in private, gave the actors suggestions about inner tensions and underlying motivations. The short play was then presented once again. This time the proceedings were much livelier and engaging. The response was positive and the author was elated. Everyone was pleased except for Albee who took Corsaro aside saying, "How dare you come in here and turn a piece of crap into something worthwhile?"

The actors eagerly went along with Corsaro's suggestions because, despite Strasberg's containment policy, they saw the loophole, the chance that new material could be revised and lead to a project. A project could break out into a small production Off Broadway, then a larger production, and then turned into a movie. Everyone knew how the game was played. The odds were high but, under the right circumstances, it was possible to work around Strasberg, use the Studio to your advantage and further your career.

Moreover, this viewpoint was based on precedent. The first incident came about in the early 1950s. Jack Garfein (who was a Studio observer at the time) convinced the writer Calder Willingham to turn his novel *End as a Man* into a play. Because the book focused on the psycho/social pressures within the confines of a southern military academy, Garfein felt the material lent itself to the kind of work Strasberg favored. Garfein was especially taken with the central character, the anti-hero with the pseudonym Jocko de Paris who used devious ploys to bully and manipulate novices who were easy prey. Strasberg permitted Garfein to explore these various behavior patterns after hours with any young members who might be so inclined.

Casting was made to order. Among those hungering for any kind of opportunity were Anthony Franciosa who was working as a short-order cook, Ben Gazzara moonlighting as an elevator operator, Albert Salmi who was ushering at a movie theater, Pat Hingle, Arthur Storch and a handful of others.

Gazzara easily related to Jocko, the bully. The rest of the contingent found no problem in being intimidated. As a case in point, Gazzara began taunting Arthur Storch over some personal matter while the cast was socializing in a local coffee shop. Storch was deeply upset over Gazzara's merciless teasing. The torment continued until the onlookers finally caught on and intervened, informing Storch that Gazzara was baiting him to give them both a taste of the bully-victim relationship. It seemed that Gazzara had a knack for cool, calculating sadism. No one in the cast ever quite knew what he was up to onstage or off. In Studio terms, the Method seemed to be paying off.

Continuing in this vein, Garfein devised improvisations to explore other aspects of thinly veiled abuse. To delve even more deeply into the life, the cast visited West Point and, subsequently, conducted close order drills. Intrigued by this whole process, Willingham (who was not associated with the Studio) incorporated the improvs into scenes and fashioned a full-length script. The results were shared with a Studio audience. A producer became interested, and a small production was mounted at the tiny Theatre DeLys on Christopher Street in Greenwich Village.

Even though Garfein had assured the cast that Strasberg would be in attendance, Strasberg waited until the reviews came in. He was reluctant to have his name and the Studio's reputation associated with a production of unknown merit. When the notices proved positive, Strasberg and Cheryl Crawford viewed the show. When the production moved to Broadway and received praise from the critic Stark Young for its edgy and tightly-knit ensemble work, Strasberg acknowledged that the play had been developed in workshop at the Studio and Garfein was awarded full-fledged membership. When the play was made into a movie under Garfein's direction with most of the original cast intact, Strasberg accepted credit for the value of the Studio's work.

In the annals of Studio-process-to-production, the most notable example was Frank Corsaro's development of *Hat Full of Rain* a year or so later. As noted, Corsaro was completely familiar with Strasberg's theories. In time he had combined them with his training and experiences as an actor and student of directing at Yale and an image of Stanislavsky training actors by day and applying the results at night to the delight of audiences. By the mid–1950s he considered Strasberg's Method to be the "work of a man of some genius" who was fostering a slow, artful process with great potential apropos of Corsaro's vision.

More specifically, to Corsaro's mind Strasberg's Wednesday/Friday sessions were designed to get at those parts of an actor's personality that were the most provocative. Strasberg was sharply critical in order to awaken individuals and make them dig deeper. Even though Strasberg indicated that the Studio was a refuge from the demands of performance, Corsaro took Strasberg's precepts to mean, How do you perform? What do you perform with? Since the aim was to bring given circumstances to life, it followed that, by necessity, an actor must stimulate the source of all expression—his personal response system—before doing anything else. Or in Corsaro's words: "My experience is the experience of the play, my anger is what I use; my this is this and my that is that; characterization and other things come later; it all comes down to my own particular reality."

At this stage, the trick was to find material the actors could respond to that would put this kind of energy to use. The answer, and the means by which his own prospects as a director took a leap forward, came in the form of a shapeless scene devised by Studio actor Michael Gazzo. By chance, Corsaro came across three young actors slumped in a darkened area of what was then the Studio's locale. Their names were Anthony Franciosa, Paul Richards and Henry Silva. They were struggling with Gazzo's dialogue, written in the vernacular of junkies under the effects of drug addiction. Adding to the problem was the fact that Gazzo hadn't indicated who the characters were or where the scene was taking place.

Corsaro offered to help. He began by looking for ways to link the behavior of addicts to the actors' individual experiences. He probed, one-on-one, into their private frustrations and desires. In Corsaro's terms, he acted as a priest and confessor.

He then transposed this information into a set of improvisations: conflicts and hypothetical situations based on Stanislavsky's basic theatrical question, "What if?" Avenues were opened up. The initial scene was expanded and more improvs were attempted based on the actors' biographies and appropriate sensory exercises. Corsaro did research, looking into the symptoms of addiction. He discovered that the effects were comparable to drunkenness, fever, and the chills and aches of pulmonary disorders. Since these experiences were so familiar, Corsaro asked the actors to recreate them. The substitutions were then used to bring about a drug "high" and a convincing foundation for their imaginary situation. This fusion of fabricated and real emotional difficulties brought them fully into Gazzo's world of the junkie and solved their acting problem.

Somewhere along the line, Corsaro then sat down with Gazzo to enlarge the scope of the piece, sensing there was a full-length play in the offing. As it happens, Gazzo had written a previous play, a formless investigation of a working-class family centering on a father who doesn't understand his two sons. The two brothers compete for the love of their remote father and find themselves also vying for the affections of a young woman. Corsaro urged Gazzo to hash out a plot. He wanted to know where this play was going, who the people were exactly, and what each of them wanted. Who is doing what to whom? Corsaro asked.

Working from midnight until three or four in the morning, Corsaro continued to improvise, adding Ben Gazzara, Eva Marie Saint and others in a structure that began to focus on a war veteran, hooked on drugs, trying to conceal the fact from his wife. The family drama opened out to accommodate the junkies, a wife who doesn't really know her husband and is torn between two brothers, and an estranged father. The new improvs revolved around these lives and relationships, arriving at the point where the play began.

Gazzo slipped Corsaro new pages, incorporated the results of the improvs into additional written material while Corsaro made certain that the improvised scenes were in keeping with Gazzo's intentions. As part of the continuing process, Franciosa (who was now playing Gazzara's brother) had to devise three distinct phases of drunkenness, and Gazzara was asked to run the gamut from a drug high to withdrawal and violent convulsions. Strasberg viewed some of the work during one of his sessions and asserted that the characters needed to be deepened. As the actors followed Strasberg's suggestions and discovered their specific relationships (plus the sensory and emotional triggers that impelled them into the imaginary circumstances), the improvised world merged with Gazzo's revisions.

Finally, after all the collaboration, this topical problem play with its tenement setting was given a preview showing for an invited audience. Everyone, it seemed, appreciated the lively results: living characters in an authentic environment; the action kept fresh, open to momentary inspiration. And an epiphany at the conclusion as the war veteran finally confesses his sins (coming full circle to the actors' initial confessions to Corsaro).

Eventually producers became interested. The original catalyst—the junkie scene—was cut down from forty minutes to fifteen minutes because it literally stopped the show and deflected from the main thrust of the plot. After more tinkering and revisions, the completed play eventually reached Broadway.

Once again Strasberg refused to be present at the opening. And once again he attended the production after it received positive notices. The play went on to have a two-year run on Broadway, did well on the road, and became a movie with Don Murray (the same Hollywood actor who appeared opposite Monroe) in the lead. Once it became firmly established, Strasberg and the powers that be at the Studio claimed the play as their own. It has since been recognized as *the* Method production: a theatrical experience based on extensive preparatory work of a certain kind, within a living environment, impelled by a timely and provocative theme.

No similar undertakings followed, no special Studio process of development was identified and refined despite Corsaro's success and Garfein's before him. Instead the Studio seemed unsure of itself, caught up in a series of distractions. Celebrity drop-ins became the order of the day. Grace Kelly, Joan Crawford, Helen Hayes, Laurence Olivier, Michael Redgrave and his daughter Vanessa, and others observed a few sessions, eager to glimpse the Method firsthand. A short time later, people were curious to learn what had drawn Marilyn Monroe to this secluded spot. The press, in turn, found that the impressions of these famous persons made good copy. They raised questions but received no answers. Was the Studio a place to get a quick Method fix? Was Strasberg a trendy guru who could instantly turn someone into a marketable personality? Was the Studio producing ensemble pieces like *Hatful of Rain* or a number of anti-social rebels? One reporter felt that, as an institution, the Studio should explain its work, disclose its aims and report its progress to avoid continued misunderstandings.

Within the inner circle different questions were raised and the misgivings were becoming more pronounced. Some finally began to openly resent the notoriety that Monroe and Dean had received as "Method people." Corsaro, who had befriended Dean, regarded him as a person who wasn't strong enough to take the kind of criticism meted out by Strasberg and was terrified of the Studio's "sophisticated and high-standard judgments." His talent was instinctual, his technique zero. He was inspired by Brando and Clift's individuality but was too rebellious and psychologically immature to be in the same league. Corsaro also found Monroe "not quite with it." She would listen to Strasberg's monologues and then whisper to Corsaro, "What does he mean?" Corsaro was also of the opinion that there were other non-representative Studio actors who dropped by for "therapy" and liked to "pick at their scabs" (wallow in their personal pain and anxieties). It was all a distortion of what he and those like him believed to be the Studio's underlying mission. The authentic membership was made up of team players who were awaiting any chance to apply the process. The true Studio people were ready and willing to perform.

The next opportunity presented itself toward the close of the 1950s. Jack Garfein, who had always been fond of 20th-century Irish playwriting, began working on O'Casey's *Shadow of a Gunman*. Another ensemble play, it concerned an isolated group, residents of a shabby Dublin boardinghouse whose lives were marred by the troubles in Ireland. As an extension of his last outing, Garfein's created improvisations centered on character relationships. He also created improvised scenes that might have taken place just before the opening beat.

This time around, however, Garfein ran into difficulty. There was no accommodating novelist at his side. The text was inviolable and complete. The loquacious dialect and Irish lyricism was outside the range of his Studio actors. To partly remedy this particular problem, Garfein added some non–Studio members to the cast and, possibly for political reasons, cast Strasberg's daughter Susan (who was also a non-member) in a supporting role.

Unfortunately, when at last it seemed likely that the project would go into production, the stumbling block that always lingered in the background manifested itself once more. After attending a run-through, Strasberg declared that the production had no reality and fell far short of his standards. He wanted "the show" recast with Studio stars like Rod Steiger and Geraldine Page. When Garfein countered by reminding Strasberg that it was the work that counted, not the stars, Strasberg replied that only well-known stars from the Studio had the ability to present work properly.

As a compromise, Kazan (who was still on the board of directors) was called in. Acting as mediator, Kazan suggested that Garfein invite Strasberg to advise in his capacity as teacher and, thereby, help Garfein ready the play for a successful run. The tactic backfired. Strasberg began to direct. He re-staged his daughter's scene, reworked the raid scene and told the non–Studio actors to "do whatever comes to you."

Much of what followed reads like a family squabble. Garfein resigned and engaged a lawyer. Strasberg stepped aside. When favorable reviews came out, Strasberg took out ads to promote his young daughter's budding career, making it appear that she had the lead instead of a supporting role. To make matters worse, Paula Strasberg notified the *New York Times* that it was really her husband Lee who had directed the play. On another occasion, she questioned Garfein's experiences during the Nazi occupation, remarks Garfein took as an attack on his character.

Shifting gears on the heels of unfavorable reviews, Strasberg offered a disclaimer to the National Theatre Conference stating that, of the eleven people in the cast, only four were members of the Studio and, even though his daughter had talent, she was still in training. A short time later, appearing to shift his position once again, Strasberg informed the members that "we have laid the basis to put into the world arena the best in ensemble theater."

By this point no one knew exactly what to make of the mixed messages: singing the praises of projects that succeeded, disclaiming any association with those that failed, and pointing the way for some kind of permanent theater. Some members like actress Carol Baker decided that all projects were rife with uncertainty because of the lack of a strong leader and sought elsewhere for fulfillment.

Undaunted, the stalwarts, the ones Corsaro characterized as "ready to perform" and able to work as a team, continued to keep their eye on the influx of writers and opportunities evolving around the playwrights unit.

By the fall of 1959 projects again appeared to be on the up-swing. Albee's *The Zoo Story* and *The Death of Bessie Smith* had been developed in workshop and were going on to positive notices Off Broadway. Corsaro managed to extract something stageworthy out of Norman Mailer's cumbersome novel *Deer Park* which, after Mailer's revisions, reached Off Broadway as well. Corsaro asked his friends William Inge and Tennessee Williams to supply one-acts for Gian Carlo Menotti's festival at Spoleto, Italy. This resulted in a tryout not only of an Inge play but a potential full-length work by Williams. *The Night of the Iguana*, featuring a cast of Studio actors, benefited from Corsaro's work-in-progress approach and was eventually expanded into a major Broadway play.

These ventures notwithstanding, the greatest cause for optimism came from the announcement that Kazan had been chosen as an associate in the development and direction of the Lincoln Center Repertory Theater. Hopes were raised that the Actors Studio would become the resident company. Talk evolved around a possible second coming of the Group: a true ensemble that would forge a national theater; an organic entity with a consistent creative vision; a company that would produce a string of distinguished American plays.

In addition, there was the assumption that Strasberg would head the training program at the future Lincoln Center. Intimations from Kazan buoyed his spirits. In Strasberg's view, prospects were unlimited: "We have twenty to twenty-five top people. The combination of actors, directors and professional experience is unparalleled. We have an unusual blend of age and youth, talent and artistic conviction and commercial awareness. It's the first time in the history of the theater. We have a unit which could make the best theater and the best movies."

Adding to the euphoria was an article which appeared in the *New York Times*. In this piece the writer declared that the Method was the dominant approach to acting and the Actors Studio was its fountainhead. The Studio thrived because its work was based on the creativity of the individual—a clear reflection of the American character.

Soon, however, the prospects of becoming the theatrical arm of a great artistic institution began to pale. Robert Whitehead, a man with an air of gentility, became the organizing director. He felt there was new ground to cover. This goal couldn't be achieved on the basis of an American theater movement rooted in realism and Lee Strasberg's overemphasis on the psycho/sexual interpretation of the subtext. In point of fact, Whitehead wanted the thrust to be anti-psychoanalytic in order to establish "a new character for our performers as well as our theater."

Differences in ideology became more apparent when Strasberg was interviewed by Dr. Stoddard, dean of New York University's School of Education and the man charged with finding suitable candidates to head the Center's training program. Stoddard inquired about Strasberg's approach to Shakespeare and the handling of language in classical drama. During the course of the conversation Strasberg was treated more like a curious individualist than an expert in his field. His hopes were dashed when the Juilliard Foundation brought in the French director Michel St. Denis to advise the Center on the formation of the theater school.

Next came an imminent split with Kazan. Upon assuming the directorship of the Lincoln Center Theater, Kazan attempted once again to convince the Studio membership to resign themselves to their workshop activities. If not, there would be a conflict of interest. Kazan would not be able to serve on the Studio board of directors and run the Center's theatrical operations at the same time.

The members, in turn, prodding a reluctant Lee Strasberg, forced the issue. There was a financial crisis which could only be solved through "long range planning," the acquisition of large grants and productions. The pressure was heightened by the fact that Kazan was forming a permanent acting company at the Center, had aligned himself with Arthur Miller and was snatching away Studio members to fill his ranks and perform Miller's plays in repertory. Something had to be done.

Strasberg continued to hedge. Aside from his troubles with the Group and his inability to sustain a career as a director a decade before, he had no track record as a successful theatrical producer on a commercial scale. On the other hand, he was still drawn to the limelight and the proposition of hit shows featuring those of his acolytes he considered "names." Still skirting the issue, Strasberg spoke of reinvigorating the Studio's responsibility to the American theater while advising the committee on financial stability that their job was limited to housekeeping. In terms of artistic matters and Studio policy, he was the sole authority.

As the Studio edged its way into the formation of a producing theater, Kazan publicly announced his differences with his old boss of the 1930s, thereby cutting his losses and citing the shortcomings he would be sure to avoid in his new position:

> The Actors Studio is now no longer a young group of insurgents. It is itself an orthodoxy. It takes particular pride in its roster of stars and names. ... My great disappointment with the work there has been that it always stopped at the same point, a preoccupation with the purely psychological side of acting. ... Regrettably, too much of the "Method" talk among actors today is a defense against new artistic challenges, rationalizations for their own ineptitudes. We have a swarm of actors who are ideologues and theorists. There have been days when I felt I would swap them all for a gang of wandering players who could dance and sing and who were, above all else, entertainers.

Switching allegiances and affiliating himself with a formidable world-class operation was not a difficult choice for Kazan. Arthur Miller would be honoring the Lincoln Center with not one but two new challenging plays. S.N. Behrman, the noted author of sophisticated comedies, was providing Kazan's newly formed company with a fresh work. There were classical plays in the offing as well.

But Kazan's tenure at Lincoln Square didn't go as planned. Miller's examination of World War II refugees awaiting interrogation in Vichy was neither compelling nor convincing. The second new offering, a portrayal of his relationship with Marilyn Monroe, was labored and made all the more unappealing by Jason Robards' disdain for his role as Miller's surrogate. Kazan was out of his depth trying to deal with Behrman's charming characters and witty banter. After these disappointing experiences he needed time to regroup and learn from his mistakes. The powers that be ("the corporation types") however weren't willing to take any more chances. Kazan had no choice but to ease away from the Center and move on.

Within this same time frame, the Studio Theater took wing for a season or two, fluttered, made its way to London and came down to earth. The details of the venture proved to be as problematic as the man in charge.

11

The Studio Theater Chronicles

On a promotional campaign, four prominent actors and a director representing the newly formed Actors Studio Theater appeared on a TV program called "Camera 3." The actors were Paul Newman, Geraldine Page, Rip Torn and Michael Wager. The director was Frank Corsaro. The year was 1963. The occasion was the opening of their first production, a revival of O'Neill's *Strange Interlude*. The host capsulized the discussion by quoting from a headline by critic Walter Kerr: "The year the actors took a fling at the moon."

The guests talked of a passion to build a theater they could call their own. They reminded the host and the viewing audience that every great theater was started by actors. Echoing this sentiment, Paul Newman commented that the impulse came from the creative people, the ones like himself and his three colleagues who were going to commit themselves and subsidize the undertaking by working for scale.

Rip Torn went on to claim that "we can serve the playwright better than any living organization." The Studio's playwrights unit was "comprised of the finest young playwrights in America today." A permanent theater run by the Studio would make possible a chamber theater for smaller productions. New works could be developed, grants would be obtained, the concern over economic matters would be eliminated. The Studio would draw the finest writers in America and enable them to flourish under its artistic control.

Warming to the subject, Torn announced that the Studio Theater expected to play all over the country and the world. It could do so because it was the only organization that could call on its unique stock of talent. Joining in, Geraldine Page declared that the Studio was legendary overseas. Its influence had spread over an enormously wide area and had infused the British theater with a new freedom. Newman added that in his travels abroad, most correspondents were eager to learn about this new phenomenon. "The theater legend of America," the others chimed in.

In explaining the means by which the Studio had reached its preeminence, Frank Corsaro argued that there had always been a way by which actors arrived at their own personal truth. The Method, therefore, was universal.

Within the space of two years, all of these claims would be put to the test. In less than that time, Page, Torn and Wager would disassociate themselves. Corsaro would change his career and try his hand at opera. Unwittingly all four may have provided themselves with a telling clue. Amid all the talk about creating their own theater, Rip Torn had mentioned that their undertaking was the culmination of "Lee Strasberg sitting in his chair."[9]

Recalling the heady formative days of the Group, it was Clurman who was the spokesman, not a committee of actors. He was not sitting back "in his chair," he was pressing forward and his cause was specific, fervent and ideal. Concerns about community and hope for the future during trying times were the order of the day, intertwined with playwrights who were like-minded and, to a great degree, committed to the same cause. With the founding of the Studio, Kazan would doubtless have come forth and spoken of the poetic realism of Williams and Miller should he (and Bobby Lewis) have ever considered creating a permanent theater. Even in his failure at Lincoln Center, Kazan had an image of the kind of theater he wanted to build and the plays he wanted his company to do.

The Actors Studio Theater had no compelling vision shared by collaborating writers. And no matter how much the actors protested, they weren't in command. In truth, their artistic director had some kind of psychological hold on them, might or might not lead, but would never relinquish the reins, preferring to act as both authority figure and Broadway showman: "In production, all that matters is that it should be well done. There should be firm artistic leadership. Authority is never questioned. ... Certain kinds of plays with hit notices will not do hit business. But if that same play has stars, it will do hit business. With the best names of the Studio you have something a production on the open market won't do."

Subsequently, just as before, circling around Strasberg became the modus operandi. The Production Board secured a large grant of over a quarter of a million dollars from the Ford Foundation. The prospectus outlined classic American plays, a primary responsibility to the American playwright, contemporary European dramas and foreign classics to alternate in repertory over a period of time. No mention was made that the plan was totally conceptual and subject to dealings with Lee Strasberg and the elements of chance.

To illustrate the tenuous nature of the prospectus, Strasberg declined to back two new major works. The first of these was a full-scale mounting of Williams' *Night of the Iguana*. Corsaro and the cast were more than ready. The artistic director was not. Nor was he ready to open the Studio season with Albee's *Who's Afraid of Virginia Woolf?* When the fund-raiser and impresario Roger L. Stevens and cohort Cheryl Crawford called the script off-color and "dull, whiny and without laughs," Strasberg passed on the opportunity. Then and there Albee ended his association with the Studio. Both plays proved to be landmark achievements in the American theater.

Even the production of *Strange Interlude* was a reflection of Strasberg's indecisiveness. Believing that the rights to all O'Neill plays were reserved for Lincoln Center, he gave Production Board chairman Rip Torn permission to try to secure the rights to the play in question, convinced there was no way Torn could succeed. Unbeknown to Strasberg, Torn had worked out an arrangement with José Quintero, the director at Circle in the Square who had won great acclaim for his staging of O'Neill's *Desire Under the Elms* along with Williams' *Summer and Smoke*. Capitalizing on his working relationship with O'Neill's widow Carlotta, Quintero obtained permission with the clear understanding that he would be at the helm. Caught in a bind, having given Torn his word, Strasberg was forced to concede, making the first offering of the Studio Theater season a product of happenstance and maneuvering.

In addition to *Strange Interlude*, the catch-as-catch-can playbill from March 1963 through June of 1964 eventually included *Marathon '33*, *Dynamite Tonight*, *Baby Want a Kiss*, *Blues for Mister Charlie* and *The Three Sisters*. In the summer of 1965, the Studio took the latter two productions abroad.

In the interim, after coming to terms with the Torn/Quintero episode, Strasberg announced to the membership that the opening of *Strange Interlude* "might well be recognized as a historic date for the American stage" and the inauguration of an American national theater. For some of those listening to his words the underlying message was "let's just wait and see."

Strange Interlude is a nine-act play of such length that it required an early curtain and forty-five minute dinner interval. Prior to the Studio Theater production, thirty-five years had elapsed since anyone had attempted to stage it. The plot centers on Nina Leeds, a willful neurotic woman obsessed by the memory of her lover who was killed in the war before their affair was consummated. The shock brings on her first nervous breakdown. This event is followed by compulsive promiscuity, a marriage to a man she doesn't love, the revelation that her husband's family has a history of insanity, her pregnancy, abortion and ploy to have a child by someone else in order to gain an untainted offspring. At the time of its creation, O'Neill was obsessed with the writings of Freud and the psychological undercurrents between fathers and daughters, mothers and sons, husbands and wives and wives and lovers. Into the mix he added the sins of the father haunting the children and the behavior patterns of a manic-depressive. Nina is calm, hysterical, lustful, cruel, sarcastic, guilt-ridden and predictably unpredictable. If nothing else, it was a vehicle for Geraldine Page who had made her mark playing similar but less overwrought roles.

The reviews were mixed. Recalling her triumph as Alma under Quintero's direction in Williams' *Summer and Smoke*, Clurman (now a drama critic) remarked that Geraldine Page was simply playing herself. Relating their high expectations vis-à-vis a Studio Theater, the critics of the *New York Times* found the event "extremely interesting ... uneven ... a giant step forward." Other critics whose expectations weren't being met pointed out the lack of ensemble work and found the production to be "star-infected and under-rehearsed." Theater critic Robert

Brustein was distracted by Page's mannerisms—"her fluttering, quavering voice, quick emotional breakdowns and curious clicking sounds." He also noted stereotypical turns like Pat Hingle's portrayal of the husband as a brash all–American simpleton and Ben Gazzara's sinister matinee heavy as Page's lover. For Brustein, the "psychoanalysis," self-absorption, stock characterizations and choice of "the worst play O'Neill ever wrote" did not bode well for this fledgling company.

In response to adverse criticism Strasberg replied that "the production, while it had our people and therefore had certain elements that were very good, was not the kind of thing that I would have wanted to be represented by."

For the theatergoing public, predicting the "kind of thing" Strasberg *was* willing to endorse was a matter of conjecture. What were the criteria? Quintero had an affinity for O'Neill and could deal with Studio actors but was not one of their own. His direction was, at times, reverential and then melodramatic, replete with screams, shouts and groans. The production was also a single outing, the results inconclusive. For those on both sides of the footlights, the play schedule seemed to be up in the air.

Ideally, material developed in the workshop and reflecting the Studio's unique process should have followed. However, the ins and outs of production coupled with Strasberg's attempts to juggle notions of what he wanted to be represented by with his big-budget visions of Broadway led to a compromise. In the final analysis, *Marathon '33* exuded a touch of Kazan and a combination of experimentation and traditional show business.

The formative stages of the project went something like this. Julie Harris encouraged her friend June Havoc to develop a work for the stage based on her (Havoc's) best-selling memoirs about the dance marathon craze. After a time, Havoc's membership in the playwriting unit led to her proposal that Harris return to the Studio for this singular engagement. Corsaro (who was slated to direct) and Strasberg were interested in the looseness of the structure and the possibilities of applying the Method. Havoc insisted on developing and directing the piece on her own. Strasberg gave in for a number of reasons. He was acquainted with Havoc; she was the sister of Gypsy Rose Lee and a movie star; her name was on the original Studio roster. According to Havoc, Strasberg was also intrigued with the idea of learning about vaudeville and comedy, subjects he knew very little about.[10] A deciding factor may have been the desire to retain the services of both Ms. Havoc and Ms. Harris. At any rate, many concessions were made including the use of outsiders and the project carried on.

Basically there were two operative elements: Havoc's special skills and experiences plus what she had learned from Kazan. From her Studio days under "Gadget's" influence she was inspired to create improvs or what she called "essence"—ways to give everyone a hands-on understanding of the marathon dancing world. The tasks were direct and tangible—e.g., what happens to you after you've stayed on your feet for hundreds of hours and how do you combat it? how do you keep your feet moving while you eat? how do you keep functioning when you're semi-conscious and a little out of your head? As she recalled from working with Kazan, there was no point in talking about technique. No one cared what you drew upon or how you got to where you were going. Her only rule of thumb was, "Just do it, for God's sake, just do it."

Moreover, Havoc was fond of mentioning her stint on Broadway with the celebrated leading lady Helen Hayes. Before her entrance Hayes would do her crossword puzzle. Just before her cue she would put the puzzle down and make her entrance. For Havoc, a Studio actor wasn't any different than any other professional. The Method was never discussed.

What was stressed was a certain vaudevillian skill and pride. In Havoc's experience one had to possess the stamina and agility of an acrobat and the ability to sing and dance four times a day. In recreating this "Olympiad" Havoc devised an entire vaudeville bill. She drilled the cast for weeks on end until they perfected the difficult marathon dance steps of the era.

She also bolstered her invention by importing comics from the borscht circuit much to Strasberg's delight. As she tells it, she caught him several times surreptitiously imitating the funny men, trying to get the hang of a triple take. But he didn't completely take a back seat. On occasion he injected opinions and gave a long appraisal after the first run-through. But Strasberg was never a factor.

At the center of what could be likened to a three-ring circus were Julie Harris' lyric intensity, comic timing, warmth and enthusiasm plus newly acquired dancing skills. Concurrently, along with Harris' portrayal of Baby June trying to make it through the contest and "hit the big time vaudeville" were the interweaving of the routines, overlapping music, mini-dramas of broken dreams, microphone announcements and multiple characters swarming on and off.

Marathon '33 was eventually nominated for a Tony award. Havoc considered it an artistic success. Some prominent Studio members, however, felt that its original virtues had been lost due to Havoc's nostalgia and control. What the public had witnessed was strictly a commercial package.

The notices were mixed. As far as the critics and the public were concerned, it appeared there was still no telling what would be presented next under the Studio banner. Those inside the workshop didn't fare any better as far as the future was concerned. It continued to be a matter of wait and see.

Somewhere in the scheme of things during this first season was a cabaret satire on the idiocy of war entitled *Dynamite Tonight*. Thanks to a Rockefeller grant to promote innovation, the piece was developed in the playwriting unit and, subsequently, became the third production of the series. In the process, Paul Sills, the leader of the famed improvisational troupe Second City was called in from Chicago along with a few of his seasoned performers. Augmented by Studio members, the effort was warmly received by a preview audience within the workshop. Cast changes were made for a number of reasons, some of them having to do with artistic differences. Whatever it was that appealed to the insiders during the first preview was apparently lost in the shuffle. "Dynamite" opened and closed Off Broadway after one performance. It became blatantly obvious that any succeeding venture would have to show a profit.

To the rescue came the Newmans (Paul Newman and Joanne Woodward). As a change of pace they wanted to do *Baby Want a Kiss*, a light comedy written by their friend James Costigan. The plan was to have Costigan play himself in the guise of Edward, a failed author; the Newmans would play visiting glamorous movie stars, and the Newmans' friend Frank Corsaro was slated to direct. Working for scale, the Newmans' names on the marquee would insure a box-office success.

Corsaro, who had begun his career as an actor with a knack for comedy, went into the project with the notion that everyone would just have fun. A few days into rehearsal he began to realize that the writing was unfinished and the whole undertaking would be better suited for a limited engagement in a small theater in the Village. But Strasberg would have none of it. It was to be the Newmans on Broadway and a successful run as planned.

What audiences and critics saw was a likable and down-to-earth Joanne Woodward and a slightly constrained Paul Newman bantering about incriminating dreams in the setting of a remote country house. The dialogue was self-mocking, verging on the absurd as the couple took turns seducing their host, Edward, floating in and out of fantasy, reveling in their beauty and fame, and fabricating not only their lives but their relationship with Edward. Whatever the author's intentions, the structure fell apart approximately ten minutes before the final curtain.

It made money. The critics hated it; all save Robert Brustein who found the Newmans engaging. The four-month run of "Baby" marked a year since the opening of *Strange Interlude*. It also marked the end of what were generally regarded as inconsequential preliminaries. In the summer of 1964 two productions emerged that finally put the question of the Studio Theater's mission and viability to the test.

To outsiders looking in, *Blues for Mister Charlie* had the potential to bring back the glory days of *Waiting for Lefty* and social relevance. It was the time of the civil rights movement in the South and the writing was based on the murder of Emmett Till, a racial incident that was fresh in everyone's mind. Outsiders saw the potential and looked forward to the opening. Behind the scenes, things weren't as promising and compelling. Once more there were fluctuations and conflict. Yet again compromises had to be made.

James Baldwin, the noted black author, had participated in the playwriting unit. He had also served as a production assistant to Kazan. It was Kazan who had encouraged Baldwin to develop the script. Hesitant at first, Strasberg was finally persuaded that Kazan was about to steal the show from under him and decided, then and there, to go along. But that was only the beginning of the struggle.

For a fourth time in a row, a major sticking point was the merits of the script. Corsaro was slated to direct and assumed he could fix things through his usual process: determining the details of the particular life in question, experimenting with the behavioral patterns and their underlying causes, and establishing definite

June Havoc (right) instructing Julie Harris on the fine points of vaudeville during rehearsals for Havoc's project for the Actors Studio Theater.

relationships. But such was not the case. Rip Torn, acting as an executive producer, had assured Baldwin that his script would be kept intact. Presently, Baldwin announced to a shocked Corsaro and Strasberg that his intention was "to go after Whitey." Any desire on their part to fashion a documentary-like look at the black and white struggle was wishful thinking. It had nothing to do with the nature and thrust of his play.

Thus Strasberg found himself in another one of his dilemmas. Should the Studio be represented by a vitriolic play rife with one-dimensional southern rednecks? On the other side of the coin, Strasberg had made promises to promote a black playwright, the work was timely, and there was a great deal of publicity surrounding the event.

After Corsaro gave up trying to deal with Baldwin's script, Burgess Meredith (a member who had several directing credits) took his place. Soon after, when all concerned finally agreed that the writing was not only incendiary but unwieldy, the Production Board voted to give the piece a minimalist staging in some performance space off the beaten track. Strasberg overruled the decision. The show was to be given the full Broadway treatment. No reason was cited.

Coming to terms with the script, Meredith's direction—replete with lighting effects and an elaborate set—turned the project into a staged epic tale: blacks pitted against the white nemesis; a mass meeting in a union hall dovetailing into a courtroom battle as witnesses drift downstage, recount past events and break into passionate soliloquies.

The indictment begins with a startling sequence. An upstart young Emmett Till goads a white southerner into killing him. This scene is followed by three long acts exploring the cause—a series of incidents centering on Till. Traveling north, he falls victim to lecherous white women, gangsters, drugs, etc.; all designed by his white oppressor "Mr. Charlie" to bring about self-loathing and, thereby, do him in. Totally embittered, he returns home to taunt the token southerner as a means of inciting his people; thus gaining revenge and making himself "well" again as he provokes the redneck into ending his life.

Of note was Diana Sands' monologue in the third act, expressing her overwhelming grief and longing for her slain lover, crouching and releasing primal moans and cries. By and large, audiences were exhilarated by her unnerving performance. To anyone who brought up the fact that even though Ms. Sands was not a Studio member she was the most expressive member of the cast, there was an explanation. She had benefited from her coaching. Besides, "all people who are naturals are Method actors without having a diploma." To any further questions about the makeup of the cast—in addition to Ms. Sands, over one-third were not Studio members—there was no response.

The reviews were, once again, mixed. Although most critics noted the manipulative hand of the author, more than a few were impressed by the sense of agitation and urgency. But in a Broadway market, these pluses and minuses, combined with many more pluses than minuses of word-of-mouth, were not enough to sustain a play of epic proportions and a cast of thirty. Special discounts were given but costs could not be met. And the question as to the distinctive nature of the Actors Studio Theater was still unanswered.

On the horizon was the production that would meet this query head on. For a year it had been common knowledge that none other than Lee Strasberg would resume his directing career. And there were no qualms or hesitations about the script. It was a masterpiece.

For all these years the artistic director had recalled the MAT's emotionally rich rendition of *The Three Sisters* in the 1920s. Since that time he had reinterpreted the MAT's production, adding his own brand of sensory realism in order to better meet what he felt were Chekhov's underlying intentions. (In point of fact, Chekhov called for comic irony, believing that humor and verve were admirable under the circumstances and any hint of self-pity would weigh the story down—a consideration that may have had some bearing on the reaction to Strasberg's directing overseas.)

At any rate, by giving the impression that the Method would be employed— thereby meeting the expectations of everyone behind the scenes—Strasberg let himself in for more difficulties. Not only was he caught at some point between his memories of the MAT and his own interpretation, he was once more juggling notions about casting and commercial success with his prescriptions for acting and theater as art.

As he readied himself for rehearsal his inconsistencies were already taking their toll. One predicament centered on Kim Stanley, the one slated to play Masha (the most histrionic of the featured roles). Stanley was widely recognized as an "actor's actor" and the one whose work was the most representative of her mentor's approach as evidenced by her remarks to the press: "The Studio is a place where you can learn under the most thoroughly trained eye how to be as free as possible so that the audience can't control your performance. Then you can have an experience that really expresses the meaning of a part and lets the audience experience it with you. That's what every good actor tries to do."

Understandably, Stanley assumed she would be given a great deal of latitude; that her uncanny ability to be in the moment and to be captivated by images and memories would be nourished. After all, the actor's creative needs were central to the Method. Yet, much to her dismay, that wasn't exactly what was in store.

At the outset, Miss Stanley required someone she could relate to as her lover Vershinin. When Strasberg chose Kevin McCarthy for the role, Stanley and Strasberg had the first of their altercations. Regardless of Stanley's protests that her work would be compromised playing opposite someone for whom she had no regard, the matter was closed. McCarthy fit Strasberg's image of the part.

Anyone familiar with the inner workings of the Group could have predicted the pattern. An intrepid actress like Kim Stanley would stand her ground just like Stella Adler. The teacher/director would then rail at other cast members like Barbara Baxley (who played Natasha, the malevolent sister) who would fight back and demand an apology. Someone more vulnerable like Shirley Knight (who played young Irina) would draw back and be protected by a person like Stanley who would step in and shout, "Why don't you yell at me? I'm the one you want to yell at." Whereupon Strasberg would back down. And that is precisely how matters went under the stress of the impending production.

Adding to the complications, Strasberg gave line readings, precise blocking and told actors like Geraldine Page (who played the spinster sister Olga) exactly how to play certain moments: "Sit behind the desk, look up at the balcony and talk loud." He even went so far as to bring in an old recording of the MAT production, playing over and over the 1920s version of the final departure of Vershinin and Masha. In defiance, Stanley took every opportunity to follow her own impulses, at one time making an entrance with her hair streaming down her back like a woman going mad.

As a direct consequence of this uneasy dynamic there were duplications of directing concepts that were four decades old; moments of understated modern naturalism; actors and actresses who were stifled because they were not permitted to explore; and the freewheeling behavior of Kim Stanley who insisted on living her role.

The production opened in late June 1964. Two of the reviewers found spontaneous truth, compassion and "inner life." The negative reviews spoke of the variety of acting styles (Kevin McCarthy's energetic all–American, Luther Adler's Yiddish accent, etc.), the failure at ensemble playing, and the display of "personal selfish needs and feelings" which, all told, made for a disjointed performance.

Every critic focused most of the attention on Miss Stanley. Some writers were quite taken with her performance right from the start: alone, reclining on a couch smoking a cigar, flipping distractedly through the pages of a magazine; then speaking in hushed tones, flashing a mocking smile and slipping into strained silences. Then later releasing outbursts of frustration, anguish and grief. Then, later still, lunging for her handsome soldier Vershinin. In effect, Stanley seemed to be responding to her real circumstances and her imaginary circumstances at the same time—e.g., her longing for Vershinin and her dissatisfactions with Kevin McCarthy and her teacher/director; her inability to leave her husband (the provincial schoolmaster Kulygin) and flee to Moscow and her frustrations with the production.

Depending on the reviewer's point of view, by using the Method Stanley was either projecting the best the Studio had to offer or demonstrating exactly what was wrong. There were comments about her Masha being out of character, possessing more than enough drive to make her way to Moscow or any other place she desired. Clurman, writing in *The Nation*, thought that she overwhelmed the character with spasms of torment far too modern and complex. Robert Brustein— after faulting Strasberg's combination of non-direction and Chekhovian clichés— found Stanley's extravagant pauses in the middle of speeches predictable. In his judgment she had become a "self-indulgent stylist," appearing to slip into a trance and then, momentarily, break out of it to employ a range of familiar responses. He had come to see the play, not personal displays of technique that left him feeling isolated.

Only Shirley Knight, in her simplicity and innocence, seemed to be in character, pulling him back into the story each time she appeared. When you add the realization that nearly one-fourth of Stanley's lines were of her own invention, it was little wonder that the controversy over the Method was still going on.

All the same, the raves for Stanley's performance attracted audiences and kept the show running for 119 performance. Shortly thereafter, the Studio Theater was invited to participate in the second annual World Theatre Festival in London. *Blues for Mister Charlie* was desired as a stimulus for the intellectual left and *Three Sisters* as a revelation of Strasberg's work applied to a Russian classic.

The reasons Strasberg readily accepted this opportunity aren't exactly clear. In his autobiography, Kazan claims that Strasberg was ravenous for personal approbation and world approval. It mattered not that Geraldine Page couldn't participate or that Kim Stanley wouldn't make the trip unless Kevin McCarthy was replaced by George C. Scott, a non–Studio actor. It seems that replacing Shirley Knight with the notoriously mannered Sandy Dennis was justified because Dennis was a name. He dispensed with Michael Wager's services (one of the four who had championed the formation of the Theater on "Camera 3") and apparently wasn't affected when Wager disassociated himself from the workshop. During these last-minute maneuvers, he discovered that Diana Sands (the leading light of "Blues") was committed to a long-running Broadway show and other featured players had to be replaced by more non-members as well. But there was no sign of dismay. He was not discouraged when Rip Torn got into a confrontation with James Baldwin and director Meredith over the cavalier way they were revamping the production. Torn was fired, he and his wife Geraldine Page severed their association and still Strasberg pressed on. The reluctant producer appeared to have drastically changed course.

On second thought, Strasberg may have been spurred by the prospect of being on the same plane as the Berliner Ensemble and the Comédie-Française who had been brought to the Festival the year before. Other factors that might have come into play are the auspices of the Royal Shakespeare Company, the words of Page, Torn, and Newman on the "Camera 3" discussion claiming world-wide influence, and Strasberg's own pronouncements: "There is enormous curiosity about the Studio in London Theater circles. ... It was a flabbergasting experience to realize how much the eyes of the world are focused on this little place here. ... I have visited the Berliner Ensemble and various theaters abroad and found immense interest and esteem for the Studio as an idealistic standard. ..."

One can also factor in his contributions to a British television special. At the request of Kenneth Tynan, the highly influential theater critic, and to legitimize the Studio as an institution and gain foreign recognition of the workshop's importance, Strasberg selected two taped segments. In the first, Geraldine Page follows his improvisational suggestions for a portion of Strindberg's *Miss Julie*. In the second, an actress by the name of Lenka Peterson goes through a private moment as though she were at home, breaking into a wild, tempestuous Gypsy dance to recorded Hungarian music and then executing a series of pratfalls.

During the live portion of the two-hour airing for England's Independent Television, the writer Penelope Gilliatt elicited responses from her fellow Brits who included the actors Brian Bedford, Rex Harrison, Robert Morley and Wendy Hiller. In reviewing this "new phenomenon," issues cropped up over language, emotion versus meaning, professional discipline, and the relationship between playwrights and actors. One of the respondents thought that the innovations might inject vitality into the English theater; another disagreed entirely. For Strasberg, the chance to vindicate his work may have been another motivating factor.

In addition, earlier extensive publicity covering Marilyn Monroe's London stint in *The Prince and the Showgirl* (as Monroe reportedly worked hand in hand with Olivier and Paula Strasberg) had fueled a great deal of interest. And, through the medium of Kazan's films, audiences throughout the U.K. had been intrigued by the raw and sensitive performances. For all their differences, Strasberg still considered Kazan a protégé who was trading on his work. Evidently for many of these reasons and more, some kind of reckoning was at hand.

Once in London, inadequate rehearsal facilities and lighting did not deter him. In May of 1965, buffeted by as many stars as he could muster, his Studio Theater went on the boards at the Aldwych.

Terry Coleman of the *Observer* reiterated that fellow critics and a number of distinguished actors, directors and avid theatergoers alike were predisposed toward the Studio Theater's performances. Peter Daubney, the artistic director of the Festival, had promoted the Studio as a national institution of international import. One British writer had portrayed the two productions in the same light as the first visit by the MAT to grace their shores. There were fond memories of the Group's mounting of *Golden Boy* and the strong effect *Waiting for Lefty* had on countless amateur troupes at the time. Everywhere you turned there were high expectations. Regrettably, none of these expectations were met.

"Blues" was regarded as an overloaded propaganda tract. The "core of true human feeling" that was promised was not delivered. It was coarsened and broadened instead. Strasberg called a press conference. He informed the media that Baldwin's play was not representative of the Studio's work. All must wait to see his production of *Three Sisters* before passing judgment. Within the ranks, his words were taken as a betrayal of the author and the company. His words also served to heighten anticipation over the second event. But once again expectations were not met. This time the reviews left Strasberg no place to turn.

Penelope Gilliatt, who had been gracious on behalf of the Method during the British TV profile and had long been an admirer of the Studio's work ethic had this to say: "The World Theatre Festival's dismal task has been to mount the suicide of the Actors Studio. ... They have turned the house of Chekhov's cultivated sisters into an expensive private asylum, trivializing Chekhov's heroines into a slob, a tiresome professional virgin, and a prison matron for junkies."

Terry Coleman observed that the Studio was "absorbed in a technique as hermetic as anything in show business, utilizing the theater as a way of flexing private neuroses. The production emerges like some terrifying psychotic doodle giving the exhibition of neuroses a solemn field day. ... One must conclude that Strasberg's teaching does not meet the public requirements of theater."

Reviewer after reviewer denigrated a production that seemed to go on for hours, resulting in boos from the audience between acts and at the final curtain (not to mention those who had taken the first opportunity to exit). One of the critics laid the blame on specific individuals: "A cluster of celebrated names rendered a death blow to the 'method' school of acting last night. No less a figure than Lee Strasberg directed this slow, sleepwalking production of Chekhov's wondrous play. ... Kim Stanley played Masha as though she were acting to her own reflection in the bathroom mirror. Miss Sandy Dennis distinguished herself as the most self-conscious actress to have visited these shores within the span of memory. ... A director who can achieve this must have a genius for destruction."

As was his custom when faced with failure, Strasberg called a meeting and chastised the cast for betraying him. George C. Scott retaliated, livid over the notion that he and his fellow actors were in any way responsible for the "fiasco." Fearing for his safety, Strasberg made a hasty retreat. Once more he went to the British press and offered explanations. The Studio was not a repertory company and had no regular actors under contract. He and his troupe had made the crossing to offer a glimpse of future possibilities, nothing more.

Back in New York, he suggested that he had been misled. And, besides everything else, he wasn't used to "trouping a show" anywhere, let alone to a world theater festival. He spoke like a disconcerted traveler who had found conditions abroad quite different than anticipated. Like someone who somehow had been misinformed.

12

World Theater and the U.K.:
A Closer Look

The Studio's claims of legendary status overseas and disclaimers over the package sent to the Festival seem to cancel each other out. Perhaps the projections of the Studio spokespeople were mixed up with the success of Kazan's movies and the lauded film careers of Brando, Dean, Paul Newman, Joanne Woodward and others. Perhaps Strasberg's projections were colored by these considerations and other motivating factors just cited. In any event, starting with the general comments made by British professionals on the BBC with regard to the Studio's imminent visit, there is reason to believe that there is a marked difference between the Strasbergian view and those of theater artists across the Atlantic. Through the latter's less fervid perspective we might be better able to examine these differences and, in the bargain, come away with a more worldly outlook and, in a sense, put the Studio in its proper place.

As a starting point, we could turn to one of the first to voice his reservations about the Actors Studio during the time frame in question—Sir Michael Redgrave. Not only recognized the world over as a distinguished actor, he was also acknowledged in theater circles throughout the British Isles as the leading proponent of the Stanislavsky system. In addition, he was acknowledged as the only one who understood and applied it properly. His qualities of equanimity and sophistication held true even when lecturing on the heated topic of Lee Strasberg's theories. Consider these two concluding statements during one of his talks: "I wish, of course, that anything I say which may sound dogmatic should be taken with the necessary pinch of salt. ... I am content to go on asking questions provided that some of those are the right questions."

In terms of the Method and the stage (he considered film acting as more of a lark), what Redgrave was questioning was the inattention to Stanislavsky's "core": the essence of a commendable play in terms of the times and events described;

161

the characters portrayed according to the author's intentions. This was the only legitimate focus, not the kind of self-stimulation Redgrave had witnessed first-hand inside the Studio and, at times, on the Broadway stage.

Taking exception to Strasberg's interpretation, Redgrave felt that by taking an imaginative leap and living through other people's lives, the fresh and effort-less state Stanislavsky coveted was readily available to any gifted performer: "Julie Harris and Marlon Brando would have been fine actors anyway, whatever class they had or had not attended." In Redgrave's view, theater was a gamut of extra-ordinary experiences that transported performers and audiences alike far from their own private worlds. He offered to reconsider his thoughts on the Studio only after witnessing a repertory of the classics featuring casts exclusively trained by Strasberg. Nothing less would do.

Shortly before her father's lectures and writings on the subject, Vanessa Red-grave had also spent some time in New York. She saw Julie Harris as Joan of Arc in Anouilh's *The Lark* and attended Studio sessions. Among her impressions of this trip was her admiration of Clurman's vigor and attention to detail in direct-ing her father in *Tiger at the Gates*; Strasberg's recognition that acting was more than repetition and sufficient practice; and a notion of the arts as a process reach-ing for some higher plane that sent forth certain reverberations.

In essence, Vanessa Redgrave was expanding on her father's aesthetics. Her extraordinary intelligence and uncanny vulnerability, her openness to all forms and seemingly limitless range as an actress coupled with her many comments on tele-vision and in print, reflect an evolving vision of what acting and theater should be.

She encountered Michel Saint-Denis, the great French director and friend of her father, at his London Theatre Centre—the same man who was later cho-sen over Strasberg to create the Juilliard theater program at Lincoln Center. Saint-Denis was a theater artist whose tastes were European and posed a threat to Strasberg's own "strictly American" approach. And here is where, through Red-grave's view, the differences in perspective become more apparent.

In her experience, Saint-Denis was compatible with Litz Pisk who studied painting, design and movement from the avant garde in Vienna. She found Pisk working at Dartington Hall with Michael Chekhov whose highly theatrical psy-chological gestures had been lauded by Stanislavsky. Returning to Saint-Denis she discovered the incorporation of animal mime, clowning, English music hall turns, Japanese Noh mask work, improvisation, the techniques of Isadora Dun-can, Meyerhold and Stanislavsky, along with the influences of Picasso and Cocteau. In short, she then realized that the desired reverberations were marked by fresh cultural achievements on both sides of the Atlantic under the shield of extraor-dinary creativity.

Using this gauge, Redgrave could appreciate a working-class experiment in the East End of London using Ben Jonson's *Volpone* as a springboard, done in semi–Elizabethan costume but tempered by Joan Littlewood's loose democratic direction. As a result, Mosca, Volpone's pimp, was free to flee through Venice and swim down the Grand Canal armed with a snorkel tube and flippers. The orchestra pit served as the waterway. As long as the production was innovative, masterly in execution and revealed something significant about the human condition, Redgrave was captivated.

As for the strickly internal approach, she noted its limitations early on. At London's famed Central School she learned that her own feelings, experiences and even her imagination could only take her and her fellow actors so far. To play the matriarch of a family of Fabian socialists in a George Bernard Shaw play, she had to read Shaw's diaries, refer to her elderly cousin Lucy Kempson's flat vowels and forthright rhythms. She attended a dinner party organized by the play's director where all and sundry were required to arrive in character, stay in character, improvise and listen to each other's tales. And that was just the beginning.

She was convinced that this total approach applied even in ventures like John Osborne's "kitchen sink" drama *Look Back in Anger*. Influenced by the American trend of psychological realism, it centered on penniless young men and women who lived hand-to-mouth in bed-sitting rooms. But there any similarity with the Method ended. The play demanded a grasp of the social/political issues of the time, especially on the part of the lead. Jimmy Porter was a highly verbal, comic and philosophically defiant character. His tirades about topics like middle-class hypocrisy and the vicissitudes of love were so challenging that any pause or act of self-absorption would disrupt the rapid-fire rhythms of the text.

Recounting her chat with Strasberg and her experiences at the Studio, Redgrave was even more convinced that naturalistic plays required the same attention to research, externals and the inner repercussions on the character, not one's self. Soon, by extension, she began incorporating the contemporaneous social and political implications of her work, which, in her view, enriched the experience for all concerned. For instance, she attributed the success of a revival of Ibsen's *Ghosts* to the spirit of the times "which stirred our audiences and made them consider aspects of our own society in a new light." In her portrayal of Mrs. Alving, she discovered a horror at lies "creeping like ghosts behind the words in newspapers which had an immediacy for the audience as well as for me." Put simply, acting that was limited to how a performer felt at any given moment without taking in the ramifications of the performance was, to Vanessa Redgrave, pointless.

These views of acting as an all-encompassing art are reflected in the work of the entire Redgrave theatrical dynasty which includes Vanessa's mother Rachel Kempson, her father, her husband and celebrated director Tony Richardson, the comic turns of her sister Lynn, her brother Corin's more reserved style, the earnestness of Corin's daughter Gemma and her own daughters Natasha and Miranda Richardson—the latter equally at home playing characters from the American South with the same total conviction, intellectual understanding and control.

From the sensibilities of the Redgraves we can look to the views of other figures from other countries as well. Liv Ullmann, for example, is renowned for performances that are unparalleled for their haunting honesty, especially in the roles she created for Swedish director Ingmar Bergman. As far as her apparent

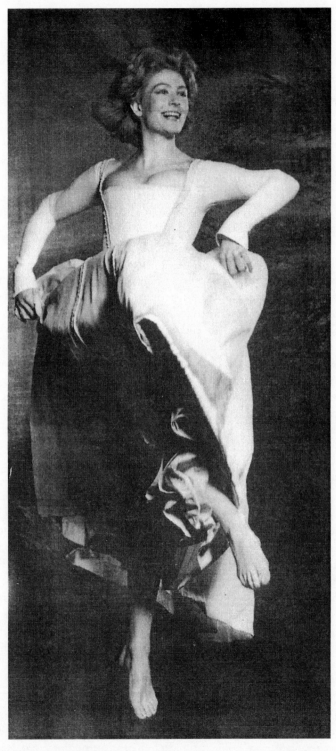

Vanessa Redgrave as Rosalind in Shakespeare's *As You Like It* **at Stratford-upon-Avon, 1961 (courtesy of Camera Press, U.K.)**

inner work is concerned, Ullmann sees the actor as a sieve. She empties herself so that she can be inundated with new emotions for each occasion, affording her character an open channel of expression. The surprise and enjoyment come from having no idea where the emotions come from. When playing Grusha in *The Caucasian Chalk Circle* she was amazed that Grusha would weep when coming upon an abandoned baby during an ordeal of poverty and revolution. However, "if the character needs to cry and your instrument is well-tuned, it will come out right. But the minute you feel private anguish or any private impulse you've lost touch." Like the Redgraves, Ullmann possessed peripheral vision, able to fully experience each moment and appreciate the implications and consequences of her craft.

Turning back to the U.K., seeing through the eyes of Olivier, Dame Edith Evans, Antony Sher, John Hurt and Glenda Jackson we find the same kind of sophistication: "At its core, acting is sophisticated pretense; the thrill is the connection with the audience, taking them on an extraordinary journey. ... It's visual, looking out at the world like Brando, having peripheral vision just as any character is peripheral. ... I seek images of the character's appearance, do research, never adhere to any one technique. ... Over-awareness of the way one works takes the place of discovery. ... I pretend, dear boy, I pretend. ..."

All the same, taken together these reflections are only pointers. Seen in a certain light they don't meet the subject head-on. There are still American actors who see no appreciable differences decades after the downfall at the Aldwych and can't understand why Strasberg's teachings aren't fully embraced overseas. As a vignette taken from personal experience indicates, in the eyes of some, the attitudes and the cultural ambiance are somewhat of a mystery.

> It is drizzling outside Porters, a restaurant nestled by the cobblestone walkway leading to Covent Garden. Inside, on a cool Sunday afternoon in early June, a lanky young bartender by the name of Royce serves mugs of tea to a couple from New England and continues his running conversation.
>
> "Had the lead in 'Streetcar'," he announces. "And in plays by Mamet, Miller—you name it. Truth, you know what I mean? It starts from you. As any of us over here from the States can tell you. As everybody knows."
>
> "If you think about it," Royce goes on, "Olivier was empty, had to fake big moments. Had to pretend. That's not it. You have to dig deeper. It's not in the words. It's in the feelings."
>
> The couple nod quietly, happy to talk to a friendly American perhaps. Perhaps just allowing themselves to act as a sounding board for a frustrated actor.
>
> "So what's the deal? Sometimes one or two of us get a bite, most of the time we get nothing."
>
> As if answering, a bespectacled woman at a far table flips a page of her *London Times* displaying an article by John Peter praising the performance of Fiona Shaw. Ms. Shaw, it seems, has opened in *Richard II* playing the leading role "as a playful, unstable child: look, now I am angry; look, now I am thoughtful; look, now I smirk and preen." Words in bold type announce that "Fiona Shaw is, happily, a portraitist, objective and unsparing, willing to mock her

own performance. Acting, after all, is about impersonation, crossing the boundaries of race, age and sex. Shaw is making theatre as it was meant to be, that
is, an adventure, a discovery of other ages, other countries, other people, other
minds."

All of this is lost on Royce. He repeats, "I mean, what is the problem?
Look at our stars. Same training, same Method, admired everywhere."

As Royce continues to shake his head, a mime dressed in a black tailcoat
and blousy white shirt goes through his paces outside, a scant thirty yards
away. Disregarding the chill and drizzle, people gather in front of the weathered Greek columns of the old Actors' Church. The mime peeps behind a column, at once surprised to see the growing crowd and delighted to appear
stupid and vulnerable as well. The spectators egg him on. Taking the cue, he
shifts into slow motion and performs tasks which are extraordinarily ordinary:
standing on one leg ... holding onto a pillar with both hands and leaning backwards ... bending over and sticking his head between his knees ... Catching
on, the audience breaks into applause.

A few minutes beforehand, the couple chatting with Royce had seen the
mime perform a similar act. They ask for Royce's comments. Royce shrugs and
shakes his head as if the mime was beside the point.

Momentarily, the couple move over to a table in the far corner as an older,
quite refined lady joins them for lunch. As it happens, she writes a column on
the arts for a London newspaper. Apparently, she is flushed with excitement
about the work of Teatro Buendia, Cuba's leading theatre company presently
based in Essex.

"No sets," she exclaims. "Just black net drapes and a few well chosen
props. One striking image after another moving forward and back in time.
Marvelous movement, ritual and Commedia improvisation—just like our own
Theatre Complicite. And Flora Lauten is stunning as the grandmother, spin-
ning on with her wheelchair, growing more and more grotesque."

As usual, the couple nods courteously. From a distance Royce peers at the
three of them, then across the crowded tables, possibly searching for some
American who will listen to his plight and finally understand.

Royce, it seems, was pressing the same selling point as the defunct Studio
Theater: the universal attraction of the Method as evidenced by its alleged use by
well-known stars. Unfortunately for Royce and his friends there is a hitch, an
imbalance of trade. The U.K. exports far more of its cultural products to the United
States than it imports. Of these imports, the kind of Studio-like process Royce
and his fellow actors were offering isn't marketable, not by itself at any rate. Keeping in mind the indicators noted so far, I set out to learn more about the reasons
why.

English Sensibility vs. Method Acting

Ken Pickering, the noted British author and theater educator, finds that "most
Americans are preoccupied with self: self-enhancement, self-improvement, that

sort of thing. By the same token, there is an obsession with personal evaluation—how am I doing? how is the next fellow doing? do I measure up? I must know how I, in particular, rate."

By comparison the British are much more self-effacing and guarded about their private concerns; believing that their true feelings are the only precious thing they own. They are, therefore, respectful of the privacy of others. They are also not easily impressed. Any emotionality foisted upon another human being is, according to Pickering, totally out of place.

Tony Craze, the London playwright who writes primarily for the working class, goes a bit further. He feels that the expression of personal feelings reveals limited communication skills. In the theater, it's intolerable: "Unless one is conscious of the audience, the social/political climate, and the layers of meaning within the text which need to be addressed, one has no business on the stage. In terms of personal feelings or being one's self in response to the theatrical circumstances, what's the point? Who cares?"

Rachel Sylvester, writing about rugby in the *Sunday Telegraph*, enlarges on this sentiment to include athletics and a way of life: "In comparison with others I need not mention, our sports figures display the best of virtues. With dignity and grace—never exhibiting self-conscious flash or private animosity—they can all be counted on to a man."

Echoing the stance of actress Fiona Shaw (the one who defined acting as impersonation), Peter Brook, the internationally acclaimed director, tends to mock all attempts to make private concerns and the cause and effects of what passes for reality paramount: "The English tend to flee from Ibsen and anything else that shows some underlying logic to life so that if one thing happens it is almost certain to cause something else. We are relying here on the arrival of happy accident. Otherwise we would flee this country, which everybody knows has no future."

When distinguished actors like Sir John Mills and Sir Alec Guinness were asked to talk about the secrets of their success on "South Bank," Melvin Bragg's noted television interview program, they sloughed off the question. So did people like Elaine Page, the star of large-scale British musicals. Nothing they attained was the result of their expressive gifts. Whatever the task at hand, "you just got on with it ... had a go."

Sir Alec took self-effacement to such an extreme that he once spoke of himself in the third person: "Deep in his heart he hankers to be an artist of some sort but he is only an actor. ... He is not at all proud of himself or his achievements and is equally attracted and repelled by the limelight, as if never quite sure how to present himself, or who he is or what he would really like to be."

It comes then as no real surprise to find an occasional attack on the Method. Around the time Royce was prodding the couple from America, the critic John Gray was lambasting those who still valued Strasberg's teachings. Writing in a current issue of *RADA* [the Royal Academy of Dramatic Art] *The Magazine*, he had this to say: "The 'Method' is nothing more than a series of private exercises with a disdain for any kind of solid technique. It is patently foolish to imagine that doing lots of naturalistic exercises about one's self and applying that futility on a stage is worth a jot."

As it turns out, Gray was writing under the ever-present shadow of the Shakespearean stage, with its fluid flow of time and space and actors who come downstage and speak directly. The notion of self-centered acting was seen as more than just inappropriate and futile. The suggestion that the text should defer to personal experience was tantamount to challenging the heritage of the British Isles. Here are others coming to the defense of language and culture:

> The opportunity to lash out with an assault of perfectly chosen words and phrases is highly prized and cherished on these shores.
>
> Any drama training program worth its salt capitalizes on a natural love of verse-speaking and song, vocal rhythms and stress, and, of course, metaphor and meaning as well.
>
> Brits are and always have been in love with language—its rhythms, the sheer delight in accurately describing something, searching for just the right word or phrase.
>
> If you're in love with language and are well-read and verbally articulate, there's a place for you on the English stage. At Harrogate, Liverpool, Cheltenham, Sheffield, Nottingham, Scarborough and Stoke—to name a few— there are always bold, adventurous seasons where the words and verbal magic of the likes of Shakespeare, Shaw, Marlowe and Coward reign.

Eclecticism, Stanislavsky, Stella Adler et al.

This isn't to suggest that the battle lines are drawn against American realism. If you put aside doctrinaire talk about a Method or the concepts of a single American guru, there is no issue. As Vanessa Redgrave intimated, eclecticism pervades the U.K. Like the world of jazz and modern painting, any notable exploration using any combination of elements is prized and welcome.

In the field of acting a good example would be the approach taken by the award-winning Welsh actor Anthony Hopkins. When he studied at RADA he grew restless concentrating solely on voice, movement and dance. He was more interested in the techniques employed by one of Stella Adler's pupils who, in turn, prompted him to read Bobby Lewis' book *Method or Madness?* and anything written by or about Stanislavsky. Soon Hopkins added to his repertoire. He incorporated Michael Chekhov's method of psychological gestures, distilling a character down to one key stance, moving into it and exploding out of it. It left the door open for inappropriate accidents. It supplied him with a certain freshness. As a matter of course, he delighted in the movies of Brando and Clift. It was all formative, grist for his inclinations and his particular mill.

Switching gears, he found himself working under Olivier at the National Theater performing in classic roles. He learned more, had more to draw on. He found another potentially useful tool during a visit to the Actors Studio while appearing in the British play *Equus*. After a time, he could recount all the influences without relying on any single one. From Olivier he learned not to break up the verse in Shakespeare but to consider each speech as both thought and action—to plunge in, risk and just do it. From variations on Stanislavsky's teachings he learned to relax, listen closely to his fellow actors and follow the rhythm of the give-and-take. He was also taken with Stanislavsky's use of the mask—finding the character's voice, shoes, way of walking, etc. From his training in Stella Adler's techniques he looked for a compelling objective that threw him up against an equally compelling obstacle: "...to needle her, to test her ... play the opposite, do the unexpected which will rattle her even more ... then go with your instincts...."

He found a use for Strasberg's emotional memory while waiting to do a take during a movie shoot. When he played a butler in the film *Remains of the Day*, he decided his action, in Adler terms, was to make each room he entered seem more empty. Everything that worked was employed. He owned his own process, a watchword that was soon taken up at the Central School, one of London's two prestigious training grounds.

The other, RADA, followed suit and adopted the same philosophy: "We take a practical, empirical approach which is mainly a question of expertly interpreting characters in a theatre which is mostly text-based and rich in language. In other words in the context of playing a role, in a play, for an audience. ... We focus on developing a responsive organism open to many demands and styles."

In this same vein, RADA now includes a staff member from the United States trained in Uta Hagen's way of "bringing a human being on stage, electric, alive and human." Anyone who has ever studied with Uta knows that she and her approach are one and the same. As she lights her first cigarette and draws in the smoke or warms her hands on a steaming cup of coffee or remembers a telling incident, she is as vibrant in class as she is living through any of her memorable roles on stage. Whatever stimulates you, heightens your responsiveness and helps you to avoid cliché behavior is valuable in her eyes. If imagining a specific cramped space and loss of privacy sparks your imagination in playing Blanche in "Streetcar," that stimulus can be used as groundwork. But in the final analysis, the only thing that counts is your performance and what you bring to the play night after night.

Which translates in the U.K. as a readiness for anything. Which, in playwright and theater educator Ken Pickering's eyes can be attributed to the practice of channel crossing—a keen interest in ideas, conflicting viewpoints, what a play means more than what happens—a result of journeying back and forth from the continent. As an example, he mentions his trips to Berlin and his experiences attending the Berliner Ensemble's productions there and in the U.K., contemplating Brecht's episodic works and appreciating their cultural and historical import.

This endless series of comings and goings is called "waves" by Graham Whybrow, the artistic director of the Royal Court, England's preeminent center for exploration in the performing arts. He lists the Studio Theater venture among the waves of productions that reach and leave British shores and, hopefully "challenge the possibilities of our time, from variations on the working class experience in the 1950s, to the surreal wave from Paris and Germany in the 1960s, and on and on to the waves centering on women's issues, black and Asian plays, to multi-cultural open-ended structures relative to the world as we now know it—fractured, highly charged and free."

If you were looking for products of this love of language, ideas, eclecticism, waves and crossings, you need only sample a few excerpts from West End reviews:

> In David Edgar's *Pentecost*, the players are busily engaged expounding the conflicting claims of art and nationalism, tourism and the needs of the poor and displaced, all within an abandoned church during circumstances akin to today's Yugoslavia. ... During the production we find actresses playing displaced refugees who sing and dance in other languages, mime exotic stories and whirl about from pillar to post brandishing weapons, tumbling, falling, roping and gagging hostages. ... Alive and kicking with their physicality, hoodlums somersault backwards off high steps, female victims struggle suspended in circus-style harnesses.
>
> In David Hare's Shavian debate *Skylark*, the actor playing Tom represents the kind of contemporary man who thinks happiness is something you purchase as symbolized by the perfect, skylit room he has created for his ailing wife. In counterpoint, the actress playing Kyra represents the dated belief that things are worth doing for their own sake regardless of material reward or career progress.

If you can take all of this in, along with everything else noted, the World Theater Festival (which is now called the London International Festival of Theatre) reflects the caliber of exploration and technique expected of any troupe that crosses the English Channel or the Atlantic.

The Actor as Internationalist

Romania's National Theatre mounts their own variation of the ancient Greek legend of Phaedra: "A silver moon hanging over a dark stage; a chorus of actors, clothed in heavy black cloaks wielding long hooked sticks approaching in sound and movement, echoing the washing sound of waves; the Goddess of Aphrodite and Artemis circling the stage in a dreamlike trance; a combination of chants, motions, incantations, reflecting the divine meddling and tragic consequences of Phaedra's growing love for her step-son."

The Cinoherni Theatre from Prague expresses the cruel absurdity of life under a totalitarian government in staging Pinter's play *The Birthday Party* in a surreal boarding house in Brighton. At the same time, an ensemble made up of British, Swedish, French and German performers are working on a group creation, exploring alienation and isolation in the dark underworld of urban life, utilizing the universal language of mime and clowning. Another group calling itself Theatre Machine is devising a comic piece—the English director having been influenced by a French director who studied with Lecog in Paris and also collaborated with the Royal Shakespeare Company.

The list of permutations, past and present, seems to go on and on. And even in the more traditional forms the actors are still referred to as players. They play. They transform. As the actor John Hurt pointed out, theater at its core is a form of sophisticated pretense designed to transport all concerned to the extraordinary.

As for realism, it's one facet of the kaleidoscope. A revival of a work by Williams or Miller must resonate on many levels. To prove her readiness, the same actress who, for instance, just portrayed Laura in a revival of *The Glass Menagerie* must be prepared to work with a group like Glasgow's Clyde Unity Theatre, playing a girl in a coma behind gauze and balloons who flits back in time, drifting through the scrim, becoming a child again and communicating her whole life's journey in mime and dance, performing the piece on both sides of the Channel. Then, at the end of the run, she may have to switch gears once again and play a role like the Eastern European, highly verbal Gabriella in *Pentecost*. During a rapid-fire fifteen-minute opening exchange with a pompous art historian, she would be frequently called upon to articulate lines like this: "I mean, during forty years we are having no great artists and all social and historic context, and this means our museums full of children's crayon drawings and old quilts and bits of colored tiles because naturally we must combat petit-bourgeois formalism and acknowledge art of heroic revolutionary masses quite as good as Michelangelo; so I tell you what I think—there is great painting and there is also less great, but if something great and beautiful comes from God or love or what-have-you-for-breakfast is defaced and made ugly and pathetic, then we must scrape clean and restore to what it was before."

All told, it takes a clear understanding of the prevailing cultural climate to embark on a world-theater venture. During the early 1960s there may have been great interest in Strasberg's theories. There was even talk in London theater circles about the Method as a possible source of revitalization. But without an awareness of the values and standards we've touched upon and adequate preparation, success, let alone global impact, would be problematic to say the least.

This isn't to say that a seasoned producer could not have employed a director with vision and assembled a gifted cast, many of whom were associated with the Studio. Given ample time to rehearse, this company might have staged a memorable production of, say, another work by Chekhov, or Miller or Williams. But as far as the realities of the Actors Studio Theater are concerned, it is understandable why, after the unfortunate experience at the Festival, the workshop restricted its activities closer to home, went through a fifth period of transition and tried to reinvent itself once again.

13

Shifting Gears

It was generally understood that major funding would not be available for any further attempts at creating a subsidized Actors Studio repertory company. There was no way to live up to the prospectus that had been tendered to the Ford Foundation, Rockefeller Foundation, etc., and no other endowed institutions were willing to take a chance.

As a consequence, many of the best talents disassociated themselves and looked elsewhere to further their careers.[11] Those who stayed on did so in varying degrees. Some had invested too much in Strasberg's process and their personal need for an artistic home. They found ways to pacify their concerns over the differences between what Strasberg practiced and what he preached.

Another coterie hadn't been involved in the formation of the theater and weren't particularly interested in the politics of production and inconsistencies of character. They had been taken seriously by their mentor and led to believe they possessed hidden gifts. They were convinced there was a deeper truth, a genuineness with a different ring than the mere appearance of reality. Their mission was to enrich every moment on stage or screen by investing their whole being, by "really seeing the moon and stars offstage" and becoming totally immersed in the given circumstances. They owed it to "Lee." And there was always the chance he might continue to confer his stamp of approval, give them a nod, a word—something. They were in the same league as Duse and Kim Stanley and nothing else mattered. The special tension of the acting sessions was all.

A third contingent regarded the workshop as a gym, a place to drop in from time to time and work out. For instance, Keir Dullea, who was soon to make a mark for himself in two notable films, had received his training from Sandy Meisner at the Neighborhood Playhouse. Meisner, like all former members of the Group who went on to teach, stressed his own version of Stanislavsky's theories, namely, being fully present in the moment. Focus on the other person, not yourself. "Don't be an actor," said Meisner. "Be a human being who works off what

Paul Newman as Frank Galvin in one of his eloquent quiet moments in *The Verdict* (1982, 20th Century–Fox).

actually exits under imaginary circumstances." It all depends on the urgency and the difficulty of the task and your natural instincts. Meisner took what he needed from Clurman, Strasberg and Stella Adler and added the theatrical truth of Michael Chekhov and the objectivity of Sudakov and Rapoport (Russian theorists who stressed the reality of doing). Dullea followed suit. There was no Method. There was a set of organic approaches. Whatever works, whatever makes more sense to you, whomever you can relate to is all that counts.

Robert Duvall, Joanne Woodward and other Studio members received the foundation of their technique from Meisner. Geraldine Page studied with Uta Hagen. Rip Torn trained in New York with Baruch Lumet (Sydney Lumet's father). Stella Adler's approach was admired even though she seemed to be coming from the opposite direction: exhorting her students to act, to be much larger than themselves, to reach for a stage tone and work for style, love of the text and the author's sense of truth. Even though she championed imagination and deplored private moments, Stella Adler emphasized action—doing. Not indicating but actually going through an experience "with your blood and your soul." Besides Brando, there were others who had studied with Stella and passed through the Studio doors. Any and all of this formative work was valid. When someone like Dullea presented work to Strasberg, he took what was beneficial, just as Anthony Hopkins had done through observation. Rip Torn considered experimenting with Strasberg's emotional exercises but was talked out of it. His instrument was regarded as a trumpet. He accepted that judgment and, from then on, simply set out to meet any challenge that came his way. In short, there was a whole camp that didn't refer to themselves as Method actors. They considered themselves professionals who encouraged one another, enjoyed the gatherings and the opportunity to work together whenever they could. Otherwise they simply went their separate ways.

As an example of this practical outlook, Brett Somers comes easily to mind. She would drop in whenever she was in Manhattan and felt the need. If Strasberg broke into a tirade, she would wait him out and then tell him whether or not she agreed. Often his approach was useable. It gave her freedom, something to do to keep her mind off such things as meeting other people's expectations, performing or worrying about the audience. If she was doing a scene from Odets' *The Big Knife*, she could focus on the heat in her house in Malibu or other aspects of the California scene she knew so well. Presently, she would fly back to L.A. and get on with her TV work or what have you.

She could also drop in at the Actors Studio West, devised as an alternative to the original workshop. In the year 1965, a number of those who had departed for one reason or another felt that the reconverted church on West 44th Street was no longer the only possible haven. The actors Martin Landau and Dennis Weaver met with the director Jack Garfein to discuss setting up a new gathering place in Los Angeles. Landau had earned a reputation as a gifted teacher, appropriating sensory work, actions and objectives and some of the emerging new theories to help individuals free themselves creatively and fully function. Among his students were Jack Nicholson, Shirley Knight, Robert Blake and the acclaimed screenwriters Robert Towne and Oliver Stone. Possibly because all of his students were working in film or TV, Landau stressed keeping the released energy just under the surface. On camera their work would then exude a certain vibrancy and immediacy: a human and honest quality of being caught in the moment; human and honest; feeling instead of trying to feel, being and becoming instead of trying to act.

As one thing led to another, an acting unit was set up within the new Studio and Landau was given the post of moderator. Strasberg came to L.A. to preside for a period of six months which prompted differences of opinion as the founders continued to press for their own operation. Without going into all the details, the Studio West finally achieved a kind of independence—associated with the original workshop but with a character and agenda of its own.

Consequently, a modest operation was set up a few blocks south of the once famous Hollywood-and-Vine where movie fans and tourists still shop for souvenirs and file past landmarks like Grauman's Chinese Theater. The property can be approached by first locating a series of narrow, quiet streets ending in a cul-de-sac. Because the L.A. workshop is hidden away in a nondescript complex of low-lying stucco buildings adjacent to a tiny public park—which, in turn, is wedged inside these art deco rectangular and box-like shapes—a first-time visitor must wend his way up a rise and drift into the setting. At that point, anyone picnicking there will be happy to identify the former garage (now converted to a small theater) and adjoining house. A little more prodding and the picnicker might add that the secluded little estate once belonged to the silent screen star William S. Hart and is now being leased to the Studio West by the city of Los Angeles.

Unobtrusively, new members and old have slipped into this retreat to try out scenes and "stretch their instruments" when not busy with film and TV engagements. Occasionally modest projects have taken place, associates from New York have joined in, and new members have been added to the rolls through audition. The place has served as an enclave far from the cold and uncertainty of its prototype and a world of theater that no longer supports new works of psychological realism as a matter of course.

The Changing Theatrical Scene

As the essayist E.B. White wrote, New York is "a city of strangers seeking sanctuary or fulfillment or some greater or lesser grail." In the late 1960s and thereafter, those seeking fulfillment in the theater had to adjust to the changing times. New workshops were cropping up everywhere, emitting the same kind of need for exploration evidenced in the 1920s in neighborhoods below and above Times Square. The notion was that the performing arts should capture what everyone at the time felt when walking the streets of Manhattan: a challenge of accepted wisdom, incorporating the new, reveling in growth and change. Art was defined as an argument with the past, a gauntlet thrown down to the known, an urgency to create something better.

As an indirect assault on the illusion of realism, Friedrich Nietzsche's words were often quoted: "Art treats appearance as appearance; its aim is precisely not to deceive. It is therefore true." Ironically, the words of Stanislavsky were also employed at the time he became interested in new forms: "It is necessary to picture not life itself as it takes place in reality but as we vaguely feel it in our dreams, our vision, our moments of spiritual uplift. ... For the new art, new actors are necessary, actors of a new sort with an altogether new technique."

Soon a great variety and intensity of experimentation was taking place mirroring the kind of experiences Vanessa Redgrave alluded to across the Atlantic. By the early 1970s, Grotowski's Polish Laboratory Theatre (which had had a great influence on the experiments of Peter Brook and Stage Two in England) was having an impact on the Open Theater and The Living Theater in New York. Like Copeau (who had inspired Clurman in Paris in the 1920s), Grotowski had returned to the essence of theater: the live relationship of actors and spectators. In Grotowski's vision the goal was to heal the audience by providing it with rituals and ceremonies and myths of its own traditions in creative response to what has happened, what is happening and what will happen. In place of the illusion of reality and a logical chain of events involving a set of motivated characters, Grotowski's happenings had to be expressed through metaphor, images, fable and the dreamlike ebb and flow of time, language, sound and movement. Appropriately, the one Grotowski was most indebted to was Stanislavsky, regarding him as a paragon of flexibility, experimentation and systematic renewal.[12] Grotowski, therefore, always kept in mind Stanislavsky's dictum that the artist must create his own methods.

Culturally in America, this quest for alternatives was openly reflected in protests against the Vietnam War, the formation of communes, a new sexual freedom, and a rambling looser style in clothing, attitudes, independent films like *Easy Rider*, rock music, folk and popular music, and pop art.

As in the U.K., on the Continent and elsewhere, permutations were the order of the day. New forms came into being: spontaneous happenings on the streets and group creations in lofts and theater spaces—a variety of venues to eliminate the separation between actors and onlookers, leaders and followers, writers and performers. Eastern philosophy filtered into the mix as the new forms called for a centered oneness, physical transformations and the ability to work collectively and give yourself over to something larger than one's self.

Off Broadway, the traditional forms of theater dissolved into the new consciousness. But traces could still be detected in the work of innovators like Daniel Nagrin and his Workgroup who were exploring the possibilities of dance-acting. Nagrin studied with Helen Tamiris, one of the pioneers of modern dance who had taught creative movement at the Group's summer workshop in 1932. In her approach (which by the late 1960s and 1970s was looked upon as very eastern), participants started from stillness and transformed into someone else. The critical element was rhythm—seeking the pulse of the character, or image, or fellow dance/actor they were asked to become. The object was to stir up deeper elements beyond their personalities and "begin to penetrate the truth." Then, echoing Sandy Meisner's technique, Nagrin asked his troupe to focus on "reading the other, moving with, to and for another" until they totally forgot about their individual selves.

Interesting enough, Nagrin studied acting in New York with Miriam Goldina who studied acting in Moscow with Vakhtangov. The techniques of Tamiris, Meisner, Goldina/Vakhtangov, group creation and the new consciousness all contributed to his philosophy of dance, theater and the arts: "We are living in a swiftly changing environment and must attune to an uncertain existence. I have devoted my life against dogmatism ... The evolving forms of improvisation are a realization that everything could have been otherwise. They open the door to use, twist, change, develop or ignore any theory or method. And even this is a way, not *the* way."

Nagrin's experiments led him to collaborate with Joseph Chaikin's Open Theater. Chaikin was both a kindred spirit and a challenging extension of Nagrin's work in that he called for an eastern loss of self in order to create poetic metaphors reflecting contemporary concerns. By necessity, participants had to be "open" which meant giving one's self over to the group vision and seeing as a child sees.

Joining this evolving arts scene—aspects of which also found their way into Broadway musicals, plays and imports from London—John Strasberg (Lee's son) and his wife Sabra Jones created their own school, synthesizing feeling and form, English and American techniques, freshly interpreting form at every turn. In so doing, John was estranged from his father who regarded this action as an affront to his life's work. Paradoxically, Lee Strasberg not only bypassed his son's work and the new wave of exploration, he too seemed to be turning his back on his life's work.

Strasberg's Alterations and Career Adjustments

According to a close associate, the only way to come to terms with Strasberg's fluctuating nature is to consider his humble beginnings starting with Ellis Island. Strasberg secretly always saw himself as a poor immigrant kid who found himself in the Lower East Side looking uptown to Broadway, craving status and recognition. He strove to be associated with something artful like a dedicated medieval guild while, at the same time, became enraptured by the presence of stars like Jeanne Eagels in *Rain* and John Barrymore in *Hamlet*. He found himself in the midst of the beckoning lights of the Great White Way attempting to "pander to all the Gods at once." Privately, according to this same source, he loved music much more than he did the theater, but there was no place for him there. He was, as they say, always conflicted.

Keeping up this balancing act—which had leaned in the direction of stars and the limelight during the days of Marilyn Monroe and the Studio Theater—he then shifted back to an emphasis on the art of acting and the nurturing of a new generation of talents. However, by the late 1960s and early 1970s, the scales began to tip again toward notoriety. In the words of actress Kim Hunter, "he became intoxicated with adulation and was publicity mad." During acting sessions, "adoring his own words and thoughts," he began taping everything he said for posterity. He brought in observers, directors and producers to hear what he had to say and to appraise his most promising new prospects. Hunter dropped from the ranks. For her and others, it was no longer a safe place to explore inner possibilities; it had become a place to audition.

Becoming more and more impressed with those who had achieved success in films or on Broadway—no matter the talent, character or level of experience—he made certain that only celebrities were on the board and added "names" to the membership list. No audition was necessary. They were made part of the workshop by dint of being heralded in the press and or being professionally powerful.

Prompted by his third wife Anna, he opened a fee-paying Lee Strasberg Theatre Institute in New York and Hollywood. Classes were given in acting for the camera, auditioning, the business of acting, professional acting, directing for film and TV, along with the traditional sensory work on a student's personal instrument. To underscore the latter, the brochure contained the statement: "Acting is the most personal of our crafts." Obviously disappointed in this new turn of events, Kazan drew attention to the gaggles of students in L.A. displaying T-shirts which read: "Actor by Lee Strasberg." The implication was that Strasberg had created stars like Brando, Dean and Marilyn Monroe. The fact that young people "of modest talent" were being enticed on both coasts to seek similar fame was perceived by Kazan not only as a dubious ploy but a misuse of Strasberg's teaching gifts and an abandoning of his traditions. In his biography, he reiterated that whereas his former mentor and boss had been dismissive of Hollywood—unhappy directing screen tests and short wartime information films, railing against false celluloid entertainments and producers who exploited actors—he had yet once again switched his position.

Still keeping his options open (although he hadn't acted in decades), in 1975 Strasberg accepted Al Pacino's intercession on his behalf and agreed to play the gangster Hyman Roth. Before he was through his credits included roles in four films and one television show. In addition to *The Godfather Part II*, he appeared in the films *Cassandra Crossing, Boardwalk* and *Going in Style* with George Burns and Art Carney. *The Last Tenant*, a story which centered on his plight as an elderly New Yorker, was his TV outing. Depending on your point of view, he was either being himself in each given situation or bringing an understated but resonant honesty to the screen. His rendition of the icy gangster with the veneer of a benign grandfather was nominated for an Academy Award.

Within this same time frame, he granted full access to Cindy Adams, a Manhattan gossip columnist, to write his biography. Filled with anecdotes, made-up conversations and imaginings about his sex life, it was difficult for longtime members of the Studio to reconcile the text of this commercial potboiler with the man who had spoken so often about acting as a high, demanding art form. A few looked upon his collaboration with Ms. Adams as a meaningless faux pas.

After his passing in 1982, some of those who had worked with him closely began issuing statements. Shelley Winters lauded him for making her aware of the honor of being an actor and of being special and possessing inner treasures.

Geraldine Page gave him credit for depriving her of everything that made her comfortable, enabling her to break out of the "fluttery spinster thing," undo and move ahead. Others talked in similar terms, grateful that he unlocked inner riches and made them part of an inner circle, permitting them to be close to the mysticism of Edmund Kean, David Garrick and Duse. Many commented on his unique X-ray vision, peering beneath their façades, unearthing their strengths and insecurities. Martin Landau spoke privately of the benefit of his harshness—it made Landau a much stronger person and actor. All who made positive comments intimated that he would be sorely missed because he alone had the power to unleash their potential. He validated their existence as they tested themselves against themselves and gained insights.

In retrospect, some of the remarks were less generous. Jack Garfein noted that his former directing teacher finally had to face his true motives: "What Strasberg discovered was what he wanted all along, to be famous in a commercial Hollywood way. Only Hollywood could give him that fame." In addition, there were longtime Studio members who described him as "completely egocentric ... occasionally kind, too often cruel ... irascible ... childish ..." One of his former protégés declared, "I hated him, I loved him."

Articulating his mixed feelings, a close associate contended that Strasberg created his own empire and his own destruction, never allowing the work to move beyond therapy. Never getting to the point where the process could be applied in active terms but, rather, housing a collection of "Method derelicts" who were content to "pick at their scabs of personal pain." Granted, Strasberg was a gifted teacher, but he never came to terms with his own slow, artful, highly idiosyncratic approach that was so dependent on vital talents who came and left. True, individuality was unlocked and people learned to be odd and interesting in their own way, but no ensemble of actors emerged who were ready to follow a like-minded director, apply the approach and produce distinctive works. *Hatful of Rain* was the first, last and only example of what Strasberg's Method was all about.

Like the Japanese story of "Roshomon," the nature and significance of Lee Strasberg's work depended on the teller of the tale. In much the same way, the tack that needed to be taken to preserve this tradition was a matter of opinion and interpretation.

Taking Up the Mantle

In his later years, Strasberg had acknowledged the aptitude of a handful of people to moderate the acting sessions and provide leadership. Among the chosen few were the directors Arthur Penn and Frank Corsaro and the actors Estelle Parsons, Ellen Burstyn and Eli Wallach. What Strasberg didn't reckon with was the resultant atmosphere of collegiality. No one took up the mantle of authority figure, no one presumed to have the last word. Reactions from observing members were fully taken into consideration as long as they weren't adamant. The moderators saw themselves solely as facilitators: those who had made it professionally and spoke the language, guiding, as best they could, those who sought input or encouragement. The tension of attempting to satisfy some elusive and almost unobtainable standard was a thing of the past.

As a moderator, Ellen Burstyn assumed a spiritual stance, implying by her demeanor that she had grasped the import of Strasberg's work through years of private study and her own intuitive nature. She touched on such matters as the sacred trust invested in those to whom Lee Strasberg granted admission. Taking risks and revealing hidden resources was both a privilege and a duty. Estelle Parsons was plain-spoken and quirky, often referring to emotional filing cabinets, using one's self totally, and focusing on what a member can do instead of struggling with tasks beyond his or her scope.[13] The director Frank Corsaro continued to be concerned with practical application, underscoring the notion that anyone who participated in the sessions was an actor performing for a critical audience despite past practices and claims to the contrary. In contrast, the other director, Arthur Penn, was soft-spoken and overly tactful. Sounding more like a visiting college lecturer, he articulated his thoughts on the acting process and shared his appreciation of unexpected and unrepeatable moments of behavior during the golden days of live television. Rounding out the roster of moderators, the actor Eli Wallach would chat amiably, drawing on familiar incidents from his life and prompting participants to do the same.

As for their credentials, Ellen Burstyn had won the Best Actress Academy Award for *Alice Doesn't Live Here Anymore* and the Broadway Tony Award for her performance in *Same Time, Next Year* along with the New York and National Film Critics awards for her supporting role in *The Last Picture Show*. Estelle Parsons won an Academy Award as Best Supporting Actress for her portrayal of the neurotic Blanche Barrow in *Bonnie and Clyde*. Arthur Penn directed such Broadway hits as *The Miracle Worker, Toys in the Attic* and *All the Way Home* and the noted films *The Miracle Worker, Bonnie and Clyde* and *Little Big Man*. Eli Wallach came to prominence as a versatile performer in screen classics like Tennessee Williams' *Baby Doll* and *The Magnificent Seven*, and had appeared with Monroe and Clift in *The Misfits*. Corsaro was still noted as the man who had developed *Hatful of Rain* and had enjoyed directorial successes outside the Studio. They were all admired and acknowledged for their longevity at the Studio.

However, at issue was the question of consistency and continuity. Especially when you add the random responses of member/observers to the mixture. Anyone offering their work would never know if the critiques would be based on developmental needs, the ability to tackle a given scene, or the ability to gratify someone's personal inclinations. Perhaps the following random sampling of differing moderator and member/observer responses may help illustrate the dilemma:

> Don't keep going back to fundamentals. Play the circumstances of the scene. Don't deny it.

But I liked the way she picked up a carrot and washed it like in real life. It's what would happen. And it was not in the script.

Never deal with a prop without it being infused with meaning. What personal association does each object in the room have?

Yes, it was very personal, easy and real. But what is going on in the scene? I wasn't focused on what your situation was.

You didn't get married to the words of the play. You brought your own reality to bear. There was no line between you and the character.

All of this will feed and enrich the final work. Use your own reference point to take you into the scene as an entry into faraway material.

It's in the word in Shakespeare, it's not in the subtext. The characters say what they mean.

Find a substitution for a queen. Go to what works for you, what's potent, what keeps it alive for you. Ease into the difficulties.

Those who needed constancy and role models for the traditional way of working—e.g. prizing one's own sensibility—could refer back to Sandy Dennis and her Oscar-winning performance as the hysterical, dim-witted Honey in the film version of *Who's Afraid of Virginia Woolf?* There they could find her so relaxed she seemed dazed, her mood shifts flitting through her as if she were a sieve, stammering and grappling with Albee's dialogue as if her thoughts and feelings were in constant battle. They could also reassure themselves by alluding to Geraldine Page as Alma Winemiller in her career-making performance in *Summer and Smoke* discovering her words as if plucking them out of the air, abruptly changing her rhythm, fluttering about and going with her instincts as she went from spinster to trollop. And there was always Kim Stanley as an ideal, always in her own personal space, suffering from a delicate state of equilibrium, trying to fend off anything and everything that threatened to overwhelm her.

For a male role model there were the films of Al Pacino, the camera lingering on his eyes, catching him brooding, concealing dangerous impulses and unspeakable thoughts just beneath the surface; about to say one thing and mean something else entirely. And then suddenly, at the first opportunity, releasing the energy and throwing himself body and soul into an action; shortly after, pulling back and letting things simmer.

The ones who had invested so much in a sure and certain touchstone could hold onto these images, Strasberg's words and anything that Burstyn et al. might say that met their need for perpetuity. It was a way to deal with the changes in the theater scene. Psychological realism was, more or less, relegated to TV (mainly specials and law and order shows), a few intimate Off Broadway plays and the occasional gritty film shot in and around New York City. The vision of the Studio as a center, home base and vital link to the profession grew more difficult to sustain.

Needing a sense of direction, the members elected artistic directors and gave them their chance to fill the gap. Frank Corsaro was one who took up the challenge. In no uncertain terms he informed the active members that the sessions were taking place in a vacuum; work on one's instrument was indulgent, merely done for its own sake. Underscoring the message he had been delivering whenever he moderated, he reminded them that Stanislavsky explored and taught by day and applied his theories on stage at night. Without this kind of application, the Studio had no real mission. Adamant statements of this kind were not, on the whole, well received. Presently, Ellen Burstyn was given a trial run. She had the opposite problem, wanting things to continue as they were, imparting her fervent interpretations of Strasberg's ideals. She too was replaced. The search went on.

Soon, outsiders were permitted to work on unrelated projects. Into the mix there were extensions of acting sessions and random staged readings of original scripts. For lack of any viable plans, the workshop struggled with the need to placate both patrons and the board of trustees and show signs of activity. Such enterprises in the past were, as they say, a mixed bag. Some projects were artistically viable and in keeping with the Studio's process like Elizabeth Stearns's *Hillbilly Women*, a lyrical theater piece based on the lives of Appalachian women.

And it should be noted that in the late seventies, due to the intercession of treasurer/benefactor Carl Schaeffer, Israel Horovitz's Playwright's Lab was housed at the Studio for a period of three years until it moved on to the Public Theater. But here is where it gets complicated again. Unlike those who had participated in the Studio's own on-again off-again playwriting unit, the writers who formed Horovitz's coterie did not welcome the creative suggestions of Studio actors. Nor did they value a reading of their initial drafts, allowing the actors to "sell" their work to them. As authors, they wanted to insure themselves that the work was structurally sound, the product of one mind, able to stand on its own merits as a piece of dramatic literature regardless of who was in the cast. In the development process they needed to keep track of the entire arc of the play, its overall style, what it was saying about life and what affect it might have on an audience. Moreover, in their judgment, Studio-like improvisations would be even more distracting, replete with personal rhythms and vocabularies and meandering behavior that lacked the power to "take you somewhere." During rehearsals, an actor's suggestion for line changes emanated from a person who only inhabits his or her character and can't tell the relationship of their part to the whole. The thought might be the right thought and that in itself had value, but, again in the minds of the playwrights in the Lab, any contribution had to serve the author's overall design.

Consequently, as far as the Lab and other projects for the public were concerned, it became more and more difficult to characterize the nature of the writing. By the same token, it was equally difficult to distinguish the quality of the acting. For instance, Horovitz had cast Michael Moriarty in the lead of *The Wakefield Plays*, his ambitious trilogy about Alfred the Great. Although Moriarty was not a member of the Studio, his highly sensitive portrayals on stage, television and film had earned him critical acclaim. When members objected to his presence on the grounds that Studio actors should be utilized whenever possible, a compromise was reached. Strasberg stepped in, evaluated the quality of Moriarty's work and granted him membership. In performance there was no way to tell that Moriarty was a product of different training or circumstances. Only that he was professional, extremely perceptive and expressive. By this stage of the game, only those who were self-absorbed stood out from all the rest.

In time, the projects ran the gamut from the venomous and embarrassing *Ladies at the Alamo* by Paul Zindel to a venture that took the workshop on an entirely different tack—the development of a flashy little musical entitled *The Best Little Whorehouse in Texas*. Infused with the brash humor of humorist and political writer Larry L. King, it began as an article in *Playboy* (King's account of the forced closing of a century-old Texas bordello). It then grew into a country-and-western musical comedy by dint of Studio member Peter Masterson's commercial inspiration. Masterson enlisted King's aid in turning his article into a series of scenes and to develop the book. He then obtained the services of Carol Hall to write the music and lyrics. The finished product enjoyed a long run on Broadway and was made into a movie starring the country pop star Dolly Parton. Before long, this particular property raised well over a quarter of a million dollars in royalties which helped defray the Studio's operating expenses.

By the early 1990s, however, neither the intervening activities or the contributions of patrons could keep the operation in the black and the workshop found itself once again in financial difficulties. Coincidentally, someone from the directors unit came up with a plan. The directors unit had, by this point, become even more of a mystery than the now semi-secret projects. Hardly anyone knew what the participants did or how those who slipped in and out were selected. Be that as it may, word had it that this particular entrepreneur had a liaison with the president of the New School for Social Research located some thirty-five blocks to the south in the vicinity of Washington Square. He proposed that if the Studio appeared to open its doors, broaden its focus and sanction a three-year MFA program, the Studio would, in turn, receive a regular income from the fees and afford some of its members jobs as teachers.

It was a sign of the times. Before long this enterpriser, whose name was James Lipton, installed himself as the dean of the school. As noted at the outset, he also produced a cable show "Inside the Actors Studio" featuring celebrities, the majority of whom were not associated with the Studio. Broadcast twice daily to 40,000,000 homes in the United States, Canada, Latin America, Europe and Asia, this program and its ubiquitous director/dean/TV producer represented itself as the voice and presence of the Actors Studio.

A faction of longtime devotees of Lee Strasberg was distressed by this abrupt change of course. Here was an individual who, according to rumor, had only one claim to fame: a stint on a daytime soap opera playing one of those generic doctors. And now he was posing as one of their own. To make matters worse, he studied with Stella Adler. According to Kazan's autobiography, Ms. Adler asked her class to stand upon hearing the news of "a man of the theater's passing." She then ordered them to sit, declaring, "It will take a hundred years before the harm that man has done to the art of acting can be corrected." Now one of her alleged pupils was representing the very place Strasberg had spent over three decades molding to his own designs, in continual conflict with Stella who was located only blocks away. And besides all of this, a television show featuring outside "names" would only exacerbate another old standing argument.

But this latest fork in the road prompted no debate. By all indications the ones who were directly involved had no qualms about Mr. Lipton's background or plan of action. Paul Newman, a frequent benefactor, stipulated that the school must teach courses in theater history. The request was granted. The curriculum was established.

All in all, the new undertaking evoked one of three responses: the combination of a school of higher learning and a cable show could revitalize the Studio's image; it was an opportunity to wrest stability out of a failing operation; the Studio as many had known it was slipping away.

14

Reinventing the Past

The TV Show and the MFA Program

As a marketing tactic, the MFA program offers graduates "an industry passport" plus a life membership in the legendary Actors Studio. The cost is $60,000 ($20,000 per year). This proposition becomes more remarkable when you consider that back in its heyday 2,000 people auditioned one year and only two were accepted: Steve McQueen and Martin Landau. Once accepted, they were members for life. No fees were attached. The only criterion was the possession of a unique sensibility and promise, distinctive enough to win the contest over all the others. McQueen was so destitute that tuition as little as ten dollars would have forced him to decline the honor. And it had nothing to do with schooling or a ticket to commercial success. It was a place to get away from all that, take your time and explore acting as an art. The MFA program is an entirely different game.

Under this new post-modern arrangement, young people from foreign lands, through the financial backing of their parents, are promised a touch of the mystique of Brando and Dean. And anyone with little or no background at all in the performing arts with a bachelor's degree in any subject from any institution is eligible to take part.

Pasting together bits of fact and employing a great deal of poetic license—omitting data, embellishing at every turn—brochures and other promotional materials were devised that played on the public's general impressions. The New School was validated as a historic site of "innovation and bold exploration" going back to the Dramatic Workshop where Strasberg and Stella Adler taught for the first time. By implication, Strasberg and Adler were associates and Brando, Tennessee Williams, Walter Matthau and Shelley Winters were under the same umbrella. From this notion, the selling pitch jumps to an illusion of a Studio roster that is a "motion picture Parnassus" and a "who's who of American theater, film and

185

television." The inference here is that anyone who has ever set foot in the Studio, including those whom Strasberg gave membership to because of their fame, power or influence, are at the beck and call of the program. Pushing this notion even further, the roster is said to be unmatched by any theatrical institution in the world and is living proof of the validity of the Studio's process.

Here again the logic becomes blurred. Strasberg is noted only in terms of the New School's beginnings. Kazan isn't mentioned at all. Adler and Sandy Meisner's techniques are touched upon and the curriculum is lauded for its broad spectrum with classes in movement, voice, text analysis, Alexander technique, theater history and theatrical styles. Switching back, the claim is made that the instructors share a common legacy and technique and the Studio's doors are opened at long last to let the Studio's method out.

Adding to the mixture, the cable television show, broadcast from the New School's auditorium, tries to sell the idea that it is emanating from the Studio and is revealing its secrets to both the viewing public and the students alike. Then again, it promotes the opposite idea that celebrities from all corners of show business have been invited in to share their thoughts and secrets. Hence the confusion over the title "Inside the Actors Studio," not to mention the continuing uncertainty over its location and what actually goes on behind closed doors.

One of the consequences of this double spin is the calls and inquiries the administrative secretary at the Studio West in Los Angeles keeps receiving. It seems that young hopefuls want to pay the same fee in the belief that they too can hobnob with famous movie stars and directors and become a card-carrying member of this special club.

In the meantime, the list of guests who have appeared continues to grow, running the gamut from comedians who poke fun at everything including the Method, to Shirley MacLaine who feels that Meryl Streep is the greatest actress because she totally abdicates her own identity, to stars of the moment who talk about conserving energy during the shooting of a scene, to older stars who bask in their own glory and are inarticulate about their own process, to other celebrities and a handful of Studio members who bring with them a plethora of anecdotes, a few insights and good will.

This brings up another reason why many longstanding members are so dismayed. The show gives the illusion that anyone with a reputation automatically qualifies as an expert on acting. And that any guest listed on the Studio's register can explain away the Method. For them, what Strasberg was trying to impart has lost its value and meaning.

The chats and discussions that follow with the students are billed as "craft seminars with film giants" who include screenwriters and anyone of interest to those on the writing, acting and directing tracks.

Graduates have no problem with this format or the course of study and couldn't care less about issues of integrity and the volatile history of the program's namesake. Their only concern is making contacts and finding work. Their quest during their three-year matriculation is the acquisition of a "toolbox" that enables them to meet any professional demands thrown their way during the 21st century.

What was imparted to them at the outset was the need for a flexible attitude: a return to a view of Stanislavsky as an evolving pragmatist, the use of Strasberg, Meisner and Adler in different combinations, and anything and everything else that might come in handy to succeed in a play, musical, television sitcom, film or what have you. No one comes to see an actor act, they are told time and again. They come to watch a story or experience an event. The performer's job is to help make that happen; help the story along, help the project meet its goal.

The tools, they are reminded, are whatever works for you. If sensory elements apply, use them. If they don't, put them aside. The precepts of Strasberg, Adler, Meisner or anyone else are not to be taken to heart. It's all about being in the moment and doing the job. If it's a Neil Simon comedy, the focus is on the words and comic timing. It has nothing to do with smelling the coffee or remembering similar moments from your life. Being professional and being in a state of readiness are the operative concerns. The more you have to call on, the better prepared.

One instructor uses an exercise in which you place the character outside yourself: imagining the person there, what they look like, etc., fully experiencing their presence and then stepping into that form. It's all pretending, never personal. Dragging your own life into the equation is not acting, it's not theater. It's dangerous.

Some students are advised that they need to lose control, break barriers and strip themselves of old habits. Beginners are advised to gain control and fashion some kind of technique. During the first year the idea is implanted that everyone on the talk show, everyone who speaks to them in the seminars, everyone they study about in theater history only seems to represent a different school of thought. In truth they are all referring to the same thing. "Method" is translated as whatever props you up and gets you to the character. Whatever gets the job done. Pragmatic flexibility is first and foremost, the only viable credo.

To underscore this basic philosophy, international students and those with heavy regional accents take courses in neutral American speech. All students take courses in voice production. There is a playwrights and directors unit that meets with those on the acting track. In this way, participants discover that they literally do not speak the same language and must make adjustments until they are all on the same wavelength working toward the same goal.

By the time they have added mask work, stage combat, accents, clowning and the components of the classics and various styles to their repertoire, they are ready, theoretically, to engage in fifteen weeks of repertory. Upon graduation, they can take advantage of anything the Studio may have to offer or tuck their membership card away for future use and move on. At this point, whether graduates bear any resemblance to those selfsame chosen few Kazan or Strasberg and his followers so admired is anyone's guess.

For a number of long-established veterans of the Studio, the MFA program has been accepted as a fact of life. Their main concern is, as always, to meet new challenges, join forces with others and evolve.[14]

Looking for Richard

In 1997, Al Pacino decided to branch out and take on the one brooding, tormented character that had always eluded him. It was written in another vernacular. The story took place during an historic period he was unfamiliar with. It was Shakespeare. It was Richard III.

His tactic was to approach it on film in bits and pieces incorporating his struggles with the text, rehearsals, encounters with people on the streets of New York and advice from experts and noted practitioners in London and Stratford-on-Avon. As in years before listening to Strasberg's circuitous comments, he would sift through all the pointers and select whatever struck a chord and was useful.

At the outset, and as a setup for the film, he assembled clips of Manhattan pedestrians responding to his queries about the title character. These became the basis of his quest: "It's very confusing. What happened before the play starts? What does this mean and what does that mean? It's not there for us. We don't know where we are or where we're going. How can we make it more accessible?"

In the next segment, Pacino goes about the business of looking for answers, interlacing the behind-the-scenes working process and the counsel of English scholars and actors and a chummy American advisor. To these sections he adds his outings in search of appropriate backgrounds in London and Stratford. Among those offering commentaries on location are Kenneth Branagh, Rosemary Harris, Peter Brook and Derek Jacobi.

Pacino digs deeper. From Sir John Gielgud he learns that part of the problem stems from the inhibitions and self-consciousness of Americans. For the most part they don't go to picture galleries, read the proper books and come in contact with experienced classical actors. Pacino nods, taking this information in stride, still looking for something more concrete.

A lady scholar explains that Shakespeare was the first to depict human beings as players and flights of the imagination as an integral part of life. The irony lies in the presentation of hypocrisy with style. Although everyone has their price, the action of the play is the search for the point beyond which people will not go. Vanessa Redgrave adds that the truth beneath all this is that those in power have total contempt for every promise they make, every reparation they have pledged.

As the project progresses (assuming the sequences, etc., were shot in some logical order), Pacino seems to be more and more excited about collaborating with noted British actors and finding some way to absorb their facility with the bard—some way to link the Method with their expertise and then meld the combination with the thoughts of his American advisor in alliance with whatever cast he can assemble: taken from old Studio colleagues, unaffiliated actors whose work he respects, and or other professionals who fit the part in question and can carry off the classic style.

Now the work becomes more detailed and specific problems are addressed. In dealing with iambic pentameter—the lines of verse containing sets of five unaccented and accented syllables—Vanessa Redgrave suggests that the meter contains

Al Pacino exploring ways to make the character of Richard III accessible to himself and viewers from all walks of life in *Looking for Richard* **(1997, 20th Century–Fox).**

the spirit and soul of the characters who have all gone through the larger than life extremes of hell, achievement and joy.

Another British expert eases Pacino's concerns over the text, assuring him that, even though he is dealing with a language of thought, he doesn't have to project. He can fall back on one of his strengths. As Richard, he can allow his inner turmoil to seep through the verse. He can say one thing and mean another. And toward the end, he can go even deeper and focus solely on his responses to the ghosts of those he has betrayed and sent to their grave. He can take his time and brood over his own self-loathing. The camera will do the rest.

From this preliminary work, Pacino determines that the orderly sequence of discussions, rehearsals and scenes enacted on location in full costume will make a connection with modern viewers. By gradually filling them in, they will be able to relate to the characters, issues and struggles Shakespeare has devised. By the same token, the gist is what is important. The cast doesn't have to understand every word. In their encounters with any given scene, they basically have to make certain they play an action commonly understood by all: "It's all about family quarrels.... Richard is stirring the pot, using the others' hatred to manipulate, divide and conquer. ... He's out to get this girl. He needs a queen and Lady Anne is perfect for the job and she needs protection. ... They got the kids, they got

Pacino applying the results of his explorations to a final scene from this Shakespearean play (*Looking for Richard*, 1997, 20th Century–Fox).

everybody. Somebody's got to go. But Hastings likes the kid and he's a tough guy. They have to cut out Hastings, get rid of him. ... "

Continuing in this casual trans–Atlantic mode, Pacino decides to rehearse the confrontation with the ghosts of his past crimes, in a London theater where the play was performed 300 years prior. In this setting he confesses that he needs the atmosphere to "get a sense of those old spirits—Method acting text style."

Alienated from his own being, barely audible, working mainly in close-up, Pacino as Richard exposes the raw feelings beneath the lines. He is equally at home in full costume during the highly filmic intercutting that make up the final battle scene.

Fittingly, the voice-over of the kindly English lady scholar filters in as Pacino as Richard tries to escape on foot, shambling up a hill: "Although he's frightfully clever, he is at the same time like a kind of boar who has subsumed into himself all these frightful animal attributes. All they have to do is hunt the boar, which they do. And they get him."

Fittingly again, as the final shots dovetail into one another and the music leads into the credits, there is a final voice-over by an English actor: "Our revels now are ended. These our actors as I foretold you, were all spirits and are melted into air, into thin air... "

Vanessa Redgrave transforms into a flamboyant American arts patron in *Cradle Will Rock* (1999, Touchstone Pictures).

Pacino would go on, exploring other classic texts, holding readings with actors of varied backgrounds, expanding everyone's understanding and range. Other veterans of the Studio would form their own acting companies, severing their bond with their former theatrical home. For them the situation was hopeless. They would have to take the process they had devoted themselves to and reapply it somehow while making accommodations for a new set of colleagues.

But there was still a nucleus who could not and would not give up their affiliation. Despite all the changes, the Studio was and always would be "the only place in the world to pursue the art of acting." Like the process they identified with, it was a matter of adapting to the given circumstances.

Continuing the Tradition

In her capacity as artistic director, Estelle Parsons altered the raison d'être a bit, taking into account the influx of new members from the MFA program. Having done so, as far as she, the Studio and the 21st century was concerned, it was business as usual.

True, Strasberg, an irreplaceable genius, was gone. But there would always be actors who wished to delve deeply into the art sheltered from commercial demands. Every artist needs a studio to work on himself. All an artist has is his

In contrast to Vanessa Redgrave's approach, Al Pacino immerses himself in the given cir-cumstances of *The Insider* (1999, Touchstone Pictures).

individuality and an abiding need to know how to best use that singular gift. Therefore, every truly gifted actor has similar desires that can only be met in this particular workshop. Individual dreams, that "individual thing ... wanting to burn up the stage like Strasberg-trained actors do," coincide with the love and appreciation of great acting. It's "scary organic work" that can only be carried out by "Method people."

Accepting the premise that the roster of moderators reflects different views that are sometimes inspiring and sometimes confusing, Parsons contends that, nevertheless, the process is cohesive. Everyone recognizes that although there are different ways to get there, they are all headed for the same place.[15] Everyone can see the difference between good work and bad work: "It's real easy to see, we all see the same thing." The only question is, When it doesn't work what would be best, what would be meaningful to help this particular person fix the problem?

Invoking Strasberg's name again, Parsons declares that the artist always tries to create something new and the great teacher prods you to use yourself and make the most of your originality. She, herself, studied privately with Strasberg, auditioned eleven times (freezing up under the pressure) until she finally reached her coveted goal and was accepted as one of the especially "smart and very gifted people" who could profit from this confirmation.

In practice, under the best of circumstances, you can then find yourself working with a director like Arthur Penn (as she had in *Bonnie and Clyde* and Ellen Burstyn had in *Alice Doesn't Live Here Anymore*). Then you are given the opportunity to inhabit the role first, relate it to your own emotional experiences, work against obstacles, absorb the outline of the action into your own system. After you've done so, after you've moved the language and the dictates of the script out of the way and made the given circumstances your own, you return to the lines, allowing for the antic, inappropriate accidents that Penn so enjoyed on live TV. This, in a nutshell, was the general idea.

With Penn as president and Parsons as artistic director, this modification of Strasberg's way of working becomes the rule of thumb. Its validation is also derived from Penn's successes that we've noted—those on television, the record of five hit plays running on Broadway at one time, and the movies attributed to his maverick sensibilities. Parsons can point to her own set of triumphs on film, television and especially the ones on stage. Between the two of them a procedure was established, a kind of grappling-with-the-text process which can best be illustrated by a sample session.

Somewhat like the days of old, members and a sprinkling of students from the New School plus two invited guests wait downstairs until the appointed hour. Then all file upstairs. The members take seats in the center and the sides of the eight or nine tiers of risers facing the playing space in front of the brick wall. A few moments later a handful of students peer down from the single row of balcony seats above.

From his chair front and center, Arthur Penn starts the session with a short greeting and announces the first of two explorations. He indicates that he has no idea what to expect.

The house darkens, the dozen or so bare stage lights come up on Parsons down left and a young black woman stage right. Parsons is dressed in matching black sweat pants and sweatshirt and carries a floppy handbag. The younger black woman is dressed in jeans and a comfortable blouse. The physical gulf between them is heightened by the fact that the young woman keeps glancing downstage, averting Parson's eyes. Parsons paces around, plucks out a pack of cigarettes, lights one, inhales deeply, flings her bag down onto the bare floor and, after another interval of more waiting, sits down on a metal chair. The young woman remains standing.

More inhalations and exhalations of smoke until Parsons finally breaks the silence. With a biting edge to her voice, she inquires as to the whereabouts of someone they are ostensibly waiting for. Growing more and more impatient, she segues into a critique about the state of the arts in comparison with the old days. The young woman's responses are brief and noncommittal.

Another cigarette lit, the first extinguished. Another pregnant pause, inhalations and exhalations of smoke. The topic drifts to the whereabouts of the young woman's husband and disappointment on the part of Parson's character over not seeing the children. The young woman's responses are still brief and noncommittal, except at the one point when she asks about Parson's appraisal of a painting. On the defensive this time, Parsons grows more secretive, suggesting that there may be or may have been political implications.

The banter continues, the smoking proliferates until, suddenly, Parsons breaks everything off, turns toward the audience and says, "And that's as far as we got."

As the house lights come back on, Penn asks them both what they were working on. The young woman confesses that she felt insecure after consenting to work on the scene and used how she felt about working with Estelle—very intimidated.

Parsons admits that she worked on the scene only because someone suggested that she try this particular piece by the English playwright David Hare. However, she soon discovered that the script didn't feed either of them, the situation was stilted, and the writing was so arch that she "couldn't get her mouth around it." They then tried doing it in their own words looking for a life and did the lines afterwards but not exactly reverting to the text.

After a little more prodding from Penn, Parsons surmises that her character was irritated because her daughter hadn't spoken to her and she hadn't seen her grandchildren for some time.

Penn replies that he sensed some kind of mistrust but didn't have any idea who he was seeing, where he was and who was doing what to whom. He turns to the members and asks, "What did you see?"

One person finds a non-use of place. If it was a museum, they should do more "place work" to relax them and reflect where they are. And what was Estelle? A mother? An expert out to judge whether something was a real Matisse? It was hard to know.

A second member states that the way Parsons smoked and waited was wonderful. She loved the way Parsons took her time and enjoyed her cigarettes which was very hard to do under pressure on stage.

Like the revelation of bits and pieces of a puzzle, Parsons discloses that the smoking came from her impression of a party member who was active during the cold war and habitually on her guard as if still wary of the KGB.

A third member, now beginning to recognize the piece, supports Parson's displeasure with the writing. Having seen the play done—announcing the title as *The Bay at Nice*—confirms that the dialogue is very arch and the acting in the London production typically external and superficially mannered.

Going off on another tack, a fourth member, addressing the younger actress, suggests that when working with Parsons the best thing to do is grab her and shake her. Not remain so physically distant. Make something happen. Another member comes up with the philosophical notion that the theme is fraud. They are both looking for fraud in the painting and each other.

Joining in the exchange that continues to flit from one point of view to another, Parsons offers more information. She only wanted to be fully present, in the moment. Surprisingly, she received so much psychic energy from her partner she suddenly became involved. This caused her to lose control and inadvertently toss her handbag onto the floor. She still didn't know who her character was—some bitter woman who lived in the past with a daughter who totally rebelled. But the main source of energy today was her partner's presence.

Penn takes the floor, amazed that Parsons was distressed over her impulses when that is the very thing he always encourages. He also is puzzled as to why neither one of them chose active waiting and the push and thrust against inertia as a much more actable tack.

Parsons counters by saying that she doesn't like to play that kind of supercilious, overbearing patroness of the arts. She doesn't want to play a character so different from herself, so pushy.

Penn answers that what she chose to do didn't take her very far and her contempt for the play kept her from investigating a whole set of behaviors beyond just being present and trying to put up with the dialogue. She needs to find strong "percolating" desires. She needs to "put the lid on the pot and put the pot on the stove boiling." She needs to make the character her own.

Parsons tells Penn that his comments don't register with her.

Getting a bit frustrated, Penn asks them both to try the scene again, physically closer, improvising and voicing their underlying frustrations.

Before they proceed, Penn goes over to Parsons, lowering his voice, talking to her privately. Like a mentor dealing with a headstrong but valued pupil, Penn advises her to declare her true feelings and take her daughter on. Parsons shakes her head and grumbles about this particular ploy which goes against her nature and intuition. Finally she agrees to try it Penn's way.

In the second attempt, the young woman strides right up to Parsons and chides her for withholding much-needed financial aid. Parsons retaliates like a mother berating an irresponsible, selfishly demanding child who has been neglectful and totally unaware of her mother's experiences and position. Free of the lines, the two go head to head, overlapping their thrusts and parries, continuing on until Penn calls an end to the fray.

Satisfied, Penn nods, praises the young woman for her charisma and poise. He remarks that it's been a long time since they've seen her work and hopes that she and Parsons will continue to develop the scene.

Carrying on in the fight against the "baggage of conforming to the text before you have earned the role through your own experience," Penn announces the second and final exploration. A man and a woman are handed a scene from *Bury the Dead*, one of novelist Irwin Shaw's vignettes about the thoughts and feelings of American soldiers slain in battle during the last world war.

The litany is the same. The text is a bare outline that has to be fleshed out by the organic responses of the creative people. To prove this alleged fact of life once again, Penn asks the couple to begin the first phase of the procedure.

Seated on metal chairs, dressed in casual clothing, the tall heavyset man and the slim, slightly older brunette start reading their lines cold. They jump on any phrase or word that gives them an opportunity to laugh, squirm or release some bit of behavior, like amnesia victims who are just starting to remember who they are and what has happened to them. It soon becomes obvious that the material is extremely dated, the characters only two-dimensional; redolent of the ingenuous newlyweds in the movies of the late 1930s and early 1940s.

They reminisce and, as was customary in the fiction of the day, readily accept the fact that one is living and the other is dead. The conflict arises from the soldier's desire to touch his sweetheart and recapture what they once had and her desire that he return to his grave. It's improper and of no use to remain a ghost.

On the second pass, Penn instructs them to add a place and improvise the scene—do something to it to bring it to life. The two confer, do some stretching exercises and move around like children who have been released from their homework and told they can go out and play. They decide that it's a nice sunny day and the soldier is painting her portrait. In the improv, he is drawn to her physically and becomes bubbly and animated. She becomes flirtatious, playing with the buttons on her blouse and flouncing around. Still rejecting his notion of picking up their lives where they left off, she gradually retreats and becomes wistful. Undaunted, on an impulse, he jumps over an imaginary space, cavorts around and announces that he's dancing on his grave, perfectly content with his ghostly situation.

Penn halts the improv. Members comment on the bravery displayed in "hitting things off on one another" and gaining so much connection in such a short space of time. Breaking into his lecture mode, Penn makes the case that actors should have no restrictions, no impositions. They need the equivalent freedom of a playwright, otherwise they become "muted behind a fence."

Penn asks the actors to read the scene again. This time they are much more animated, building on the relationship they discovered in the improv and the encouragement they've just received.

Rephrasing the same litany, Penn, the lecturer/moderator, argues that only when actors are given time for invention and the opportunity to infuse material with their personal impulses can they arrive at "behavioral and emotional treasures." Actors should not be encumbered by anything that stifles their "breadth, lift and spontaneity."

As with his encounter with Parsons, all is not acceptance, joy and light. A wiry young woman wearing thick glasses takes exception. Speaking from the top row, she questions the insistence on placing the playwright in a secondary position. "What about Irwin Shaw's intentions?" she asks. "What about what he had in mind?"

Penn backs down a little, trying to placate this member. "Of course," he says. "What I mean is, a marriage of the words and the actor's process. A marriage of the two."

A greater disturbance is caused by a gray-headed man seated in the third row. His face turning red, he contends that neither of the two actors dealt with the essentials, the realities, the sensory things. "What does it feel like to be dead?" he shouts. "What does the wet clay do to you? What do you see? What do you smell?

Where does the clamminess and all those awful sensations take you? And how does a young girl deal with something that isn't there but has that smell and feeling around it?"

There is a silence. Penn is thrown off guard. Presently, others come to the defense of the acting partners, complimenting them on the fine job they did given absolutely no time to prepare; how far they came in such a brief span, establishing a relationship it would have taken weeks to acquire in rehearsal in the commercial theater. And how it was all due to their wonderful "well-tuned instruments."

Recovering his composure, Penn asks the older man if he's all right. Perhaps something has been troubling him, causing him distress. There is another long pause. The older man declines to answer.

Later on it is revealed that the person who was so distraught has been attached to the Studio for decades and has nowhere else to go. He's been waiting impatiently for some kind of second coming, a return to the old days, what the place once stood for or what it once had and lost. He can't put a name to it. But he hungers for it all the same.

Epilogue

At the beginning of the 21st century, the Tony for best play was awarded to *Copenhagen* by British author/philosopher Michael Frayn. The timeliness of the work revolves around an imaginary meeting in theatrical space between two giants of quantum physics, Werner Heisenberg and Neils Bohr, with Margrethe Bohr acting as facilitator. In their encounters the characters collide, separate and realign themselves like so many particles and waves—e.g., weighing issues while postulating that nothing can be "quite located or defined"; struggling over past relationships and key events while, at times, getting lost in their own personal orbits. And then, ultimately, grappling with questions of value. For instance, was the application of the theoretical work, especially in 1941 and during the latter phase of World War II, and all the decisions "great and small" worth the risk? What of the consequences? Or, in Heisenberg's terms, is everything and everyone governed by the uncertainty principle? Moreover, what is truly of significance and deserves to be preserved? If one had to choose a paradigm for assessing the nature and merit of the historic Actors Studio, the "Copenhagen" model would surely be apt. Nonetheless, the Studio of the future may be sidestepping its provocative legacy and the kind of questions Frayn raises in favor of aligning itself with the celebrity culture and resting on its laurels.

Consequently, the fervor and contradictions that fueled this phenomenon and gave it distinction seem, on the face of it, to have been forsaken. The satirical review "Saturday Night Live" did a parody of "Inside the Actors Studio" as a venue where viewers can learn the trade secrets of their favorite sitcom stars. In almost the same superficial vein, president Arthur Penn appeared on the actual Studio TV show and talked of a congenial place where interested writers and MFA graduates were all part of "the loop." When Strasberg's name was brought up, he was simply noted as a tough moderator who could rid people of conventional habits. Consistently, anything that might be deemed problematic on this cable show continued to be quickly brushed aside. Behind the scenes at the New School, issues pertaining to the Group, Strasberg, Adler, Kazan, and the Studio Theater venture, etc., also continue to be modified to the point where all and sundry are depicted as, basically, pursuing the same goal. And, when everything is said and done, the only thing that matters is acquiring that identical all-purpose tool kit—whatever gets you there, whatever works. Behind the famous closed doors on Forty-fourth Street, the official version seems to concur, proclaiming that there were never any real disagreements to speak of. And members go on extolling the virtues of Method people guiding the gifted in a way that is universally admired.

Interestingly enough, however, the benign façades can't quite hide the reverberations beneath. Just like those selfsame subatomic particles and waves that form the basis of quantum physics, the restless energy is always there, the uncertainty principle still pertains. We've already touched upon the fact that former active members are disturbed, old-timers are waiting for some kind of revitalization, altercations are taking place pitting the writer against the actors' creative needs, and moderators are still trying to dislodge whatever stubbornly is hiding underneath.

And in the outside world there are signals that the old agitation continues to manifest itself as well. On the Studio's taped celebrity talk show, Christopher Walken (a guest who is actually listed on the Studio roster) responds affably to questions about his colorful career. Elsewhere he reveals that his primary task is to create chaos on the set, to literally get in trouble and work his way out. On the continent, Theo Angelopoulos, winner of the Palme d'Or at Cannes for directing, complains about the self-indulgent antics of his leading actor "who comes from the Actors Studio which is not a school but a religious sect." In an interview for a noted film quarterly, Edward Norton, the "genius-touched chameleon," contends that Strasberg's internal method is useless and only Stella Adler's maxim that an actor's greatest gift is his imagination has any cachet. Simultaneously, another article in another noted film quarterly appears in tribute to Al Pacino, indicating his debt to Strasberg and his disdain for the age of relentless promotion and interviews (ostensibly referring to the Studio talk show). Refusing to reveal any of his own secrets, he offers a quote from the Flying Wallendas instead: "Life is on the wire, the rest is just waiting." Seemingly by extension, a few weeks later an acting coach on a major movie shoot praises a teenager for his "fearless, naked and truthful" self-exposure. Elaborating, he describes a cathartic scene: the eleventh grader inside Yankee Stadium alone with Sean Connery on the pitcher's mound, calling upon a deep personal loss, "following the Lee Strasberg Method of getting to the bottom, finding the real emotion—like Brando!" At the same time yet another piece reaches the newsstands detailing Paul Newman's struggles to escape from Brando's shadow and the meaninglessness of celebrity. And so it goes. The struggle over what passes for truth goes on, as does the battle over maintaining integrity and dealing with the trappings of success.

And even while disregarding this uneasy interplay and the invaluable controversies, triumphs and follies that brought them to this pass, the Studio leadership can't resist leaving little hints of its significance despite itself. In the preface to the MFA catalogue, Erwin Piscator's Dramatic Workshop of the 1940s is cited as a forerunner. As it happens, Piscator was a German émigré who worked with Bertolt Brecht, fostered an external approach to keep audiences critically awake, and invited Strasberg to teach in order to promote debate. As a direct result of his experiences in World War I, Piscator saw objectivity as the only antidote to the pitfalls of romanticism and unchecked emotions. Since the New School's credo of artistic freedom was instituted to secure the right to disagree in the face of rampant nationalism circa 1918, others whom Piscator disagreed with, like Stella Adler, were invited to teach as well. Moreover, on the next page of the catalogue, billing the MFA program as "a manifesto of a revolution," the dean of the school invokes the self-dramatizing tone of bohemian New York and the value of disputes and confrontations. As though following suit, Arthur Penn once reminded the students who were issued the catalogue that the Studio's process is steeped in risk and anarchy.

And now, irrepressibly, the pointers lead us just around the corner to Washington Square and Emma Goldman, the Russian immigrant who preached the anarchists' credo of a self whose creative powers are released through revolutionary ferment. Her talks, in turn, mark the time and place that shaped the lives of Clurman, Strasberg and Stella Adler: the Village as a vital crossroad for a cast of diverse and radical characters—theater people and intellectuals emanating from the Yiddish Theater nearby; expatriates from the continent and eastern Europe; authors and artists of every stamp from Chicago, Davenport, Iowa, etc., adding to the stir; everyone seeking transformation in the one American city where "something considerable may happen."

The parallels and intersections filter back to Moscow and return, transmute, proceed up the Great White Way and crisscross continually until they reach into the next century. The fervor, messiness and contradictions can't be overlooked, not for long. Neither can the highs and lows if this story is to have any meaning. As we've seen, in the process things were lost. The notion of recreating the MAT in America never came to pass, especially in terms of experimentation. Save for Bobby Lewis' special sensibility and fascination with style, there was hardly a trace of Vakhtangov's theater of joy and playful communion with the audience. Nor is there much evidence of Michael Chekhov or Meyerhold's audacious brand of theatricality and no sign at all of Suler's worldly ease and transcendental explorations. Also lost to the passage of time was the social conscience and camaraderie of the Group, its crusade to help people survive.

But the Group still has merit as a forerunner and an ideal. In turn, at its best, the evolving Studio serves as a link to an ever-widening chain of provocative associations. For instance, in *The Dream Life of Angels* a French actress by the name of Natasha Régnier exudes the same scruffy, desperate vulnerability reminiscent of James Dean's portrayal of Cal in *East of Eden* over four decades earlier. Gabriel Byrne, an Irish actor who earned critical praise in American movies, takes to the Broadway stage playing the leading role of James Tyrone, Jr., in Eugene O'Neill's *Moon for the Misbegotten*. He learns to trust the play and the words from this work of the 1940s. At the same time he faces down his own demons from "a tough and private place," his emotionality impelled by "a primitive need for us to tell each other our transgressions and to be forgiven." His acting partner Cherry Jones relates the costs, the dividends and how exhilarated she and Byrne felt that never once did they cheat the audience or O'Neill and still managed to live through the experience till the very end. Taken together, these examples and countless others remind us of the debt we owe to all the edgy ventures that preceded.

All told and put simply, a compelling turbulence runs through this story and binds it together. Individually and collectively, members of the Group, those who worked with Kazan, actors who were chosen in the early years of the workshop and those who legitimately gained entrance during the Strasberg years, kindred souls, playwrights like Odets, Miller and Williams and scriptwriter/novelists like John Steinbeck and Bud Schulberg—all are part of the synergism, drawn to the junction of life and art, magnetized by its dangers. On those occasions when the vital elements were in place and the dividends outweighed the costs, something singular came into being. In their own special way, actors captured Stanislavsky's beloved spirit of the moment and the lives of theatergoers and movie audiences respectively were enriched and profoundly changed.

Notes

1. Because the topic of the Method and the Actors Studio is so fraught with contradictions and hyperbole, the only recourse is to seek a balanced perspective, one akin to Ric Burns' documentary of New York. In this treatment, Manhattan is depicted as a port of call, enabling us to view the historic influx of immigrants, changes in the cultural climate from era to era as the metropolis began to challenge London as the center of the world. From this vantage point you can readily envision a city of desires and sense the ceaseless energy and perpetual expansion, the limitless horizons where everything seems possible—a region of ambition and success. The segment on the 1920s is especially helpful with its evocation of F. Scott Fitzgerald's response upon arriving from St. Paul, captivated by "the racy, adventurous feel of it at night, and the satisfaction that the constant flicker of men and women and machines gives to the restless eye." As a newcomer he found it the epitome of the American dream. Later on he realized that it had limits, that it was just a city after all, not a universe. And it's all these things—the enchantment and disenchantment, the sophisticated pretense at its core while striving to extend its commercial and cultural reach, being both cosmopolitan and provincial, embracing émigrés who identified with the proletariat of the Russian revolution plus all the other excesses and contrasts that provide a backdrop for the actions of figures like Clurman, Strasberg and Stella Adler. In a word, just like the interplay suggested by Burn's photographs and moving pictures, the dynamics can be viewed as a montage. Moreover, the encounters and events can be seen through the eyes of a cinematographer: using a wide-angle lens, changing lenses and zooming in when needed, holding steady then cutting, panning and moving off and away, never mired in one locale or limited by some insistence that you have to take sides in the controversy.

2. Excerpts from conversations between Vakhtangov and his disciples Zahkhava and Kotlubai indicate that, theoretically, the issue of performing vs. playing with the utmost inner conviction was resolved by the second decade of the 20th century. In these exchanges Vakhtangov clearly asserted that inner experience had to be conveyed through theatrical means. He also stated that the audience should never be deceived into believing that actors are not acting. In his view, realism and naturalism must be histrionic in order to be of any value. Only theatrical methods can impart genuine life on the stage hence the necessity for "fantastic realism." This reconciliation, however, was never accepted by some practitioners of Strasberg's teachings. Even by the late 1950s, actress Mildred Dunnock still

thought in terms of polarities as illustrated by her judgment of James Dean: "He was constantly at war with his own theatrical temperament, torn between the desire to be theatrical and the desire to be truthful."

3. Stella Adler's background in the Yiddish theater had a profound influence on her concept of theater. Beginning at the age of three under the guidance of her father, the legendary Jacob Adler, and her mother, a flamboyant actress in the company, she found the Yiddish language warm and soulful, infused with an emotional blend of pleasure and pain. The plays were classic stories, much larger than life, which sustained the audience of émigrés through noble ideas. By the time she was in her early twenties, she was totally convinced that the actor's task was to feed the particular world of the play and the soul (which was much richer and deeper than the self). Years later, as a teacher, she was fond of saying that Americans had such difficulty acting because life had beaten them down and crushed their souls. They needed great plays to inspire them to reach emotional heights. Size, power, courage and heroism were watchwords integral to her technique. As for self-expression, her favorite quote came from the ancient Greek philosopher Heraclitus: "Don't try to know who thou art. Long has this idea tormented thee. It is much better to know what thou can do, and do it like Hercules." She listed Stanislavsky, Sarah Bernhardt and her father among her spiritual teachers and considered her mother the Bernhardt of Yiddish theater because of the great range of her characterizations. She continued to take exception to Strasberg's view of the imagination as secondary, always fostering a dramatic sense of the author's vision and the author's characters. After a noteworthy effort in one of her classes she would call for applause for the playwright as well as the actors.

4. At times this history seems like a puzzle constructed of opposite pairs. Starting with the instruction at the American Laboratory Theater, which should have been called the Russian Laboratory Theater, the list of dualities in uneasy juxtaposition seems endless: an aloof martinet calling for more spontaneity and passion (see Ouspenskaya's incredibly wooden performances in movies like *Waterloo Bridge*); an American theater founded on a Russian model fueled by a Russian technique; a commune made up of highly individualistic participants many of whom had an aversion to groups; anti-capitalistic sentiments dependent on the free enterprise of show business (Stella Adler said that she would put up with communism only if she were queen); self-absorption within an ensemble; drawing the audience in by pretending they aren't there; a sanctuary away from commercial pressures which places participants in emotional and psychological jeopardy; an actors theater in which the actors are subservient; extolling the virtues of art and theater while coveting success in Hollywood, etc.

5. In my conversation with Arthur Bartow, the artistic director of New York University's graduate professional theater program, I was reminded that the fervor I experienced in the late 1950s was linked to a special set of circumstances. There were only a few approaches to acting, and forms of American realism were thriving on Broadway. Marilyn Monroe's decision to study privately with Strasberg and attend exclusive Studio sessions drew great media attention. All of this synergistic activity promoted the idea that acting required dedication and organic verve. The Studio, therefore, was regarded as central in providing the stage, live television dramas (which to a great extent depended on actors who could behave naturally in extreme close-up) and film with this special commodity. With the advent of new forms, the realization that Method acting was highly idiosyncratic, and the near extinction of the hit realistic play, the media began to lose interest. Variations on Method acting and the activities of the Studio then became a small part of a much larger picture. Yet, as one more irony, even though the list of optional techniques continues to grow and the old guard remain captive of their own impressions, what goes on twice-weekly behind the closed doors may represent a last bastion of dedication and tireless devotion.

6. It appears that only those members who identified exclusively with Strasberg's teaching used the term Method or referred to themselves or their colleagues as "Method people." Others simply shared a preference for going through an experience rather than faking it or indicating. As Geraldine Page put it, "as an actor you must do the fullest, best, most interesting interpretation of the character and not the fullest, most wonderful exposition of your own discoveries of yourself." Even someone like Dustin Hoffman who spent his early years working on Strasberg's sensory exercises and attempting to be private in public, models the characters he plays on people he knows and relies on make-up and the imitation of people's voices, attitudes, values and prejudices. As always, there are tendencies and one can describe what seems to be the process during Studio sessions, but, as June Havoc put it, no one knows how someone might be applying something Lee said to them. Everyone is different and no one wants to talk about it. Rip Torn considered looking for a lucky coin, something he could quickly slip into his pocket just before he performed.

7. While working on a screenplay based on the life of James Dean, Israel Horovitz shared his thoughts about actors, especially those who championed the Studio's process. As an avowed Freudian, he suggested that the artist is found in the suffering child and that many who were drawn to the Studio were dysfunctional well before they passed through its doors. With playwrights claiming the ultimate authority and producers, directors and others dictating to them at every turn, it was perfectly understandable why they wanted their unique impulses and response patterns validated. It is little wonder they would seize any opportunity to lead the way in the outside world and then retreat by "moving into a room with their friends."

8. As for the controversy over gurus, some seventeen years after Strasberg's passing, Robert Brustein (as dean of the school of theater at Harvard) was still troubled about Stansberg's continuing influence. In 1998 he created a play entitled *Nobody Dies on Friday* and produced it at the American Repertory Theater in Cambridge. The script and the production excoriated Strasberg, portraying him as a nervous little man, mothering Marilyn Monroe in his own New York apartment (while she remains offstage as a disembodied voice numbed by sleeping pills), clinging to her as a passport to money and fame. As a direct result, his children—especially his son—suffer from psychological abuse while his wife Paula goes on justifying his machinations. The work is purportedly based on John Strasberg's memoirs and satirizes both the man and the Studio. However, although Strasberg's teachings may continue to have some effect through the offerings at the institute that bears his name, facets of the New School's acting program, and the efforts of those who spread his word, it seems unlikely that Mr. Brustein has any cause for alarm. The notion of an all-knowing patriarch, or matriarch for that matter à la Stella Adler, has little cachet in a society in transition with its new styles of interaction between people of different ages and sexes; one that regards authority figures as an artifact of a distant past.

Moreover, the file of guests on "Inside the Actors Studio" who are passed off as authorities by dint of the fact that they've attained some degree of commercial success is further proof that the social pattern has changed drastically since the age of the great teachers. As new generations became consumer oriented, no single Method had much chance of holding sway. The thought of seeking out a mentor as a source of inspiration, especially one associated with a great theater tradition has become passé in an age that regards an efficient tool kit as de rigueur.

9. The more time you spend with insiders, the more apparent it becomes that the old adage is true: talk to any three people associated with this subject and you'll come away with at least four contradictory answers. When, for example, Phoebe Brand tells you that in her eyes the Strasberg she worked closely with as a member of the Group was impossible to work with "but we learned a lot from Lee," that discrepancy marks the pattern: a

set of circumstances experienced by individuals with distinct backgrounds who came together when the timing was right and then went their separate ways. And it's this mix of judgments that both provides invaluable insights and helps circumvent the simplistic myth about a preeminent group of artists under the leadership of Lee Strasberg who made an indelible contribution to American culture. It was June Havoc's tough experiences in vaudeville that enabled her to oversee her own work and regard Strasberg as a harmless friend with an interest in neuroses who had little knowledge of comedy. In the late 1960s, the members I encountered were concerned over those who thought of the Studio as a substitute family and Strasberg as a stern patriarch who might one day show them some love. From yet another perspective, Rip Torn viewed events in terms of his upbringing in Texas, believing that every undertaking should be done with all your heart, thus making his dismissal from the "Blues for Mister Charlie" project more devastating. When you factor in the words members use to describe the workshop—"Lee's candy store … a gym … a wonderful place at that particular time … home of the greatest dysfunctional family in the world… " it's readily apparent that any take on the Studio as an ongoing cohesive institution has missed the mark.

10. Although the Studio has never been attuned to comedy, there appears to be an approach to turning malaise and suffering into laughter not dissimilar to the process favored at the Studio. For instance, according to actress Linda Lavin, there is no distinction between comedy and drama. During an interview in the *New York Times* she described her axiom as "if it ain't real, it ain't going to be funny and if it ain't funny, it ain't real." By asking herself Kazan-like questions about her character—What does she want, need … what stands in her way … how is she going to get out of it?—she was able to make a seemingly outlandish comparison between her role of Marjorie (who thrives on chaos in *The Tale of the Allergist's Wife*) and Ibsen's *Hedda Gabler*. To Lavin, both women are aliens in their own environment. As is the case in most of Neil Simon's plays, Ms. Lavin seemed to be suggesting that laughter is derived from the audience's recognition of the truth, not from an actress' timing and comic style.

11. The list of former active members who have started their own theater companies has continued to grow, along with the fact that many, if not most of the actors chosen are not associated with the Studio. The criteria for casting centers mainly on versatility, range, experience, compatibility, stage presence and the ability to sustain a performance level night after night.

12. Long before he was laying plans for a new theater dedicated to the plays of O'Neill and the development of new works and playwrights and shortly after the demise of the Studio Theater, Frank Corsaro was inspired by yet another facet of Stanislavsky. He came upon the fact that in 1918 Stanislavsky was commissioned to create an opera studio theater to raise the cultural level of the actor-singer and form a working ensemble with a unified approach. Stanislavsky's notes about his productions of Tchaikovsky's *Eugene Onegin*, Rimsky Korsakov's *The Tsar's Bride*, Puccini's *La Boheme* and Moussorgsky's *Boris Godounov* revealed his pursuit of "the extraordinary contained within the ordinary." His notes on mounting Verdi's *Otello* made a special impression on Corsaro and, all told, prompted him to capitalize on his own multi-talents and love of music in a new and challenging way. Working with many major opera companies in the United States, he re-examined the content of the operas, utilized multi-media technology for modern works, and appropriated his organic technique and applied it to the opera singer's craft. In Corsaro's view, this inner approach was fully validated by Maria Callas' debut in *Lucia di Lammermoor*. During the famous sextet in Act II while her colleagues jockeyed into traditional positions front and center and projected their voices directly at the audience, Callas closed her eyes, remained in place and sang quietly to herself. According to Corsaro, Callas was faithful to the given

circumstances (six people alone with their thoughts) and the only one on stage who was truly there.

13. Decades after Strasberg's passing there were still actors closely identified with his teachings. Reviewing Jane Campion's *Holy Smoke!* Andrew Sarris found Harvey Keitel totally predictable with his usual "brand of hard-edged Actors Studio sensitivity." In comparison, he praised the extraordinary range of British actress Kate Winslet who, unlike Mr. Keitel, "continues to amaze with her change of accents, expression and physical postures" starting with her debut as a homicidal nymphet through her portrayals in *Sense and Sensibility, Jude* and other projects like *Titanic.* In *Holy Smoke!* he felt she offered a startling rendition of an impressionable young woman in "what passes for the modern cinema in all its post-censorship sensations."

14. In February 1998, the MAT celebrated its 100th anniversary. While on tour, the troupe visited the United States for the first time since the 1960s. One stop was the Actors Studio where representatives of the MAT held a summit on the future of Stanislavsky's heritage. According to theater director Andre Gregory who was present, in Moscow, Grotowski—apropos of his experimental work in the 1960s and early '70s—is considered the true heir. Whereas Strasberg's work is linked to a style in vogue prior to the 1920s, Grotowski appreciated Stanislavsky's entire oeuvre, including his later technique of physical action, and appropriated his controlling metaphor of exploration: ongoing testing that enables one to find one's own way in the spirit of the times.

15. By the 21st century it was commonplace for Academy Award winners like Britain's Michael Caine and America's Hilary Swank to praise those kindred spirits who "inhabit their roles" and live their character's life during preparation. In Ms. Swank's case she spent over a month experiencing what it would be like to be a male, mirroring the real Teena Brandon who transformed herself into Brandon Teena in *Boys Don't Cry.* In other words, in the Hollywood lexicon, acting honors connote the mastery of some difficult challenge—a role that requires the subordination of one's personality and type. On Broadway, the Tony Award for a dramatic role is generally awarded to those who have sustained a high performance level in the portrayal of a physically, emotionally and stylistically demanding role over a period of time. On balance, the intimate kind of work still promoted during Studio sessions is more appropriate for a play like *Dinner with Friends* with its quiet scenes in a Connecticut country kitchen, the table laden with canisters of beans, tricolor pasta on the counter, decaf brewing, and the action evolving around a change of relationships. In this case, the issues cut into actors' private lives and prompt them to rethink values and priorities. Yet, even though an actress may be actually making a marinade and the physical details like the smell of garlic and scallions on her fingers anchors her performance, there is still a distance. The rule of thumb in most cases is to gain perspective, to respond to the character, pity her at times, admire her and forgive her and give considerable thought to what urges her to make the choices that she makes. During a production in New York, one actress went so far as to allow the audience response to affect her nightly performance, to hear things through their ears and use those reactions, let them filter through her mind as she altered her understanding of the part. At the same time everyone in the cast experienced a degree of introspection which, in turn, affected their performance in different ways. But it's not clear what would have happened if "Method people" had joined any of the casts in New York, Louisville, California and Paris and brought that process to bear. The practice of personalizing and improvising around the circumstances first and dealing with the text later might have met with resistance. But then again, except for those who insisted on that way of working, they would, in all probability, have adjusted to the director's wishes. There might not have been any appreciable difference at all.

Bibliography

Books

Adams, Leith, and Keith Burns, eds. *James Dean: Behind the Scenes*. New York: Birch Lane Press (Carol Publishing Group), 1990.

Alexander, Paul. *Salinger*. Los Angeles: Renaissance Books, 1999.

Baldwin, James. *Blues for Mister Charlie*. New York: The Dial Press, 1964.

Bates, Brian. *The Way of the Actor*. Boston: Shambala, 1987.

Bogdanovich, Peter. *Who the Devil Made It*. New York: Alfred A. Knopf, 1997.

Boleslavsky, Richard. *Acting: The First Six Lessons*. New York, Theatre Arts, 1949.

Brustein, Robert. *Seasons of Discontent*. New York: Simon and Schuster, 1965.

Chekhov, Anton. *Best Plays of Chekhov*. New York: Modern Library, 1956.

Chekhov, Michael. *To the Actor*. New York: Harper, 1953.

Ciment, Michel. *Kazan on Kazan*. New York: The Viking Press, 1974.

Clurman, Harold. *The Fervent Years*. New York: Hill and Wang, 1945.

_____. *Lies Like Truth*. New York: Grove Press, 1958.

Cole, Toby (ed.). *Acting: A Handbook of the Stanislavsky Method*. New York: Crown, 1955.

Corsaro, Frank. *Maverick*. New York: The Vanguard Press, 1978.

Easty, Edward Dwight. *On Method Acting*. New York: HC Publishers, 1966.

Edgar, David. *Pentecost*. London: Nick Hern Books Limited, 1995.

Edwards, Christine. *The Stanislavsky Heritage*. New York: New York University Press, 1965.

Funke, Lewis, and John E. Booth (ed.). *Actors Talk About Acting*. New York: Random House, 1961.

Garfield, David. *A Player's Place*. New York: Macmillan, 1980.

Gassner, John. *Producing the Play*. New York: Holt, Rinehart and Winston, 1953.

Gazzo, Michael. *A Hatful of Rain*, in *Famous American Plays of the 1950s*, selected and introduced by Lee Strasberg. New York: Dell, 1962.

Gelman, Howard. *The Films of John Garfield*. Secaucus, N.J.: The Citadel Press, 1975.

Gordon, Mel. *The Stanislavsky Technique: Russia*. New York: Applause Theatre Books, 1987.

Guinness, Alec. *Blessings in Disguise*. New York: Alfred A. Knopf, 1985.

Hare, David. *Skylight*. London: Faber and Faber, 1995.

Havoc, June. *Marathon '33*. New York: Dramatists Play Service, 1969.

_____. *More Havoc*. New York: Harper and Row, 1980.

Hethmon, Robert H. (ed.). *Strasberg at the Actors Studio*. New York: The Viking Press, 1965.

Hirsch, Foster. *A Method to Their Madness*. New York: DaCapo Press, 1984.

Holley, Val. *James Dean: The Biography*. New York: St. Martin's Press, 1995.

Hornby, Richard. *The End of Acting*. New York: Applause Theatre Books, 1992.

Hoskyns, Barney. *James Dean: Shooting Star*. New York: Doubleday, 1989.

Howlett, John. *James Dean—A Biography*. U.K.: Plexus Publishing Ltd., 1997.

Inge, William. *Four Plays*. New York: Grove Weidenfeld, 1990.

Kazan, Elia. *Elia Kazan*. New York: Alfred A. Knopf, 1988.

Lewis, Robert. *Method or Madness?* New York: Samuel French, 1958.

_____. *Slings and Arrows*. New York: Stein and Day, 1984.

Mailer, Norman. *Marilyn*. New York: Warner Books, 1975.

McCann, Graham. *Rebel Males*. New Brunswick, NJ: Rutgers University Press, 1993.

Meisner, Sandford. *On Acting*. New York: Random House, 1987.

Miller, Arthur. *Death of a Salesman*. New York: Penguin Books, 1996.

_____. *Timebends*. New York: Grove Press, 1987.

Moore, Sonia. *The Stanislavsky System*. New rev. ed. New York: Compass Books, The Viking Press, 1974.

Morella, Joe, and Edward Z. Epstein. *Rebels*. New York: The Citadel Press, 1971.

Munk, Erika (ed.). *Stanislavsky and America*. New York: Hill and Wang, 1966.

Nagrin, Daniel. *Dance and the Specific Image*. Pittsburgh: University of Pittsburgh Press, 1994.

Odets, Clifford. *Six Plays of Clifford Odets*. New York: The Modern Library, 1963.

O'Neill, Eugene. *Plays of Eugene O'Neill*. New York: Random House, 1954.

_____. *A Moon for the Misbegotten*. New York: Samuel French, 1958.

Page, Tim. *Dawn Powell*. New York: Henry Holt, 1998.

Redgrave, Michael. *Mask or Face: Reflections in an Actor's Mirror*. New York: Theatre Arts Books, 1958.

Redgrave, Vanessa. *Vanessa Redgrave*. New York: Random House, 1994.

Rigdon, Walter (ed.). *The Biographical Encyclopedia and Who's Who of The American Theatre*. New York: James H. Heineman, 1966.

Roose-Evans, James. *Experimental Theatre*. New York: Universe Books, 1970.

Ross, Lillian. *The Player*. New York: Simon and Schuster, 1961.

Ryan, Paul. *Marlon Brando*. New York: Carroll and Graf, 1992.

Salinger, J.D. *The Catcher in the Rye*. Boston: Little, Brown, 1951.

Schneider, Alan. *Entrances*. New York: Viking Penguin, 1986.

Schulberg, Budd. *On the Waterfront*. Carbondale, Ill.: Southern Illinois University Press, 1980.

Silverberg, Larry. *The Sanford Meisner Approach*. Lyme, NH: Smith and Kraus, 1994.

Smith, Wendy. *Real Life Drama*. New York: Alfred Knopf, 1990.

Stanislavsky, Constantin. *An Actor Prepares*. New York: Theatre Arts, 1946.

_____. *Building a Character*. Translated by Elizabeth Reynolds Hapgood. New York: Theatre Arts Books, 1949.

_____. *Creating a Role*. Translated by Elizabeth Reynolds Hapgood. New York: Theatre Arts Books, 1961.

_____. *My Life in Art*. New York: Routledge, 1975.

Stansell, Christine. *American Moderns*. New York: Henry Holt, 2000.

Strasberg, Lee. "Acting and the Training of the Actor," in *Producing the Play*, by John Gassner. Rev. ed. New York: Holt, Rinehart and Winston, 1953.

Tynan, Kenneth. *Show People*. New York: Simon and Schuster, 1979.

Vakhtangov, Eugene. "Fantastic Realism," in *Directors on Directing*, ed., by Toby Cole and
    Helen Krich Chinoy. Rev. ed. New York: The Bobbs-Merrill Company, 1963.
Williams, Tennessee. *A Streetcar Named Desire*. New York: The New American Library
    (Signet Books), 1947.

Newspapers and Periodicals

Alpert, Hollis. "Autocrat of the Sweat Shirt School." *Esquire*, October 1961.
Atkinson, Brooks. "Strange Interlude." *The New York Times*, June 18, 1963.
_____. "Three Sisters." *The New York Times*, July 28, 1964.
Boleslavsky, Richard. "The Laboratory Theatre." *Theatre Arts Monthly*, July 1923.
Bosworth, Patricia. "Geraldine Page Wants to Flip Her Wig." *The New York Times*, November 24, 1968.
_____."Kazan." *Vanity Fair*, September 1999.
Brustein, Robert. "Keynes of Times Square." *New Republic*, December 1, 1962.
_____. "Are Britain's Actors Better Than Ours?" *The New York Times*, April 15, 1973.
Coleman, Terry. *The Observer*, May 10, 1965. London.
Douglas, Reid. "A Little Madness in the Method." *Contemporary Review*, December 1961.
Ewing, Sherman. "Wanted: More Stars, Less Method." *Theatre Arts*, January 1961.
Eyre, Richard. *Evening Standard*, June 8, 1995. London.
Fuller, Graham. "Getting Out of My Head: An Interview with Edward Norton." *Cineaste*,
    vol. XXV No. 1, 1999.
Gussow, Mel. "Turning Your Troubles into Comedy." *The New York Times*, March 21, 2000.
Guthrie, Tyrone. "Madness in the Method." *The New York Times Magazine*, September 15, 1957.
Harrity, Richard. "School for Stars." *Cosmopolitan*, January 1960.
Hewes, Henry. "Strange Interlude." *Saturday Review*, March 23, 1963.
_____. "Marathon '33." January 11, 1964.
_____. "Baby Want a Kiss." May 2, 1964.
_____. "Blues for Mister Charlie." May 9, 1964.
_____. "Three Sisters." July 18, 1964.
Hirshhorn, Clive. *Sunday Express*, July 5, 1995. London.
Jones, Ellis. "Is There Life Still Out There?" *RADA The Magazine*, Spring 1995. London.
Kazan, Elia. "Candid Conversation." *Show Business Illustrated*, February 1962.
_____. "Theatre: New Stages, New Plays, New Actors." *The New York Times Magazine*, September 23, 1962.
Lahr, John. "Bombs and Qualms." *The New Yorker*, May 1, 2000.
Lane, Anthony. "Winging It." *The New Yorker*, April 5, 1999.
Marriott, R.B. "Strasberg Explains." *The Stage*, May 20, 1965. London.
Murphy, Kathleen. "Al Pacino." *Film Comment*, March/April, 2000.
Oliver, Edith. "Strange Interlude." *The New Yorker*, March 23, 1963.
_____. "Marathon '33." January 4, 1964.
_____. "Blues for Mister Charlie." May 9, 1964.
_____. "Three Sisters." July 4, 1964.
Peck, Seymour. "The Temple of the Method." *The New York Times Magazine*, May 6, 1956.
Peter, John. *Sunday Times*, May 31, 1995. London.
Pogrebin, Robin. "At the Junction of Life and Art." *The New York Times*, March 3, 2000.
_____. "Facing Down Demons." *The New York Times*, April 26, 2000.

Raab, Scott. "The Graceful Exit." *Esquire*, May, 2000.

Rogoff, Gordon. "Lee Strasberg; Burning Ice." *Tulane Drama Review*, Winter 1964.

_____. "The Moscow Art Theatre: Surprises After Stanislavsky." *The Reporter*, March 25, 1965.

Romney, Jonathan. "Make It Yellow." *Sight and Sound*, May 1999. U.K.

Ross, Lillian. "Talk of the Town." *The New Yorker*, June 12, 2000.

Sarris, Andrew. "Holy Smoke!" *The New York Observer*, October 18, 1999.

Sherwood, Robert, Harold Clurman and Norris Houghton. "An Actor Prepares: A Comment on the Stanislavsky System." *Theatre Arts Monthly*, March 1937.

Shtier, Rachel. "Dispensing with Dogma." *The New York Times*, August 2, 1998.

Siegel, Ed. "Broadway Opens to Everyone." *The Boston Globe*, March 12, 1999.

Strasberg, Lee. "View from the Studio." *The New York Times*, September 2, 1956.

_____. "On Acting." *Texas Quarterly*, Summer, 1960.

_____. "Studio Theatre Plans," May 26, 1964.

Sylvester, Rachel. *Sunday Telegraph*, May 31, 1995. London.

Taubman, Howard. "Marathon '33." *The New York Times*, December 23, 1963.

_____. "Baby Want a Kiss." April 20, 1964.

_____. "Blues for Mister Charlie." April 24, 1964.

_____. "Three Sisters." June 23, 1964.

Theatre Record, April 23–May 6, 1995. London.

Weatherby, W.J. "The Art of Acting Inside Out." *The Guardian*, October 15, 1959. London.

Zolotow, Maurice. "The Stars Rise." *The Saturday Evening Post*, May 18, 1957.

Other Sources

The Actors Studio. Interviews by the author. Spring 1968 (in order): Don Fellows, Marcia Haufrecht, Hildy Brooks, George Furth, Lee Strasberg, Penny Allen, Patricia Gilbert, Alice Hermes, Liska March, Delos Smith, Lane Smith.

Actors Studio MFA Program. Catalogue, New School University, School of Dramatic Arts. New York, 1998–2000.

Actors Studio Tape Recordings of Lee Strasberg's critiques, discussions, talks, etc., over a period of eleven years (1956–1966). Wisconsin Center for Theater Research. The University of Wisconsin.

"American Theater Conversations: The Actors Studio." Creative Arts Television. 1995.

Barter, Nicholas. Personal Interview. June 10, 1995. U.K.

Brockway, Merrill. "Stella Adler: Awake and Dream." RM Arts, American Masters. WNET, New York, 1989.

Brustein, Robert. "Nobody Dies on Friday." Unpublished play. American Repertory Theatre, Loeb Drama Center, Cambridge, MA, October 4, 1998.

Burns, Ric. "New York: A Documentary Film." PBS. WGBH, Boston, November, 1999.

Campbell, Ken. Personal Interview. May 30, 1995. U.K.

Castro, Tony. Personal Interview. June 1, 1995. U.K.

Chekmayan, Ara. "Forever James Dean." Documentary. Warner Home Video. 1988.

Colman, Jeff. Personal Interview. January 18, 1999. U.K.

Conversations and interviews conducted between March 1999 and November 2000 with Arthur Bartow, Phoebe Brand, Robert Brustein, Frank Corsaro, Keir Dullea, Dick Franchot, Andre Gregory, Julie Harris, June Havoc, Israel Horovitz, Fred Kimball, Martin Landau, N. Richard Nash, Estelle Parsons, Bob Reynolds, Sam Schacht, Brett Somers, Elizabeth Stearns, Rip Torn.

Craze, Tony. Personal Interview. June 5, 1995. U.K.

Dunning, Alan. Personal Interview. June 2, 1995. U.K.

Firsthand observations at the Actors Studio. Spring 1968; Fall 1999.

Foster, Jill. Personal Interview. June 7, 1995. U.K.

Frome, Sheldon. "Strasberg and the Studio Actor." M.A. thesis, The University of Florida, 1969.

"Inside the Actors Studio." A series of interviews on the Bravo cable network featuring Lauren Bacall, Alec Baldwin, Matthew Broderick, Carol Burnett, Ellen Burstyn, Glenn Close, Robert DeNiro, Faye Dunaway, Sally Field, Danny Glover, Lee Grant, Anthony Hopkins, Dennis Hopper, John Hurt, Martin Landau, Nathan Lane, Jack Lemmon, Jerry Lewis, Sidney Lumet, Shirley MacLaine, Paul Newman, Mike Nichols, Estelle Parsons, Arthur Penn, Anthony Quinn, Julia Roberts, Susan Sarandon, Neil Simon, Steven Spielberg, Sylvester Stallone, Meryl Streep, Donald Sutherland, Christopher Walken, Eli Wallach and Anne Jackson, Shelley Winters. Aired in varying sequences. 1995–2000.

Interviews with Alec Guinness, John Mills and Elaine Page hosted by Melvyn Bragg. The South Bank Show. Thames. Aired on the Bravo network. 1999.

King, Jane. Personal Interview. May 31, 1995. U.K.

Kinloch, Maggie. Personal Interview. June 3, 1995. U.K.

"Lee Strasberg." *Biography*. Arts and Entertainment Network. April 1, 1999.

The Lee Strasberg Theatre Institute. Catalogue. New York, 2000.

London International Festival of Theatre. Brochure and pamphlet. The Arts Council of England. 1995.

"A Long Time Till Dawn" by Rod Serling. Kraft Television Theater. 1953. Distributed by Hollywood Attic, Burbank, California.

"Looking for Richard." 20th Century–Fox. 1997.

Mercier, Mary. Mimeographed brief history of the Actors Studio and the Actors Studio West. June, 1999.

Nagrin, Daniel. Personal Interview and observation of his Work Group. Fall 1976.

Pickering, Ken. Personal Interview. June 6, 1995. U.K.

Ranger, Paul. Personal Interview. June 14, 1995. U.K.

Rogoff, Gordon. Personal Interview. January 2, 1969, Yale University.

Index